GW01417523

Les Liii
Transgression and French Literature

Edited with an Introduction by

Larry Duffy
and
Adrian Tudor

THE
UNIVERSITY
OF HULL
PRESS

Cottingham Road
Hull
HU6 7RX

A CIP catalogue record for this book is available from the British Library.

© 1998 University of Hull Press
Text© Larry Duffy and Adrian Tudor and all authors sited in the Contents list

Published 1998

Paperback ISBN 0 85958 672 3

Printed by
LSL Press Ltd, Bedford, England

Les Lieux interdits: Transgression and French Literature

Edited with an Introduction by

Larry Duffy
and
Adrian Tudor

UNIVERSITY OF HULL PRESS

Contents

Notes on Contributors

Sue Bedry, a graduate of the State University of New York, has recently completed an MLitt at the University of Glasgow on French and Russian fiction of the nineteenth century.

Patrick Crowley, after graduating from University College Cork, did a DEA at the University of Lille III, and is now studying for his PhD at Royal Holloway, University of London. His particular area of research relates to contemporary fiction, critical theory and the articulation of fictional identities through the interplay of autobiography, history and myth.

Mark Darlow, who graduated from the Universities of Kent and Lyon II, is in the first year of a PhD, at the University of Kent, on the eighteenth-century librettist, music critic and journalist Nicolas-Etienne Framery. He is currently based at the Ecole Normale Supérieure, Paris.

Véronique Desnain is a graduate of Goldsmiths College, University of London, and is now working on her PhD at the University of Bristol. Her research examines feminist criticism of some of Racine's tragedies and considers the importance of gender in terms of characterisation and audience response. She has lectured at the University of the West of England, and now teaches at the University of Bristol. She has published in *Seventeenth-Century French Studies* and has co-authored three of the BBC *Select* French language textbooks.

Larry Duffy is a graduate of the Universities of Manchester and Dijon, at both of which he has subsequently taught. Having worked initially for a year at the University of Hull on the manuscripts of *L'Education sentimentale* in the capacity of research assistant, he is now in the second full-time year of a PhD on the fictional exploitation of changing patterns of mobility in nineteenth-century France, centred on the work of Flaubert and Zola. He has contributed to a forthcoming volume entitled *Fin de Siècle?*. He teaches in the French Department at Hull.

Jacqueline Eccles is completing her MPhil on Marie de France and the role of Henry II in Medieval French Literature at the University of Liverpool. She teaches in the French Department at John Moores University.

Anne Frémiot is currently completing her doctorate in French Studies at the University of Nottingham, of which she is a graduate. Her research explores the discourses of identity and difference offered by the dandy in the novels of Barbey d'Aurevilly. She is the editor of a forthcoming volume entitled *Fin de Siècle?*, to be published by Nottingham University Press, and the author of an article which will appear shortly in *Dalhousie French Studies*.

Angela Kershaw obtained her BA and MA at the University of Nottingham, where she is now in the final stages of a PhD on the representation of gender in the French political novel of the 1930s. Her research interests include gender in literature, women's writing, the interface between politics and writing, and the politics and culture of the interwar years (particularly in terms of the contribution made to it by women).

Benjamin Noys has completed a DPhil on the reception of Georges Bataille in Anglo-American Theory at the University of Sussex. He has published articles in *Popular Music* and *Theory, Culture and Society*, on subjects ranging from contemporary dance culture to Bataille and Habermas. His research interests also include the use of deconstruction in the analysis of the internet.

Shona Potts graduated from the University of Aberdeen in 1993 and taught at the University of Savoy, Chambéry, for a year, before returning to Aberdeen to start a PhD on the questions of history and narrative voice in the contemporary African novel in French. She also teaches in the French Department at Aberdeen.

Fabienne Reymondet is completing her doctorate at the University of Kent. Her research focuses on the prosaic dimensions of the work of the contemporary poet Jacques Réda. Interested also in the question of the nature of lyricism in twentieth-century fiction, she has written on Hervé Guibert, and has contributed to the forthcoming proceedings of the conference on Contemporary Writing in Switzerland held at the Institute of Romance Studies in July 1997.

Paul Scott is a graduate of the Séminaire St Curé d'Ars, Paris and of Durham University, where he has recently completed his MA in Seventeenth-Century Studies. He is currently studying for a PhD in Seventeenth-Century French Theatre.

Adrian Tudor is currently completing a PhD on the first Old French *Vie des Pères*. A Hull University graduate, he taught for four years at the Universities of St-Etienne and Savoy and at the Ecole Nationale des Mines. He has published articles on Marie de France, the *Vie des Pères*, the medieval toad and paedagogical methodology. Conference papers include those given at the International Medieval Congress, Leeds, 1996, and the 12th Colloquium of the Société Internationale Renardienne, Turin, 1997. He is currently Visiting Fellow at Harvard University following the award of a one-year scholarship by the Kennedy Memorial Trust.

Preface

This book comprises thirteen essays, ten of which are based on papers given at a Postgraduate Research Day which took place at the University of Hull Graduate Research Institute on 15 March 1997, supplemented by three further submissions by conference delegates. The conference was generously sponsored at University level by the School of European Languages and Cultures and the Department of French. The essays represent a variety of approaches to a single theme by a new generation of scholars working in an impressively wide range of areas of critical enquiry.

The editors would like to acknowledge the invaluable help and support of the following: Dr Alan Bower, Director, Graduate Research Institute; Pat Escreet, School Secretary and Dr Alan Best, Dean, School of European Languages and Cultures; the Department of French, in particular the Head and Acting Head of Department, respectively Dr Alan Hindley and Mr Douglas Jamieson, and Professor Tony Williams and Dr Brian Levy for their enthusiastic and continued encouragement and support. We should also like to thank Glen Innes of The University of Hull Press for his advice and assistance during the production of this volume.

Larry Duffy
Adrian Tudor

Volume publié avec le concours du Service Culturel de l'Ambassade de France à Londres.

Introduction

Larry Duffy and Adrian Tudor

A volume entitled *Transgression and French Literature* might initially and easily be misread as being solely concerned with transgression's literary potential, rather than with, to an equal extent, the transgressive potential of literature. French writers seem to be resoundingly aware of both these related but distinct elements of the transgressive, as the following essays would appear to illustrate. The variety of the approaches and methodologies employed here suggests that there is in fact a multiplicity of perceptions of the meaning of transgression and of its roles in literature, either as fictive subject-matter or purpose. In some of the chapters of this volume, attention is focused on transgressive behaviour and the reactions it engenders as represented in French literature. Often the representation of such behaviour is not transgressive at all in itself, and is complicit with the conventions which are being transgressed (consider for example Drieu La Rochelle's attitude to homosexuality, as discussed by Angela Kershaw). On other occasions, what is being represented is utterly commonplace and unthreatening. Eugene Savitzkaya and Jacques Réda, for example, exploit the ordinary as subject matter. Their unusual manner of exploiting it, however, transforms it, so that ultimately the mundane becomes as disrupted as the generic conventions which are disrupted in representing it.

Broadly speaking, then, most of the work assembled here could at first be naïvely pigeonholed into one of two categories: either that of the representation of the transgressive act in literature, or that of generic transgression by literature. However, this is only a question of emphasis; a wide variety of approaches is represented in this book, and the subject of transgression is so problematic that there will always be some overlap between the respective transgressivities of content and genre. Often the question of whether transgressive subject-matter implies transgressive literature is directly addressed. This question is in fact

1

central to Benjamin Noys's discussion of Georges Bataille. In a controversial, indeed polemical essay, the conventional view of Bataille as high priest of transgression is questioned precisely on account of the stated transgressivity of the content of Bataille's work. To dwell on the transgressivity of Bataille's work, as Bataille himself has done, is perhaps to impose limits on that transgressivity.

On the other hand, of course, it could be, and is, argued that transgression would be impossible without limits. That transgression should disrupt limits and at the same time reaffirm them is not as contradictory as might initially be apparent. Indeed, this is central to Bataille's understanding of transgression. Taboos, to an extent, exist for the purpose of being broken. Human societies, in fact, sanction, or rather, to be more precise, sanctify transgression of taboos in practices such as marriage and war, and thus keep it under control. This is of particular relevance to Angela Kershaw's discussion of *Gilles*. In Drieu's novel, society's codes on homosexuality (and by extension male sexuality) are transgressed to their utmost to provide, paradoxically, the ultimate expression of masculinity. Transgression is sanctioned in order to further the greater good as Drieu sees it. A dissenting practice, since socially useful in that it reinforces a higher conformity, is permitted. As with the socially encouraged expression of pro-creation and hunting in Bataille's view, 'the taboo cannot suppress pursuits necessary to life, but it can give them the significance of a religious violation'.[1]

This gives rise to the question whether transgressions are necessarily subversive. Kenneth Graham, with reference to the Gothic narrative, suggests that transgression 'might be a shout against an imposed silence or an assertion of truth to counteract prejudice - or, more subversively, it may affirm a constraint while quietly transgressing it. However it responds, the Gothic experience grows out of prohibition'.[2] This is perhaps the case for all creativity and literary exploration. A work does not necessarily need to transgress a prohibition to be influenced by it, since a reaction to an interdiction may still extend literary or cultural boundaries. Just as for Bakhtin women break out of their boundaries in sexual intercourse and menstruation, having a body that is 'never finished, never completed; is continually built, created and builds and creates another body', so is the literature of transgression one of constant renewal.[3]

In the biblical context, the transgression of Adam gives rise to original sin, which in turn imposes upon the believer the need to repent. The 'rebirth' of repentance will lead to confession and salvation, the ultimate Judæo-Christian goal. Every essay in this book demonstrates that the same can be said for transgressions of a literary type: generic, sexual, literary, religious, political, spiritual, social, spatial, moral or parental transgression can be the catalyst in the creative process, 'transgresser pour se créer autre'.[4] Just as transgression of the Ten Commandments is a necessary step to salvation, so transgression is perhaps necessary if literary or political change is to be achieved. The concept of transgression goes far beyond the simple transgressive act: pornography and erotica may shock through their explicit sexual content but they conform in both manner and form to that particular genre. In blasphemy and violence both spiritual and physical limits can be reached, but it could be posited that it is in the challengeing or breaking of these limits that an action becomes truly transgressive. Transgression can be a productive force that gives rise to creativity and innovation through its position on 'the fringe of official culture'.[5]

The present volume on the theme of transgression, by graduate scholars working across the disciplines of French literary studies, seems to show that this driving force of creativity cannot be pinned down to one, all-inclusive definition. The sociological and literary context, the period that sees the production of a work, and the politics and economics that surround it, can contribute to making transgression all things to all people: marital fidelity may have been a major moral issue in the novels of the nineteenth century, but for Marie de France the question was rather one of legality, social justice and practicability. This book seeks not to define transgression, nor to examine transgressive behaviour; its goal is to explore a number of methodologies and approaches to a universal literary phenomenon. The following essays provide, to borrow an expression from Naomi Segal and Nick White, 'analytical snapshots at symptomatic moments' in the French literary history of transgression.[6] The multiple authorship of the present volume ensures a multiplicity of viewpoints towards this complex but universal topos.

Transgression is generally held to imply the breaking or the by-passing of a rule. A legal or moral transgression of an older form may be necessary, as is the case with the Foire plays examined by Mark Darlow, in order to overcome new political constraints. Herein lies a paradox: from the chapters that follow one might easily conclude that transgression is almost a pre-requisite for creativity. However, in order to transgress there must be barriers or constraints, and the restriction of the means of expression can harm the quality of the newly created product. Vercors's *Le Silence de la Mer* is a literary masterpiece born out of the constraints of the Occupation, but the very desire to transgress moral norms can ultimately render works such as Cyrille Collard's *Les Nuits fauves* unlikely or unable to satisfy completely the reader's expectations. Of course, what may appear to be carnivalesque transgressions – the cross-dressing, biting parody, drunkenness and general lewdness of medieval theatre or the abusive and boisterous behaviour of a football crowd – are simply a cleverly presented and licensed catharsis. Michael Camille sees this as an 'unfettered freedom of expression often served to legitimate the status quo, chastising the weaker groups in the social order, such as women and ethnic and social minorities. We have to face up to carnival's complicity with the official order played out in the supposed subversion of it'[7].

The notion of transgression in literature runs parallel to the religious ideal of salvation: in order to be saved the sinner must repent, and in order to repent he must be a sinner. So, from the very beginning of the Christian tradition some of the greatest penitential literature centres on the very worst sinners who perform spectacular spiritual recoveries. As Jean-Claude Payen points out with regard to the medieval pious tale, the whole point of the exercise was that 'les pénitents [...] soient de très grands coupables, qui reviennent de loin et ont besoin d'une grâce exceptionnelle'.[8] Transgression is the overstepping of a boundary that can lead to new perspectives or methods, a profane equivalent to the saved soul of the sinner. The seventeenth-century martyr-plays examined by Paul Scott would appear to set this dilemma in a real, historical context.

In the early sixteenth century there was a very tangible coming together of real and literary transgression in a form that conformed completely with the accepted rules of the period. A convicted felon, sentenced to die in a prolonged and agonising manner, was given the opportunity to be swiftly executed by the sword in a dramatic representation of a mystery play. The felon accepted this offer, since he believed that the person entrusted to perform the execution, a minor criminal sentenced to banishment but offered clemency through his accomplishment of the execution, would not dare do the deed. But he did, and he did. Putting aside the argument over theatre's literary status, the modern reader can see here, more clearly perhaps than in any other literary moment, a convergence of literary and literal transgression.[9] Two centuries later, Rousseau's *Du Contrat social* was to be at the confluence of political and literary transgression, arguing that each individual's liberty finds its limit when it transgresses the liberty of another.

To transgress is in essence to challenge or go beyond a physical or a metaphysical boundary. Edmund Leach illustrates how difficult it is to pin this down more explicitly: 'A boundary separates two zones of social space-time which are *normal, time-bound, clear-cut, central, secular*, but the spatial and temporal markers which actually serve as boundaries are themselves *abnormal, timeless, ambiguous, at the edge, sacred*.'[10] Walls and barricades, genres and forms, anticipations and expectations, all expressions of marginality invite trespass, all obstacles will eventually be violated. Boundaries may be simple and physical – a fence or a hedge as highlighted by Fabienne Reymondet in her discussion of Jacques Réda's poetry – or they may be a complex web of conceptual barriers established by the ruling classes in order to exclude a particular section of society, or by the implied author to determine the nature of transgressive actions which occur within particular spaces. Shona Potts notes how Ousmane Sembène's challenge of existing geographical and political boundaries after independence transgresses the limits 'which were designed to safeguard the colonial population both physically and in terms of authority'.[11] Peeking over a wall in residential Paris, entering a particular room because of its suitability for transgressive behaviour, or claiming the right to be in a formerly prohibited area of a post-colonial city can amount to very much the same thing in that each is a transgression of an established power structure. In each case the setting up of boundaries, and the occurance of transgressive acts within, though or across these boundaries, are essential parts of the creative process. Perhaps here, with the exception of Zola where transgression occurs in the semi-public space of the *serre*, at once public and private, we are not too far removed from Bakhtinian carnival: 'The public square and the streets adjoining it are the proper place for carnival. The public square brings what is marginal or borderline in ordinary life to the very centre of the community.'[12] The social disruption of carnival menaces or challenges the order of the city, and whilst neither of the texts studied by Reymondet or Potts lend themselves easily to a Bakhtinian reading, it is in the lifting of spatial restrictions – a vital element of carnival – that transgression is able to take place. On the other hand, however, in Zola's *La Curée*, as Larry Duffy indicates, it is only within certain socially-defined physical boundaries that transgression of moral and social codes can occur. That is, spatial restrictions are central to transgression.

Fabienne Reymondet shows further that a literary form

that transgresses convention is in fact a way of moving limits and of exploration rather than violating fixed forms: Jacques Réda's poetry does not conform to poetic convention, being neither narrative, didactic, anecdotal nor descriptive. By unsettling poetic and generic categories this hybrid poetry challenges the taboos of the pre-eminent post-Mallarmean poetics. The *nouveau roman*, the result of 'a questioning of the aesthetic basis of creativity', represents another form of transgression in literature, one that blurs the distinctions between 'the familiar and unambiguous codes of literary convention', such as prose and poetry or narrative and description.[13] But, as the development of the twentieth-century novel from long before the *nouveau roman's* emergence until almost half-a-century into its aftermath shows, stylistic transgressions will inevitably become conventions themselves. This is borne out especially by the essay in this collection most overtly about the transgression of genre and of readers' expectations of it. By the end of the twentieth century, especially in the post-*nouveau roman*, postmodern era, writing which disrupts writing is almost conventional. Some such writing, however, remains transgressive; Eugène Savitzkaya cannot be pigeon-holed as being merely a ('conventional') transgressor of genre: he transgresses generically but also thematically, and, what is perhaps especially significant, in terms of the mixture of genres which Patrick Crowley demonstrates as existing in his work. A desire to explore and to create may push the author towards a flouting of the rules of composition of a particular period, for example away from the ideals and into a violation of Aristotelian unity, resulting, in the case of the *nouveau roman*, in a form that perhaps shocks twentieth-century sensibilities. This is what Evans terms 'the transgressive impulse of modern art',[14] but in fact the chapters of the present volume suggest that there is nothing 'modern' about this impulse; all that changes are the rules that are bypassed or broken.

The apparent breaking of taboos is frequently the lot of the author, although all is not always what it seems. Sade may well describe acts that overstep the mark laid down by society, but it might be argued that he does so in a recognisable form that transgresses few if any of the primary rules of literature (in some ways, might Raymond Queneau's *Exercices de Style* not be more transgressive, given its emphasis on style rather than content?). This again raises the question of whether to portray transgressive acts is itself to transgress. Benjamin Noys suggests that it is Bataille's very need and will to shock that in fact makes him something of a conformist. In quite another field, Adrian Tudor illustrates the remarkable creativity of a medieval author that has its roots in the very strong antisemitism of the age, an anti-semitism whose origins lie in the perceived 'ultimate' transgression of the Jewish people. The form, however adroit, corresponds closely to an established literary type, and the content arrives at conformity, both literary and thematic, by way of an examination of the worst possible transgression. The theme of the transgression of the Jews is further taken up by Véronique Desnain in her study of *Athalie*. Desnain argues that the Jewish god of wrath is a cornerstone of the patriarchal system and that the literary struggle of the Jews – who, incidentally, will subsequently need to overcome the consequences of their perceived, collective transgression – is taken to be political rather than religious.

It is as much the recording of transgressive behaviour as transgression *per se* that at present holds our attention. Again, it is essential to question whether the act of recording transgressions is itself an act of literary transgression. The issue of how literature comes to terms with transgression is of prime importance and much can be learned from examining both a transgression and a reaction to it. Transgressions can be described in ways which are not in themselves transgressive but which at the same time affirm that taboos can become desirable. Véronique Desnain's essay illustrates this by stressing that Athalie is transgressive in the eyes of the audience if not in actual fact, her gender being the only basis for transgression. Mark Darlow describes how the form of the *écriteaux* plays was carefully established and modified; in retaining a semblance of the appearance of conventional theatre, these plays proved an effective vehicle for political expression. An oblique critique of growing absolutism is to be found in the martyr plays discussed by Paul Scott, in an essay that confirms that authors and playwrights may at times have to appear to conform in order not to threaten their own personal security. Martyr plays, at the time of civil unrest, are 'a radical reassertion of the accountability of those in power'. As public order and central authority reassert themselves, so do martyr plays decline in popularity. Scott astutely comments upon Corneille's dilution of Polyeucte's transgression and links this to Louis XIV's actual presence at a performance of the play. Marie de France's *Lais* may not be innovative as far as form is concerned – indeed, was this ever a concern of the author? – but they constantly depict images of fidelity and transgression, be it social, political, amorous or religious. Jacqueline Eccles highlights the fact that the political transgressions of Lanval are examined in a conventional narrative whose only claim to individuality, at first sight, is that the author is a woman. The transgressions of Arthur's court would create a potentially serious situation when transferred from the realm of literature to the actual royal court of twelfth-century England.

This potential of literature as political critique is echoed by Sue Bedry and Angela Kershaw, both of whom stress the notion of political transgression. However, the political can be expressed in different and distinctive ways. Whereas the super-fluous man's political transgression is communicated through his attire and air of superiority, through his exploitation of his imagined endowment with exceptional intelligence and sensibility (and, interestingly, the crime – *prestuplenie*, literally overstepping, transgression – of the superfluous man's most famous literary descendant, Dostoevsky's Raskolnikov, is one which is non-political yet inspired by the same conceit as that which encourages the superfluous man to believe himself to be superior to others), in the fiction examined by Angela Kershaw, the political is sexual. Different, and in Gilles's case 'superior', sensibilities are expressed through homosexuality rather than through superficiality. George Stambolian and Elaine Marks, highlighting French writers' 'profound understanding of the value of homosexuality as a transgression', state that 'because it perpetually questions the social order and is always in question itself, homosexuality is other'.[15] What is interesting about *Gilles* is that otherness is exploited in the furtherance of an extreme brand of conformity; and in other homosexual fiction, such as that of Louise Weiss, the sexual transgressor remains ultimately powerless in her otherness.

This is in contrast to the dandy figure as represented by Barbey d'Aurevilly. Power and transgressive status may in Louise Weiss be seen as being mutually exclusive, but Anne Frémiot suggests that in Barbey, and in other nineteenth-century discourses of *Dandysme*, otherness is both goal and means of empowerment. The social structure which isolates the dandy paradoxically makes him more powerful within it precisely on account of his isolation. Again, the paradox central to Bataille's view of transgression would seem to be in operation, in that the social and moral codes which bring taboos into action are exactly what facilitate their being breached. Reinforcement and disruption occur simultaneously. In the context of the dandy, this simultaneity is most interesting when seen in the context of the transitory nature of the dandy's era. Both the fall of the aristocracy and the rise of the bourgeoisie play into his transgressive hands; he can exploit and subvert both. Social inversion is crucial to his behaviour (even if this be merely his turning inside-out of his waistcoat) and again brings to mind the Bakhtinian notion of carnival. As with Zola, Réda and Sembène, spatial factors are also in evidence. In *Les Diaboliques*, moral and social transgressions are accompanied, as in Zola, by geographical uses.

These chapters offer no heuristic consensus, no simple definition nor any single answer to the question of transgression. Although this volume is the work of different authors with diverse interests, all address a common subject and collectively present some of the problems connected with a universal theme. From this presentation, aimed at a wider audience than might normally read such essays if individually presented, emerge a number of insights into – if not solutions to – the problems posed by the theme of transgression in French literary studies. Some new questions are raised by giving direct attention to some of the issues shared by contributors, and despite the wide range of topics covered, certain features involved in the study of transgression are consistently suggested. The distinction between transgression in literature and transgression by literature is an extremely important starting point in this book, and before further issues are broached this distinction must be addressed. But in order that a deeper understanding of the wider issues might be reached, this distinction itself needs to be accepted and yet transgressed.

University of Hull

1 G. Bataille, *Death and Sensuality* (New York: Ballantine, 1962) p. 68.

2 K. Graham, *Gothic Fictions* (New York: AMS, 1989), p. xii.

3 M.M. Bakhtin, *Rabelais and His World*, trans. by H. Iswolsky (Cambridge, MA: MIT Press, 1968), p. 317.

4 Expression employed by Anne Frémiot in her conference paper on Barbey, Hull, March 15 1997.

5 J. Kristeva, *Desire in Language*, ed. by L.S. Roudiez (Oxford: Blackwell, 1981), p.86.

6 *Scarlet Letters. Fictions of Adultery from Antiquity to the 1990s*, ed. by N. Segal & N. White (Basingstoke: Macmillan, 1997), p. 4.

7 M. Camille, *Images on the Edge* (London: Reaktion, 1992), p. 143.

8 J.-C. Payen, *Le Motif du repentir dans la littérature française médiévale* (Geneva: Droz, 1971), p. 534.

9 See Henri Rey-Flaud, 'Comme sur une autre scène', *Europe*, 654 (1983), 93-101 (p. 101).

10 E. Leach, *Culture and Communication: the Logic by which Symbols are Connected* (Cambridge: Cambridge University Press, 1976), p. 35.

11 See p. xxx, below.

12 D. LaCapra, 'Bakhtin, Marxism and the Carnivalesque', *Rethinking Intellectual History* (Ithaca - London: Cornell University Press, 1983), 291-324, (p. 301).

13 M. Evans, *Claude Simon and the Transgression of Modern Art* (London: Macmillan, 1989), pp. xi-xii.

14 ibid., p. 248.

15 *Homosexualities and French Literature. Cultural Contexts / Critical Texts*, ed. by G. Stambolian and E. Marks (Ithaca and London: Cornell University Press, 1979), p. 26.

PART ONE

Pre-Modern Literature and Theatre

Marie de France and the Law

Jacqueline Eccles

Throughout the course of history women have 'transgressed', in as much as their fight for equality has involved the defiance of 'tradition'. Women who seek freedom of expression and have independence of mind have often turned to writing. One such woman is Marie de France and the fact that she chose to write in a manner which challenged well-established social conventions makes her an ideal subject for a study of the theme of transgression. My aim here is to examine her treatment of the law. Marie's *Lais* – in particular *Lanval,* on which I shall concentrate in these pages – contain many references to legal matters and they frequently use legal vocabulary. I intend to comment on the legal situation in Marie's day, and on her own preoccupation with the law.

Many scholars accept that Marie wrote at least some of her *Lais* in England, given her knowledge of that country.[1] There is in fact much to connect her with England, and in particular with the court of Henry II.[2] Her knowledge of English law, as we shall see, is exceptionally accurate and it links her to Henry, whose interest in the law is well documented.[3] She was writing at a time when the population had begun to enjoy the stability brought about during the early years of Henry's reign. England had emerged in this period from the turmoil of King Stephen's rule, and the English court must have been a challenging audience for an author like Marie, given her strong views on socio-political issues. We cannot know precisely how her stories were received, but Denis Pyramus gives us some indication of their popularity when he says in the prologue to *La Vie seint Edmund le Rei* that her work won her the praise of knights and barons, who loved to hear her stories over and over again.[4]

Henry II is renowned for his interest in the law, and his most significant achievement in this area is undoubtedly the Assize of Clarendon of 1166. The Assize was the greatest innovation ever known in Criminal and Land law and it this still forms the basis of the British justice system today.[5] Any of the English nobles in Marie's audience would have been aware of the wider implications of the Assize and also of Henry's reputation in dealing personally with legal matters. This makes the trial scene in *Lanval* especially interesting, as its detailed description of legal proceedings is full of significant links to contemporary legal practice. As Elizabeth Francis has observed in her article on the trial scene in *Lanval*, Marie's knowledge of the English legal system is remarkably accurate:

> Many of the terms [Marie uses] are of course common to other mediaeval writers dealing with similar subject-matter, yet if the passages are compared with those used by Béroul and in the Renart, it will be found that the lai of Lanval gives a much greater impression of precision. It is difficult not to infer that many of the phrases are intended to bear a technical value. [6]

Although *Lanval* is based on a well known plot structure, the story is presented in a way which challenges social conventions.[7] Marie uses the setting of the Arthurian court, a setting which would undoubtedly have intrigued Henry. As a young boy he had spent time in the Welsh Marches with his uncle, Robert of Gloucester, who, amongst other things, is known to us as the dedicatee of Geoffrey of Monmouth's *Historia Regum Britanniae*,[8] and it is here that Henry probably came into contact with Arthurian legends. The Arthurian court was subsequently presented by other writers as a virtual utopia, yet in *Lanval* it shows obvious signs of strain and corruption.

What did Marie wish to say to Henry and why? Firstly, it is clear that she was reacting to some of the changes made by the Assize. One of its advantages was that it favoured criminal trials rather than the more traditional trial by ordeal.[9] John Bowers remarks that 'the passing of the ordeal as a judicial spectacle marked an important transition for early modern England, a transition to which Marie's *lais* contribute a critique of past practices as well as intimations of future developments'.[10] Marie was undoubtedly aware that in reality the Assize took power away from the Church only to hand it over to the State, or more accurately, to Henry and his advisors. She may therefore have felt strongly about the lack of significant progress towards a fairer judicial system. The power to administer the trial by ordeal had previously been held only by the Church; since God was the judge, it had seemed only right that his representatives on earth should look after technicalities. The Assize changed this completely, giving the sovereign (Henry) the right to administer justice. Marie's lays are permeated by a strong defence of the individual and collective right to privacy in the eyes of the law and society, and the change in the law effected by Henry's Assize did little to improve these rights in criminal matters.[11] It became a means for the State to abuse the law just as the Church had previously done for years. Indeed, although suspicious of the ordeal as an instrument of justice, Henry II himself still used it as a judicial tool when it suited him to do so.[12]

Throughout her *lais*, Marie questions aspects of the law, and in *Lanval* she deals with the moral dilemma of criminal trials. It would be consistent with her less dogmatic conception of right and wrong to offer her patron a work which both acknowledged his successes and indicated potential failures. As Bowers remarks of *Lanval*, 'the legal drama represents the dark side of the jury trial under direct royal supervision'.[13] Marie is not afraid to comment on what she sees as weaknesses in the system. To have questioned the most significant innovation in a previously highly unjust legal system shows the level of Marie's integrity as a writer. The Assize was in fact revolutionary for the medieval justice system, but, as we have seen, there was certainly room for improvement, and it is to this conclusion that Marie's presentation of the legal system in England leads us.

In *Lanval* the reader's attention is quickly drawn to the fact that Lanval is a foreigner, forgotten by his king and without relatives or friends to support him (vv. 18-20, 27-28, 398-99).[14]

There also seems to be some doubt as to whether he can stand trial, as he is not English. It is worth noting here that Henry II, who had limited political ambitions outside England and France, was not renowned for his hospitality towards foreigners:

> Many people came to Henry II for help in their own troubles. They were received politely and refused with courtesy. Gerald of Wales made so bold on one occasion to upbraid Henry for his lukewarm response to the offer of the throne of Jerusalem brought to him by Patriarch Heraclius in 1185... 'If the patriarch or others come to us' [Henry] replied, 'it is because they seek their own advantage rather than ours'.[15]

Marie may perhaps have been making a cautious comment on the way she had been treated in England, or the treatment of others at Henry's court. It is certain that the way she handles the story, however she intended it to be received, would have raised eyebrows at the English court.

Henry II's particular skills lay in the organisation and government of the law reforms which he insisted on instigating. He was not, in fact, an expert in legislation, but he found new ways to administer an otherwise flagging and unjust system, beginning in 1164 with the Constitutions of Clarendon which were simply a declaration of the customs of the monarch. According to Pollock and Maitland, Henry's chief innovations in Criminal Law were the Jury and the Writ.[16] This would again seem to lead us immediately to Marie de France's *Lanval*, and it may date the work definitively as post 1166. This is an important fact, for although much more precise dating of this and the other lays has been proposed, it provides us with a definite link between Marie and the court of Henry II. It suggests that she was in fact familiar with the English Justice system, and what better place to become acquainted with such a complicated system than the court itself? Elizabeth Francis notes how the trial scene in *Lanval* has more in common with actual trials than, for example, with that of the *Roman de Thèbes*:

...it appears probable that [Marie] was affected also by models of legal procedure of a different kind. It is noticeable how little her legal vocabulary corresponds to that of the Thèbes model and how closely to that used by Maitland in description of actual trials.[17]

This link between *Lanval* and the Assize of Clarendon becomes particularly significant when one considers that scholars such as Jean Rychner date the *Lais* to the 1160's.[18]

In *Lanval,* the jury and the oath-helpers, that is, those who act as guarantors, are important for many reasons. As we have seen, Henry's chief innovation was the introduction of the jury, and the fact that it is present in *Lanval* cannot be ignored. The medieval jury was essentially a body of local people, summoned by a public officer to decide a 'question' on oath. This was not the same as delivering a judgement, as modern juries do. The 'question' could have been a point of law or simply a matter in which the truth must be ascertained. The jurors had to declare the truth, something known as *recognoscere veritatem.* Other judicial bodies made up of laymen were the doomsmen and the compurgators (or witnesses), who were assigned by the accused, or indeed, the accuser, in order to prove his case. It was customary for the accused to provide some guarantee that he would re-appear at court to hear the charges brought against him (to 'stand bail'), and for him to have a selection of 'oath-helpers'. These would be men of good standing in the community who would swear under oath as to the character of the accused. They were, in effect, character witnesses. Lanval is no exception, he too must provide men of good character to speak for him:

> Li reis ad plegges demandé
> Lanval fu sul e esgaré
> N'i aveit parent në ami.
> Walwain i vait, ki l'a plevi,
> E tuit si cumpainun aprés.
> Li reis lur dit: 'E jol vus les

Sur quanke vus tenez de mei,
Teres e fieus, chascun par sei.' (vv. 397-404)[19]

The words of the king here are very specific: he not only expects
Gauvain and the other knights to put up everything they have
obtained in his service, but he also stipulates that each man's
land be counted separately (*chascun par sei*). There is no plausible
explanation for Marie's accuracy here other than her familiarity
with the post-1166 justice system in England. The king's
demand for judgement at the opening of the trial is also accurate
as the law stood:

Li reis demande le recort
Sulunc le cleim e les respuns:
Ore est trestut sur les baruns.
Il sunt al jugement alé,
Mut sunt pensifs e esgaré
Del franc humme d'autre païs
Quë entre eus ert si entrpris. (vv. 424-30)

In this case, it is perhaps surprising that Arthur should adhere to
the letter of the law as, in reality, he would not as king have been
obliged to *request* anything. The Assize stated that the plaintiff,
the 'appellant', must appeal (*appellare*) for a judgement to be
made. The king, however, held what Pollock and Maitland call
the 'reserve of justice',[20] which meant that he could quite legally overrule any decision made at his court. He was also the one
who determined the punishment. The text of *Lanval* correctly
states that the king himself, not the court, must banish Lanval if
he is found guilty of the charges brought against him. It is no
coincidence that banishment was Henry II's preferred punishment, even if the accused succeeded in the ordeal.[21] If Arthur
does 'appeal' for a decision to be made, it is not because he has
to do so, but because he too wishes to see that justice be done,
and specifically that it be done according to the law. That the
king should be presented in this way is significant. He is shown
to have been negligent of Lanval, and it is implied that he has

also neglected his wife. He wishes harm to come to Lanval, (vv. 431-32), yet he shows that he wishes the trial to proceed according to the law. Could this have been a pointed, yet respectful reminder that even a king is not above the law?

The fact that Marie's knowledge of the machinery of justice is so incredibly accurate suggests that any apparent inaccuracies are deliberate. One example would be the use of the character of the Count of Cornwall as Justiciar. At the time Marie was writing, the actual Justiciar was not the Count of Cornwall but, depending on the date, Richard de Lucy or Ranulf de Glanvill.[22] These men both originated from the lower landed classes and the justiciarship was their reward for loyalty to the king. Until 1175, the Duke of Cornwall was Reginald de Dunstanville, an illegitimate son of Henry I, and therefore Henry II's uncle. After his death the Dukedom reverted to the throne as Reginald left no male heirs. If Marie was seeking favour in the English Court, then she could not have failed to impress Henry with her choice of the Count of Cornwall as Justiciar. What is more, Urban T. Holmes's contention that Marie de France may have been Marie de Beaumont is also supported by the Duke's presence.[23] Marie de Beaumont's older brother was married to Reginald of Cornwall's daughter, providing yet another possible family connection.

No *lai* has a conclusion more dramatic than that of *Lanval*, as the future happiness of the hero hinges upon the successful outcome of his trial. The appearance of his fairy mistress at court is essential, and her dramatic entrance transforms what was a desperate situation into a certain victory for Lanval. It is worth noting here that Lanval's comments to the queen do in fact constitute a breach of the law, as this insults his overlord, the king. (There should never be one more beautiful than the wife of one's king!) Marie presents her audience with a difficult problem, as she sets Lanval's trangression of the law against the queen's own misdemeanour. She makes the point that any defiance of the law should be treated as an individual case, and that the circumstances of the individual should be taken into consideration. She thereby defends the rights of the individual, just as does the fairy mistress when she enters court to help in the acquittal of her lover. The use of an element of the *merveilleux* reflects Lanval's hopeless situation. He has acknowledged his guilt at having boasted about his beloved, thereby shaming the queen, and this could lead to his being banished, burned to death or hanged (vv. 327-28, 457-60). His fairy mistress has told him that should he reveal their relationship to anyone he will never see her again. He has, therefore, lost his only witness, and is unable to 'defend himself in court' (S'il ne s'en peot en curt defendre, v. 327) without the aid of the supernatural. Lanval's lover is able to tell the king that his wife has lied to him, thereby proving his innocence, solely because she is from the realms of the *merveilleux*. The legally-minded Henry II would certainly have been aware of the dilemma this presented.

Stephen G. Nichols, speaking of Marie's dedication of the *Lais* to King Henry, says that the last lines of the prologue (En mun quoer pensoe e diseie/Sire, ke[s] vos presentereie) 'associate Henry II both with Marie's affective life and with the intentionality of her poetic production'.[24] We see then a quite intentional use of her stories to convey her ideas to Henry and his court. As we have seen by his continued use of the ordeal, he was a king known to change what he felt was unjust, though not without a certain level of hypocrisy.

We can be sure that Marie's trangression of these traditional ideas and values did not go unnoticed. Her treatment of the law in a country undergoing massive change in that area can only have greatly aroused the interest of her audience, and her talent in presenting the legal aspects of her stories with such accuracy, particularly in the case of *Lanval*, provides us with an excellent description of legal procedure. The works of contemporary historians are often tainted with their desire to please their patrons, or in the case, for example, of Geoffrey of Monmouth, so steeped in political propaganda that they can in no way be considered 'truthful'. It is thanks to writers like Marie that we have a fairly accurate picture of the social conventions of the time. It would be true to say that Marie 'transgresses' simply by having written. Her gender immediately sets her apart from other medieval writers, and her treatment of the issues about which she writes defies many of the acceptable views of the time. One only has to consider the prologue to the *Lais* to realise that Marie saw her writing as a duty, in order to serve and educate future generations:

> Ki Deus ad duné escïence
> E de parler bon' eloquence
> Ne s'en deit taisir ne celer,
> Ainz se deit volunters mustrer (vv. 1-4)

She goes on to say:

> Li philosophe le saveient
> E par eus memes entendeient,
> Cum plus trespasserunt le tens,
> Plus serreient sutil de sens
> E plus se savreient garder
> De ceo k'i ert, a trespasser. (vv. 17-22)

It was clearly her aim, therefore, to present her audience with challenging situations which might enable them to learn more about the inadequacies of their own society. Her defiance of traditional ideas was, for her, nothing less than a responsibility, as we read here in the Prologue. We may say, therefore, that although writing in the romance mode, Marie should be recognised, through her transgressions, as one of the most accurate observers of her time.

Appendix : Text of the Assize of Clarendon

(MS. Bodl. Rawlinson, C. 641)

Also published in: William Stubbs, *Select Charters and Other Illustrations of English Constitutional History from the Earliest Times to the Reign of Edward the First* (Oxford: Clarendon Press, 1895).

Incipit Assisa de Clarenduna facta a rege Henrico, scilicet secundo, de assensu archiepiscoporum, episcoporun, abbatum, comitum, baronum, totius Angliae.

I.   Inprimus statuit praedicus rex Henricus de consilio omnium baronium suorem, pro pace servanda et justitia tenenda, quod per singulos comitatus inquiratur, et per singulos hundredos, per xii. legaliores homines de hundredo, et per vi. legaliores homines de qualibet villata, per sacramentum quod illi verum dicent: si in hundredo suo vel villata sua sit aliquis homo qui sit rettatus vel publicatus quod ipse sit robator vel murdrator vel latro vel aliquis qui fuerit receptor robatorum vel murdatorum vel latronum, postquam dominus rex fut rex. Et hoc inquirant Justitiae coram se, et vicecomites coram se.

II.   Et qui invenietur per sacramentum praedictorum rettatus vel publicatus quod fuerit robator vel murdator vel latro vel receptor eorum postquam dominus rex fuit rex, capiaturet eat ad juisam aquae et juret quod ipse non fuit robator vel murdator vel latro vel recepto eorum postquam dominus rex fuit rex, de valentia v. solidorum quod sciat.

III.   Et si dominus ejus qui captus fuerit vel dapifer ejus vel homines ejus requisierint eum per plegium infra tertium diem postquam captus fuerit replegiatur ipse et catalla ejus donec ipse faciat legem suam.

IV.   Et quando robator vel murdator vel latro vel receptores eorum capti fuerint per praedictum sacramentum, si Justitiae non fuerint tam cito venturi in illum comitatem ubi capti fuerint, vicecomites mandent propinquiori Justitiae per aliquem intelligentum hominem, quod tales homines ceperint; et Justitiae remandabunt vicecomitibus ubi voluerint quod illi ducantur ante illos: et vicecomites illos ducant ante Justitias; et cum illis ducant de hundredo et de villata ubi capti fuerint, duos legales homines ad portandum recordationem comitatus et hundredi, quare capti fuerint, et ibi ante Justitas facient legem suam.

V. Et de illis qui capti fuerint per praedictum sacramentum hujus Assisae, nullus habeat curiam vel justitiam nec catalla, nisi dominus rex in curia sua coram Justitiis ejus, et dominus rex habebit omnia catalla eorum. De illis vero qui capti fuerint aliter quam per hoc sacramentum, sit sicut esse solet et debet.

VI. Et vicecomites qui eos ceperint ducant eos ante Justitiam sine alia summonitione quam inde habebant. Et cum robatores vel murdatores vel latrones et receptores eorum, qui capti fuerint per sacramentum vel aliter, tradantur vice-comitibus, et ipsi recipiant eos statim sine dilatione.

VII. Et in singulis comitatibus ubi non sunt gaiolae, fiant in burgo vel aliquo castello regis de denariis regis et bosco ejus si prope fuerit, vel de alio bosco propinquo, per visum servientium regis, ad hoc ut vicecomites in illis possint illos qui capti fuerint per ministros qui hoc facere solent et per servientes suos custodire.

VIII. Vult etiam dominus rex quod omnes veniant ad comitatus ad hoc sacramentum faciendum, ita quod nullus remaneat pro libertate aliqua quam habeat, vel curia vel soca quam habuerit, quin veniant ad hoc sacramentum faciendum.

IX. Et non sit aliquis infra castellum vel extra castellum, nec etiam en honore de Walingeford, qui vetet vicecomites intrare in curiam vel terram suam ad videndos franceos plegios, et quod omnes sint sub plegiis: et ante vicecomites mittantur sub libero plegio.

X. Et in civitatibus vel burgis nullus habeat homines vel recipiat en domo sua vel terra sua vel soca sua, quos non in manu capiat quod eos habebit coram Justitia si requisti fuerint, vel sint sub francoplegio.

XI. Et nulli sint in civitate vel burgo vel castello vel extra, nec in honore etiam Walingeford, qui vetent vicecomites intrare in curiam vel terram suam vel socam suam, ad capiendum illos qui rettati fuerint vel publicati quod sint robatores vel murdatores vel latrones vel receptores eorum, vel utlagati vel rettati de foresta; sed praecipit quod juvent illos ad capendium eos.

XII. Et si aliquis fuerit captus qui fuerit saisiatus de roberia vel latrocinio, si ipse fuerit captus diffamatus et habeat malum testimonium de publicamento, et non habeat warentum, non habeat legem. Et non si fuerit publicatus, pro saisina quam habet eat ad aquam.

XIII. Et si alinquis fuerit recognoscens coram legialibus hominibus vel hundredis de roberia vel murdro vel latrocinio vel de receptione eorum, et postea negare voluerit, non habeat legem.

XIV. Vult etiam dominus rex quod illi qui facent legem suam et mundi erunt per legem, si ipsi fuerint de pessimo testimonio, et publice et turpiter diffamati testimonio multorum et legalium mare transibunt, nisi aura eos detinuerit; et cum prima aura quam habebunt postea mare transibunt, et ultra in Angliam non revertentur nisi per misericordiam domini regis: et ibi sint utlagati; et si redierint capiantur sicut utlagati.

XV. Et prohibet dominus rex ne aliquis vaivus, id est vagus vel ignotus, hospitetur alicubi nisi in burgo, et ibi non hospitetur nisi una nocte, nisi ibi infirmetur, vel equus ejus, ita quod monstrare possit monstrabile essonium.

XVI. Et si ibi fuerit plusquam una nocte, capiatur ille et

teneatur donec dominus ejus venerit aad eum plegiandum, vel donec ipse habeat salvos plegios; et ille similiter capiatur qui hospitatus fuerit.

XVII.   Et si aliquis vicecomes mandaverit alii vicecomiti quod homines fugerint de comitatu suo in alium comitatum pro roberia vel pro murdro vel latrocinio vel receptione eorum, vel pro utlagia vel pro retta forestae regis, ille capiat eos: et etiam si per se vel per alios sciat quod tales homines furgerint in comitatum suum, capiat eos et cusodiat donec de eis habeat salvos plegios.

XVIII.   Et omnes vicecomites faciant inbreviari onmes fugitivos, qui fugerint de suis comitatibus; et hoc faciant coram comitatibus, et illorum nomina scripta portabunt ante Justitias cum primo ad illos venerint, ut illi quaerantur per totam Angliam, et eorum catalla capiantur ad opus regis.

XIX.   Et vult dominus rex quod ex quo vicecomites susceperint summonitiones Justitiarum errantium, utipsi cum comitatibus suis sint ante illos, ipsi congregabunt comitatus suos et inquirent omnes qui de novo venerint in suos comitatus post hanc assisam; et illos mittent per plegios, quod erunt coram Justitias, vel illos custodient, donec Justitiae ad eos venerint, et tunc habebunt coram Justitias.

XX.   Prohibet etiam dominus rex ne monachi vel cononici vel aliqua domus religionum recipiant aliquem de populo minuto in monachum vel canonicum vel fratrem, donec sciatur de quali testimonio ipse fuerit, nisi ipse fuerit infirmus ad mortem.

XXI.   Prohibet etiam dominus rex, quod nullus in tota Anglia receptet in terra sua vel soca sua vel domo sub se, aliquem de secta illorum renegatorum qui excommunicati et signati fuerunt apud Oxenforde. Et si quis eos receperit, ipse erit in misericordia domini regis; et domus, in qua illi fuerint, portetur extra villam et comburatur. Et hoc jurabit unusquisque vicecomes quod hoc tenebit, et hoc jurare faciet omnes ministros suos, et dapiferos baronum, et omnes milites et franco-tenentes de comitatibus.

XXII. Et vult dominus rex quod haec assisa teneatur in regno suo quamdiu ei placuerit.

University of Liverpool

1   G.S. Burgess, *The Lais of Marie de France: Text and Context* (Athens, Georgia: University of Georgia Press, 1987), pp. 18-19, 95, and Jean Rychner, *Les Lais de Marie de France* (Paris: Champion, 1966), p. viii.

2   Burgess, pp. 18, 19, 30, 83; R.R. Bezzola, *Les Origines et la formation de la littérature courtoise en Occident (500-1200)*, 3 vols, (Paris: Champion, 1958-63), I, p. 305; John Bowers, 'Ordeals, Privacy and the *Lais* of Marie de France', *Journal of Medieval and Renaissance Studies*, 24 (1991), 1-31 (pp. 1, 6-7, 8.); Michelle A. Freeman, 'The Power of Sisterhood in Marie de France's "Le Fresne"', *French Forum*, 12 (1987), 5-26 (p. 1). There are many other studies which examine this aspect of the *Lais*, too numerous to list here. For a complete bibliography, consult G.S. Burgess, *Marie de France: an Analytical Bibliography*, Research Bibliographies and Checklists, (London: Grant and Cutler, 1977, Supplement no. 1, 1986, and Supplement no. 2, 1997).

3   See F. Pollock and F.W. Maitland, *History of English Law before the Time of Edward I*, 2 vols, (Cambridge: C.U.P., 1895, I, chapter 6).

4   Piramus, Denis, *La Vie Seint Edmund le Rei, poème anglo-normand du XIIe siècle*, ed. by H. Kjellman, (Slatkine Reprints: Geneva, 1945).

5   For an explanation of the implications of the Assize, see Pollock and Maitland, pp. 144-68. The text of the Assize can be found in my appendix, also see William Stubbs, *Select Charters and Other Illustrations of English Constitutional History from the Earliest Times to the Reign of Edward the First* (Oxford: Clarendon Press, 1895).

6   E.A.Francis, 'The Trial in *Lanval*', in *Studies in French Language and Mediaeval Literature presented to Mildred K. Pope* (Manchester: Publications of the University of Manchester, 1939), pp. 119-20.

7   See D.D.R. Owen, *Eleanor of Aquitaine: Queen and Legend*, (Oxford: Blackwell, 1993), pp. 164-65.

8   Geoffrey of Monmouth, *History of the Kings of Britain*, trans. by Lewis Thorpe (Harmondsworth: Penguin Books, 1966), pp. 51-52.

9   Trial by ordeal was the form of judgement favoured by the Church. The Assize favoured more conventional methods of justice and formed part of the famed dispute between Henry II and the Catholic Church.

10   art.cit., p. 2.

11   This is dealt with in much more detail by Bowers, in ibid.

12   On the apparent contradiction in Henry's reforms, see ibid., p. 10, who

cites Paul R. Hyams, 'Trial by Ordeal: The Key to Proof in the Early Common Law', in *On the Laws and Customs of England*, ed. by Morris S. Arnold et al., (Chapel Hill: University of North Carolina Press, 1981).

13   Bowers, op.cit., p. 21.

14   Marie de France, *Lais*, ed. by Alfred Ewert, with an introduction by G.S. Burgess (Bristol: Bristol Classical Press, 1995).

15   W.L. Warren, *Henry II* (London: Eyre Methuen, 1973), p. 221.

16   Pollock and Maitland, op.cit., pp. 146-54.

17   Francis, p. 123, referring to the work of Pollock and Maitland, op. cit.

18   ibid., pp. vii-xii.

19   Marie de France, *Lais*, p. 68.

20   ibid., p. 154. In 1178 a permanent court was established by Henry to enable all the complaints of the kingdom to be heard in his absence. He retained overall control over its decision making. Previously he had been personally responsible for the judgements made. Every citizen had the right for their case to be heard in the king's court, and the king had the right to veto any decision.

21   See Bowers, pp. 8-9, who cites the *Gesta Henrici II*, 2:152, and Henry C. Lea, *Superstition and Force: Essays on the Wager of Law, the Wager of Battle, the Ordeal, Torture* (2nd ed., rev. Philadelphia: the Author, 1870; repr. New York: Greenwood, 1968). The latter notes that Henry II was so satisfied with the Assize of Clarendon that he renewed the policy when these laws were revised at Northampton in 1176.

22   On the question of the dating of the *Lais*, see G.S.Burgess' recent introduction to *Marie de France: Lais*, pp. vii - viii. (See also note 14).

23   See Urban T.Holmes Jnr., 'New Thoughts on Marie de France', *Studies in Philology*, 29 (1952), 1-10; and 'Further on Marie de France', *Symposium*, 3 (1949), 335-39; P.N. Flum, 'Additional Thoughts on Marie de France', *Romance Notes*, 3 (1961), 53-56; Yolande de Pontfarcy, 'Si Marie de France était Marie de Meulan', *Cahiers de Civilisation Médiévale*, 38 (1995), 353-61; and Peter R. Grillo, 'Was Marie de France the Daughter of Waleran II, Count of Meulan?', *Medium Aevum*, 57 (1988), 269-73.

24   Stephen G. Nichols, 'Marie de France's Commonplaces', *Yale French Studies*, 79 (1991), 134-48.

La Légende de l'enfant juif : peinture des personnages, mouvance d'épithètes

Adrian P. Tudor

Cette légende fort populaire au Moyen Age, concernant l'enfant juif qui, jeté dans un fourneau par son père est miraculeusement sauvé des flammes, se trouve dans de nombreux textes médiévaux.[1] Les trois versions les plus anciennes en langue française sont celles d'Adgar,[2] de Gautier de Coinci[3] et de l'auteur anonyme de la *Vie des Pères*.[4] Ce dernier ouvrage est un important recueil de contes pieux et de miracles de la Vierge dont les 42 premiers datent de la première moitié du treizième siècle. La version anglo-normande d'Adgar a retenu notre attention pour son antériorité à toute autre version en français, et celle de Gautier de Coinci, pour l'auteur lui-même, qui reste l'un des plus renommés de son époque. Cependant, c'est surtout dans *Juitel*, deuxième conte de la *Vie des Pères*, que le récit atteint son apogée en raison de la vivacité exceptionnelle et l'extraordinaire détail dramatique du récit. Ce texte contient d'ailleurs des exemples de mouvance d'épithètes qui rajoutent plus de *senefiance* à un conte déjà complexe. Le conte pieux étudie tout naturellement les transgressions, puisqu'une chute est necéssairement le prélude au salut. D'après la mentalité chrétienne médiévale, ce sont les Juifs qui sont responsables de la transgression la plus terrible, c'est-à-dire la crucifixion. C'est par une étude comparative de quelques éléments de ces trois versions de la légende de l'enfant juif que deviendront plus claires les attitudes médiévales, parfois contradictoires, envers les Juifs; et, en étudiant *Juitel* de près, que se révéleront le génie de l'auteur de la *Vie des Pères*, comme celui de son conte.[5]

Adgar composa son conte en Angleterre au cours de la deuxième moitié du XIIe siècle. En fait, *Le Gracial* est en grande partie une traduction d'un *essamplaire* latin:

Cest escrit fine, Deu merci,
Selunc le livre mestre Albri
Ke de Saint Pol oi, de l'almarie   (Epilogue, vv.1-3[6])

Kunstmann note les divers textes latins qui furent à l'origine de
cette source perdue, dont notemment les miracles de Dominique
d'Evesham, d'Anselme le Jeune (?) et surtout de Guillaume de
Malmesbury, et remarque que 'je, Adgar, est un autre... et le
lecteur sera bien avisé de se rappeler que la moitié des *je* du
Gracial sont des *ego* traduits'[7]; mais cet érudit essaie quand
même d'attribuer certains passages à Adgar, tout en soulignant
qu'il n'a pu les retrouver dans les sources latines principales, et
donc admettant implicitement que les passages qu'il cite
auraient bien pu été tirés d'autres sources inconnues. Ce problème
est omniprésent dans les études médiévales, mais nous en faisons
ici la remarque pour souligner le fait que le travail d'Adgar, aussi
talentueux et méritoire soit-il, fut en grande partie un travail
de *traduction*. Sa version de l'histoire est brève:

Un certain Pierre de l'abbaye Saint-Michel de Cluse (Chiusa),
au Piémont, a raconté une histoire déjà très connue. Il s'agit
d'un enfant juif qui accompagne des enfants chrétiens à
l'église un jour de Pâques et qui communie avec eux. A ce
moment-là, le petit Juif remarque une statue de la Vierge et
il croit que cette personne aide le prêtre. Il croit que c'est la
statue qui donne l'hostie. Quand son père apprend qu'il a
communié il est tellement furieux qu'il jette son enfant dans
un fourneau qu'il vient d'apercevoir. La Sainte Vierge protège
l'enfant des flammes. Entre temps, la mère de l'enfant juif se
met à crier à tel point que toute la ville, et Chrétiens et Juifs,
se rassemble autour du fourneau. Tout le monde s'étonne de
voir l'enfant sain et sauf, et ce dernier raconte l'intervention
de la dame qui avait aidé le prêtre à la messe, c'est-à-dire la
Vierge. Le père se fait jeter lui-même dans le fourneau et
périt; et depuis lors, Chrétiens et Juifs de la région dédient
leur vie à Notre Dame.

Dans ce petit miracle de 103 vers Adgar raconte l'essentiel du récit, sans insister sur beaucoup de détails. On est à Pâques, l'enfant juif communie, il raconte tout à son père, ce dernier se met en colère. Ce dernier tombe par hasard sur un fourneau et jette l'enfant dedans, mais Notre-Dame le protège. La mère crie et toute la ville y accourt, l'enfant raconte comment la Vierge l'a sauvé, on tue le père, et tout le monde loue la Vierge. Notons quand même que la mise en scène et la déclaration des autorités occupent un pourcentage important – 8 vers sur 103 – d'un conte court et plein d'action:

> En Biture, une cité,
> Avint un fait mult renumé
> Ke uns moines cunter soleit
> Ki de Cluse moines esteit.
> Cil moines ert Pieres numez,
> De bone vie mult loez.
> Bien dist ke il en la cité fud
> E k'il i vit ceste vertu.   (Miracle 14 du *Gracial*, vv.1-8)

Nous ne rencontrons le père qu'au moment où la colère le pousse vers l'infanticide, et il n'y a aucun lien logique entre lui et le fourneau. D'ailleurs, il est possible que le motif de la statue offre à Adgar la possibilité d'éviter un péché de la part du prêtre: donner la communion à un Juif non-baptisé, cela n'aurait-il pas représenté un crime contre la loi de Dieu? En plus, cet enfant va à l'église *pur enveiser* (v.18) et il se fait emmener par les enfants chrétiens. Adgar ne présente donc pas d'arguments solides pour que la Vierge sauve l'enfant juif, à l'exception du fait qu'il va à l'église et y communie. (Comme nous allons le voir, l'auteur de la *Vie des Pères* prend grand soin de peindre l'enfant juif sous un jour favorable avant de raconter le miracle). Or, pour revenir au propos principal de cette étude, Adgar – ou bien ses sources latines – ne se préoccupe pas des détails des épithètes, son conte étant de toute façon très court. Il n'y a pas de noms propres dans cette version du conte, mis à part le moine (Pierre) qui avait raconté l'histoire, la ville de Bourges, *Pasches*, Jésus et la Sainte Vierge, c'est-à-dire, aucun protagoniste humain. Les personnages d'Adgar restent anonymes. La façon dont Adgar décrit ses personnages est donc très importante, mais en fait nous n'en apprenons pas grand-chose. L'enfant juif est *fiz a un jueu* (v.13), *li enfes al jueu* (v.22) et *fiz al jueu* (v.26), ou bien *li enfes* ou *l'enfant* (vv.17, 31, 40, 45, 54, 56, 70). Ces termes sont tous assez neutres. Notons quand même qu'Adgar ne le décrit jamais comme *jueu*, ce qui établit une sorte de distance entre l'enfant et la foi juive. Quant à son père, méchant représentant du peuple juif, Adgar n'en dit pas trop: *sis peres* (vv.32, 39) devient *le giu* (v.89) quand la ville apprend sa félonie, puis le *pere al enfant* (v.91) quand il est pris par la foule, et dans le four il meurt enfin comme *li dolenz* (v.94). Il y a ici une certaine mouvance – la dégradation *sis peres* → *li dolenz* – mais le conte est trop court et le personnage du père trop peu présent – nommé 5 fois seulement – pour y voir un schéma défini de la part de l'auteur. Il faut noter à ce propos que dans une enluminure du XIVe siècle – c'est-à-dire de deux siècles postérieure à Adgar et un siècle après Gautier de Coinci et la *Vie des Pères*, mais qui raconte toujours la même légende – il y a une différence physique entre le père et le fils: 'Le père est nettement orientalisé [...] mais son fils, qui reçoit l'eucharistie avec les autres enfants, [...] rien ne le distingue comme enfant juif.'[8] Dans nos trois versions du miracle, les traits distinctifs du Juif sont plutôt des caractéristiques – père anti-chrétien et violent – que des différences physiques, même si l'enfant chez Gautier a une apparence physique exceptionnelle, et si il y a une sorte de métamorphose, voire tranfiguration, après la communion de l'enfant juif dans *Juitel*. Il nous semble qu'Adgar, comme pour les enlumineurs dont parle Blumenkranz, voulait souligner non pas les traits éthniques du père mais plutôt 'une idée théologique en rapport avec le problème du salut'.[9] En ce qui concerne les autres personnages, la nomenclature n'est guère plus révélatrice: la mère de l'enfant est simplement *la mere a l'enfant* (v.55) ou *la mere a ceste enfant* (v.63), et elle crie après son fils *Cume custume est de mere pieuse, / Seient crestienes u jieues* (vv.57-8); les enfants chrétiens sont décrits ainsi au vers 11, et ne sont plus que *les enfants* au vers 18. A deux reprises les chrétiens et les juifs sont même décrits ensemble:

> Tute la gent de la cuntree,
> Crestiens, gieus ensement   (vv.66-7)

> Tuit ensemble en la cuntree,
> crestien, jieu ensement   (vv.96-7)

On peut donc en conclure que les noms ont peu d'importance pour Adgar – ceci est un conte dont la courte durée ne permet d'ailleurs pas le développement de motifs 'littéraires' (ce qui n'enlève rien, bien sûr, à l'intérêt de ce petit miracle). Enfin, nous signalons également l'absence d'antisémitisme chez Adgar. D'après ce conte, Bourges est une ville où les chrétiens et les juifs vivent ensemble avec bonheur,[10] et il n'y a pas d'exclamations véritablement antisémites:

> Avint mut gloriusment
> Ke enfant crestien alerent
> A mustier e od els menerent
> Un enfant, fiz a un jeue,
> Ki folement reclaiment Deu   (vv.10-14)

> La gent vers le giu se pristrent,
> De li malfere s'entremistrent   (vv.89-90)

A la fin du conte les chrétiens et les juifs *servirent Deu omnipotent / et sa mere, la dame sainte / Ki fist e fait merveilles meinte* (vv.98-100), mais Adgar ne parle pas de leur conversion: son conte démontre l'amour et la pitié de la Vierge plutôt que la vilenie du peuple juif. En effet, Adgar composait ses miracles dans un climat apparement moins hostile vis-à-vis des Juifs que celui de Gautier et de l'auteur de la *Vie des Pères*.[11] Certes, les relations entre les deux confessions étaient loin d'être faciles, mais les historiens modernes s'efforcent de peindre une image moins sombre que celle, traditionnelle, d'un antisémitisme fanatique (ou bien d'un 'anti-israélisme forcené'[12]): 'If the legal status of Jews were our sole criterion, the picture of their relations with medieval Christians would need to be painted in very sombre hues. Laws, however, were made to be broken, and the actual relations between Jews and Christians were for long periods far different to those which the Church Councils and, to a less degree, the Jewish ritual code tended to produce. Jews and Christians often defied the laws which sought to keep them asunder.'[13]

Ceci dit, il est important de se rappeler le fait qu'Adgar fut poète *anglo-normand*. Or le 12e siècle connut lui aussi des excès d'antisémitisme, surtout en Angleterre. Les communautés juives n'y étaient pas très nombreuses, mais leur influence financière croissante auprès des rois d'Angleterre, et les sentiments anti-juifs inspirés par les croisades, y provoquèrent des vagues de violence. C. Roth souligne les conditions favorables des Juifs en Angleterre sous le règne d'Henri II (1154-89), notant au passage que 'there was no pretext [...] for Englishmen to imitate the massacres which intermittently continued on the continent'.[14] Pourtant R.B. Dobson constate que 'within England also, although less dramatically than in northern France, there is evidence of growing hostility towards the Jews during the 1170s and 1180s'.[15] Les calomnies antisémites contre le Juif assoiffé de sang se propagèrent rapidement après la mort de Guillaume de Norwich en 1144. Même si de nombreux habitants de Norwich ne voulaient pas croire que Guillaume fût victime d'un rite meurtrier juif, 'within a generation [...] it seems likely that large sections of the English population had been predisposed to accept ritual murder accusations at their face value.'[16] Même si le *boy-martyr* chrétien le plus célèbre est le saint Hugues le Petit de Lincoln, qui trouva la mort en 1155[17] et qu'évoquera Chaucer dans *The Prioress' Tale*, le culte persistait bel et bien jusqu'à la fin du 12e siècle: Harold de Gloucester (1168), Robert de Bury St Edmunds (1181) et Adam de Bristol (vers 1183) furent tous trois canonisés grâce à la conviction populaire que les Juifs les avaient sacrifiés. Cette ambiance d'hostilité envers les Juifs – politique, économique[18] et populaire – fut entretenue par les décrets de Latran III (dans lesquels le pape Alexandre III [1159-81] indiqua les dangers des rapports sexuels entre

Chrétiens et Juifs), et par les assauts meurtriers qui ravagèrent
les communautés juives en Europe (surtout après le massacre de
Blois en 1171). En effet, Dobson rajoute que 'the series of savage
acts of persecution against Jewish communities in northern
France [...] until at least the atrocity at Bray-sur-Seine in March
1191 seems to represent a particularly significant and sinister
development in the history of European anti-semitism. The
effect within England of these gratuitously sadistic massacres, at a
period in this country's history when relations with the north of
France were unusually close, is bound to have been considerable'.[19]
Adgar vivait donc à une époque où les habitants de l'Angleterre
devenaient de plus en plus hostile envers les Juifs. Peu après la
composition du *Gracial*, au moment du couronnement de
Richard I, il y eut des émeutes anti-juives dans de nombreux
centres urbains: 'A phase of vindictive Jew-baiting led almost
inevitably to murder and then to a concerted attempt by the
mob at the complete extermination, usually by arson, of the
urban Jewries'.[20] En mars 1190, le soir du *Shabbat ha-Gadol*, eut
lieu à York le plus meurtrier des massacres, où quelques 150
Juifs se donnèrent la mort plutôt que de se voir livrés à la haine
de la foule.

Il nous semble utile, avant notre étude des textes de
Gautier et de la *Vie des Pères*, de nous rappeler les décrets antisémites, de notoriété publique, de Latran IV (1215):

- no.67 se proclamait contre les 'lourdes injustices' pratiquées
  par le Juifs et les obligeait à 's'acquitter envers les églises
  des dîmes et offrandes qu'elles recevaient'.

- no.68 préscrivait aux Juifs de se distinguer par le port d'un
  habit différent pour éviter les unions sexuelles entre Juifs et
  Chrétiens, et interdisait aux Juifs de 'paraître en public' les
  jours de lamentation / le dimanche de la Passion.

- no.69 interdisait qu'on confie des charges publiques aux
  Juifs;

- no.70 rappellait qu'après leur bâpteme les Juifs convertis ne pouvaient pas retourner à des rites judaïques;

- no.71, en prêchant la IV Croisade, supprimait les intérêts sur les dettes des croisés depuis leur départ jusqu'à leur mort / leur retour. [21]

Comme nous allons le voir, ces décrets devaient influencer, peu à peu, tous les aspects de la vie des Juifs en Occident, y compris dans les oeuvres littéraires.

Les Miracles de Nostre Dame de Gautier de Coinci connurent un grand succès et sont conservés dans de nombreux manuscrits. Composé entre 1218 et 1233, ce recueil ne représente plus une traduction assez littérale de sources latines mais plutôt un ensemble de contes racontés d'une façon personnelle et personnalisée.[22] Gautier voue une fervente dévotion à la Vierge et décrit ses interventions miraculeuses dans le monde du treizième siècle. Son mîracle *De l'enfant a un gìu qui se crestìena* compte 142 vers pleins de détails supplémentaires par rapport à la succincte version d'Adgar:

A Bourges, le fils d'un verrier juif est le plus intelligent et le plus beau de tous les enfants juifs. Estimé par les écoliers de la ville[23], il souffre des corrections fréquentes que lui inflige son père. A Pâques, le petit juif fait comme ses camarades et communie à l'église; mais, au lieu du prêtre, c'est la bellissime statue d'une dame, la tête voilée et portant un enfant, qui prend l'hostie et la donne à l'enfant juif. Ravi de cette vision de douceur et de beauté, il rentre à la maison le visage rayonnant. Quand son père le voit si beau, il lui demande d'où il vient, et l'enfant répond honnêtement : il vient de communier avec ses camarades écoliers. Pris de colère, le père jette son fils à terre, et lui dit qu'il est tombé dans le piège des chrétiens et qu'il va le punir de façon exemplaire. Il prend l'enfant par les cheveux et le jette dans son fourneau; ensuite, pour mieux faire brûler son fils, il cherche du bois sec et remplit le fourneau. Les cris désespérés de la mère de l'enfant attirent une foule de plus de dix mille personnes. Tout le monde s'étonne de voir, en ouvrant le fourneau, que le petit juif n'est pas seulement sain et sauf mais couché à même la braise comme s'il était sur un lit. Son père, lui, est roué de coups et jeté à son tour dans le fourneau. Alors, les flammes se raniment et le père meurt. L'enfant raconte comment la dame qu'il avait vu à l'église l'a couvert de son voile et l'a sauvé du feu et de la fumée et comment, se sentant si bien, il s'est endormi. On baptise l'enfant et sa mère ainsi que de nombreux juifs qui avaient assisté au miracle. Ils serviront la Vierge toute leur vie.

Comme de coutume, Gautier remplit son conte de détails humains et de commentaires sociaux. Moins soucieux qu'Adgar de préciser ses sources – *ce truis lisant* (v.1)[24] – il se jette tout de suite dans le récit, expliquant que le Juif était verrier (v.2). En ce qui concerne la vraisemblance, ce fait rend l'action de ce miracle plus satisfaisante que dans la version d'Adgar. (En effet, comme remarque Benjamin de Tudèle vers la fin du XIIe siècle, la fabrication du verre était l'un des métiers pratiqués par les communautés juives.[25]) Mais, Grayzel note que 'local councils [...] forbade the public appearance of Jews during Holy Week, from Friday to Sunday inclusive. They also forbade Jews to do any public work on Sundays and holidays, for the work itself was interpreted as a blasphemous infraction of the day sacred to Christianity.'[26] Or nous sommes à Pâques, et le fourneau du Juif est déjà allumé. Cela veut-il dire que le père travaillait en public, et se trouvait donc en violation d'éventuels réglements locaux? Notons aussi les détails 'humains' que rajoute Gautier: le père qui court après son fils et le couvre de baisers (vv.38-40);[27] sa cruauté quand il apprend que son fils a communié (vv.47-63); la souffrance de la mère qui croit son enfant brûlé vif (vv.64-69); et le sort douloureux mais mérité du père (vv.84-88). Gautier fournit également des détails 'surnaturels': la beauté sublime de la statue de la Vierge (vv.20-34); le changement physique chez le garçon juif (vv.36-37 – comme dans *Juitel* et dans l'iconographie médiévale, la beauté du garçon a une valeur symbolique); le miracle (vv. 76-80); et ce même miracle raconté par l'enfant (vv. 94-104). Quant à la peinture des personnages, Gautier décrit à la fois les caractères et les actions; et la mouvance onomastique, que nous allons étudier dans la version de la *Vie des Pères*, y figure aussi, mais elle n'est pas très subtile et plutôt passagère. La mère de l'enfant juif est toujours un personnage très neutre : le lecteur ne la rencontre que quand elle est témoin des actions horribles de son mari,

> La mere aqueurt, qui brait et crie   (v. 64)

et nous la retrouvons au dénouement du conte:

> Sa mere aprés lui se baptoie
> Ou non de Sainte Trinité.   (vv. 112-13)

Au demeurant, ces vers ne sont pas sans ironie, quand on se souvient du caractère et du sort de son mari! La mère ne joue donc qu'un rôle secondaire. Son mari, lui, est l'un des protagonistes du conte, mais Gautier ne recherche pas le suspense en le nommant, dès le deuxième vers, *un giu verrier mesdisant*. [28] Une fois *uns gius* tout court (v. 5), c'est plus à travers les actions de ce personnage que le lecteur découvre sa personnalité. Par exemple, il est violent envers son fils:

> La char, qu'avoit tenrete et mole,
> Sovent ses peres li batoit
> Por ce qu'avec aus [*les écoliers*] s'embatoit   (vv. 12-14)

Bien sûr, selon Gautier le fait d'être Juif était déjà accablant,[29] et les actions de ce Juif ne servent qu'à renforcer un sentiment antisémite acharné. La tendresse que montre le père en voyant son fils plus-beau-que-jamais est un outil dramatique qui présente un contraste frappant avec le vrai caractère du personnage. Son fils l'appelle alors *biaus pere* (v. 42), mais les rapports entre père et fils ne seront plus les mêmes. Le fils a en effet péché contre le père et contre la loi juive (comme vue par

Gautier), le père le déteste déjà et est entièrement conscient de ses actions:

Tu iez cheüs en maus liens!
En despit de toz crestiens
Et en viltance de lor loi
Grans merveilles ferai de toi!   (vv.51-54)

Notons en passant l'ironie de ce dernier vers: en effet, le père n'a pas tort, puisque son fils voit bel et bien une merveille, mais une merveille différente de celle à laquelle songe le père ! Ici l'auteur répète le mot *merveilles,* l'ayant employé au début du miracle:

Or entendez fines merveilles.   (v.3)

En reprenant ce terme, Gautier crée un effet de 'résonnance' très ironique et très frappant.

Ayant déjà décrit ce qui s'est passé à l'église, Gautier met maintenant Chrétiens et Juifs en opposition. Le père devient *li chiens* (v.62) quand il est en train d'alimenter le fourneau, terme répété la dernière fois qu'il est nommé directement par l'auteur:

L'enragié chien mout tost saisirent   (v.84)

Le motif du Juif-chien-diable se trouve dans la Bible.[30] Le chien (et la hyène et le loup et le renard) étaient impurs et symbolisent dans l'Ancien Testament les ennemis de l'Homme et de Dieu. Pourtant, dans l'iconographie chrétienne, le chien est souvent symbole de la fidélité et figure sur de nombreux gisants médiévaux. Dans les Bestiaires on trouve également une image plutôt positive de cet animal; nous remarquons pourtant que le chien retourne à son vomissement et ainsi symbolise 'cil qui repairent a lor pechié dont il eurent confés'.[31] Cette idée reprend presque mot-à-mot quelques versets bibliques (Proverbes 26 : 11). D'ailleurs, Block fait mention d'un miséricord à Aarschot où se trouve l'image d'un Juif qui embrasse un chien: 'The legend told of Jews who kissed dogs and ate them, since they were forbidden to eat pork.'[32] Notons aussi, en passant, le parallèle entre les sons non-humains – l'aboiement d'un chien, le langage guttural des arabes, les sons peu familiers de l'hébreu – et le diable. J. Voisenet note que 'les bruits et les sons inarticulés, comme ce qui est inorganisé, appartiennent au monde du désordre sur lequel Satan étend son emprise.'[33] Nous retrouvons cette même image dans la Bible à propos de ceux qui complotent contre Dieu :

> Ils reviennent le soir, ils grondent comme le chien (Psaume 59 : 7)

Chez Dante, ce sont les démons et les damnés qui aboient :

> Cerbero, fiera crudele e diversa
> con tre gole caninamente latra
> sopra la gente che quivi è sommersa   (*Inf.*, vi, 13-15)

> urlar li fa la pioggia come cani   (*Inf.*, vi, 19)[34]

En fait, l'image du chien convient très bien dans le conte de Gautier (et aussi dans *Juitel*): l'auteur nous a déjà montré que le père est capable d'affection envers son fils, mais celui-ci retombe aussitôt dans le péché, juste comme le chien qui retourne à ce qu'il a vomi. D'ailleurs, d'après Pierre de Beauvais, la hyène, cousin du chien, symbolise les fils d'Israël: 'Cesti sanble les fius Israel qui au commencement servirent Dieu et apres se donerent es delices du monde et a luxure et continerent les mahomeries; et por ce dit li prophetes que signagogue resanble cele orde beste.'[35] Ce n'est pas seulement dans la littérature édifiante que l'on trouve cette image; Chrétien de Troyes, entre autres, s'en sert:

> Li faus juïf par lor envie,
> c'on devroit tüer come chiens,
> Firent als mal et nos biens
> Quant il en la crois le leverent;
> Als perdirent et nos salverent...(*Perceval*, vv.6292-96[36])

Enfin, il est intéressant de noter que, chez Gautier comme chez
Adgar, le père est brûlé vif. Il n'y a pas de changement dans son
état depuis le début du miracle, pas de mouvance d'épithètes, et
la tendresse qu'il montre envers son fils, suivie tout de suite
d'une tentative de meurtre, peint une image fort négative de ce
personnage.

Quant à l'enfant lui-même, Gautier le décrit comme *un
giutel* (vv.5, 24, 42, 50) et ensuite comme *l'enfant* (vv.56. 76, 89).
Le diminutif le distance de la foi juive, mais c'est surtout dans
son caractère et ses actions que le lecteur comprend qu'il s'agit
ici d'un Juif atypique:

> Mielz entendant et mout plus bel
> De touz les autres giuetiaus   (vv.6-7)

Mieux encore, il est apprécié des enfants chrétiens :

> Por ce qu'il ert plaisans et biaus
> Tuit li clerçon de la cité
> Le tenoient en grant chierté.   (vv.8-10)

Il est beau physiquement,

> La char, qu'il avoit tentrete et mole   (v.12)

d'autant plus après que la Vierge l'ait béni :

> Toute sa face resclaira
> De la grant joie qu'il avoit.   (vv.36-37)

Le lecteur est témoin de la haine qu'éprouve le père à
l'égard de l'enfant (vv.46-54) et de la cruelle violence dont ce
dernier est victime (vv.55-63). Ce ne peut être qu'une bonne
chose qu'on se fasse haïr d'un Juif...[37] Gautier ne laisse traîner
aucun doute quant au fait que l'enfant, bénéficiaire d'un miracle
si glorieux, est digne de ce qui lui arrive. Le père, lui, mérite bien

sa mort douloureuse. La véhémence de l'appel de Gautier à l'extermination des Juifs contraste vivement avec le ton du miracle d'Adgar. Dans son étude sur la communauté juive nîmoise, J. Simon note un processus de dégradation des conditions favorables des juifs de cette ville vers le début du XIIIe siècle: 'les populations [chrétiennes] perdirent peu à peu les sentiments de tolérance et de fraternité dont elles avaient été animées jusqu'alors envers les juifs',[38] ce changement de sentiment ayant été causé par la propagande de l'Eglise et la croisade contre les Albigeois. Simon ajoute que 'l'Eglise força le peuple, malgré lui, à s'éloigner du Juif, à le considérer comme un être abject'.[39] Donc, entre l'époque d'Adgar et celle de Gautier de Coinci et de la *Vie des Pères*, il y a eu un changement d'attitude et de politique: 'The powerful position of the Church in the first half of the Thirteenth Century made the western Church cognizant of its unity under the Catholic Church. In this unity the Jews found no place, in fact they seemed a source of danger to it. Innocent III thereupon gave them a place outside of Christian Society, marking their exclusion by means of the Badge. Relentlessly he and his successors drove them into the place assigned them. It was a policy which eminently fitted in with the other political and economic conditions, and was therefore enthusiastically adopted and carried to its logical conclusions.'[40]

Il n'y a pas de nomenclature en mouvance chez Gautier, et les caractéristiques des personnages se révèlent dans leurs actions plutôt que par l'intervention directe de l'auteur. Gautier ne s'intéresse pas à la *motivation* de l'enfant juif. Il se concentre sur le miracle et l'après-miracle, et aussi sur le personnage du père : à la fin du miracle, quelques 14 vers – soit 10% du miracle – sont consacrés à un appel à l'extermination des Juifs. Ce miracle démontre la pitié de la Vierge, certes, mais Gautier voulait-il que le lecteur retienne le fait que même le plus mauvais pécheur peut s'attendre au salut éternel – ce qui n'est pas tout à fait le cas dans son conte, puisque le *guitel* est distancé de la foi juive – ou bien, tout bonnement, que *Vers aus sui durs si durement / Que, s'iere rois, por toute roie / Un a durer n'en endurroie* (vv. 140-142)?

Juitel, deuxième conte de la *Vie des Pères*, est plus ou moins
contemporain de la version de Gautier de Coinci.[41] Composée en
trois temps par au moins deux clercs, ce recueil de 74 contes
pieux reste une riche source de miracles et de légendes largement
inexplorée par les philologues. Comme la plupart des contes que
contient la première *Vie des Pères*[42], *Juitel* est précédé d'un
prologue et suivi d'un épilogue, tous les deux importants,
réciproquement de 71 et de 22 vers.[43] Mais, même si on ne tient
pas compte de ces vers, le récit proprement dit est toujours deux
fois plus long que les versions d'Adgar et de Gautier, faisant
quelques 271 vers :

> En Egypte vit un verrier juif qui a une femme et un
> enfant de sept ans. Ce dernier n'aime pas les enfants juifs,
> préférant jouer avec les enfants chrétiens[44]. Son père
> désapprouve et le bat en conséquence, mais l'enfant continue
> à jouer avec les enfants chrétiens qu'il aime tant. A Pâques les
> enfants chrétiens sont pleins de joie parce qu'ils vont
> communier, mais leur camarade juif est triste, croyant qu'ils
> iront à l'église sans lui. Ils promettent de l'emmener avec eux
> et le petit Juif en est très content et très excité. Le lendemain
> il les accompagne à l'église et communie avec eux, mais
> quand il rentre à la maison son père est soucieux : l'enfant
> s'est levé et est sorti sans lui en parler, et maintentant il rentre
> radieux. Il demande à son fils de s'expliquer, et l'enfant
> raconte tout. Le père, furieux, veut se venger. Il jette son fils
> dans son fourneau et ferme la porte; cependant, à son insu, Dieu
> protège l'enfant. Entre-temps, la mère crie désespérément et ses
> voisins arrivent; à leur grande surprise, à l'ouverture du
> fourneau, ils trouvent l'enfant sain et sauf. Ils amènent
> l'enfant à son père et celui-ci se repent, loue Dieu et dit qu'il
> veut se convertir; avec lui et sa femme, beaucoup d'autres
> Juifs deviennent chrétiens. Son fils reçoit une bonne éducation
> et devient prêtre.

Nous ne sommes plus à Bourges mais en Egypte, comme ailleurs
dans la *Vie des Pères* (n'oublions pas que le recueil se veut inspiré

des *Vitae Patrum...*), et il n'existe plus cette ambiance tolérante que le lecteur retrouve chez Adgar. Cette version de la légende apporte beaucoup d'éléments nouveaux, surtout au niveau de la peinture des personnages. La longueur du conte permet à l'auteur de peindre ses personnages, et donc d'ajouter à l'aspect 'humain' du récit. C'est ainsi que l'auteur rend ses personnages moins anonymes, même s'il s'agit d'un genre où, dans l'ensemble, les personnages ne sont pas nommés. Il lui est possible de déployer également les noms d'une façon précise selon la situation: Globalement, cet usage suggère une mouvance d'épithètes voulue, outil littéraire qui donne au conte une autre couche de *senefiance*.

La mère reste un personnage assez neutre, mais notons toutefois sa réaction humaine au sort de son fils. L'auteur ne la considère pas comme une Juive :

> Come mere, ki ne set feindre
> la dolor qu'il covient plaindre...   (vv.589-90)[45]

En effet, l'auteur ne parle jamais de 'la mère du juif', mais de 'la mère' tout simplement. Les enfants juifs (v.424) et chrétiens (vv.435, 465) sont qualifiés de ces adjectifs par nécessité. Déjà, au cinquième vers du conte, l'auteur commence à décrire la *motivation* de l'enfant juif et prépare la *justification* du miracle à travers sa description du garçon :

> Cil enfançons cure n'avoit
> des juïteax, ainz reperoit
> avec les enfans crestïens.   (vv.433-35)

Au début du conte, le fils n'est pas Juif du tout, mais *enfançons* (v.433) ou *fil del juïf* (v.463) et a, symboliquement, 7 ans.[46] Qui plus est, ce n'est pas seulement une question de symbolisme chrétien. Innocent IV allait légiférer, en 1246, contre les baptêmes forcés des enfants juifs : *Prohibeas etiam quantum in te fuerit ne in baptizandis eorum filiif ipsis violentia inferatur, cum*

sacrificium voluntarium esse debeat, non coactum.[47] Or, Erler a noté
que les enfants juifs pouvaient se faire baptiser sans la permission
de leurs parents à partir de 7 ans.[48] Une seule fois l'auteur
désigne-t-il l'enfant comme *juïtel* :

> Par l'usaige et per art set l'en
> la raison del monde et le sen:
> sans le juïtel ne savoient
> rien fere, quant il ne l'avoient;
> et cil toz esgarez estoit
> d'autre part, quant il nes veoit. (vv.471-76)

Ici deux choses distancient l'enfant de la foi juive: le diminutif et
le contexte. Nous sommes toujours au début du conte et l'auteur
est toujours en train de faire la mise en scène; il n'a pas encore
décrit le miracle. Il donne l'impression que les enfants chrétiens
parlent eux-mêmes par l'intermédiaire du narrateur. Ensuite,
l'enfant est à trois reprises *li juïs*. Chaque usage de ce terme nous
semble intentionnel ou, au moins, rationnel:

> Longuement lor amor maintindrent
> et tant k'a une Pasque vindrent
> que li enfant s'ajoïssoient
> de ce qu'acommigier devoient
> le jor de Paske, par matin.
> *Li juïs tint le chief enclin*
> et dist: 'Iroiz i vos sanz moi?
> - Nenil, firent il tuit, avoi !' (vv.477-84, nos italiques)

La valeur symbolique de cette scène est évidente – un Juif, à
Pâques, la tête baissée et exclu des cérémonies, du sacrement
et de la joie qui accompagnent cette fête chrétienne... La tête
baissée ne signifie pas seulement la honte mais aussi la soumission.[49]
Alors, l'enfant juif devient ici un personnage symbolique; et le
coté humain de ce personnage ne fait que rajouter au symbolisme:
son inquiétude est mise en opposition avec la joie et l'excitation
de ses camarades chrétiens. Mais c'est aussi un enfant, et il ne

veut pas être exclu. En employant le terme *juïs*, l'auteur donne à ce passage plusieurs niveaux de *senefiance*. La deuxième occurence de l'emploi du terme *juïs* se trouve quelques vers plus loin:

> Mout s'en parti *li juïf liez*,
> mout fu la nuit esmanvelliez
> por ce ke perdre ne voloit
> ce ke l'en promis li avoit.   (vv.499-502, nos italiques)

Voici un rare exemple d'une application positive du nom 'Juif'.[50] Il est peu commun de trouver l'adjectif *liez* qualifiant le substantif *juif*;[51] le lecteur se serait attendu normalement à un adjectif ou à un contexte négatif (*un ort juïf vil et malvais* [v.659]; *quant Jhesucrist crucifierent / en Mont Calvaire* [vv.443-44]).[52] Il y a peut-être un peu d'ironie dans le fait que l'enfant sait qu'il va à l'église avec ses amis; de toute façon, l'emploi de cet adjectif, tout en rappelant le lecteur de la polémique Juif / Chrétien, distancie encore plus cet enfant juif de la foi juive / du peuple juif. Le troisième et dernier cas où l'auteur nomme l'enfant *li juïs* est quand il est à l'église:

> Li juis avant se ficha
> come anfes ki tot vuet veoir
> et qui de tot vuet essaier.(vv.516-18)

La scène nécessite, encore une fois, l'emploi du terme *juis*: sur le plan dramatique / logique, parce qu'un enfant chrétien n'aurait pas eu les mêmes sentiments; et sur le plan didactique, puisque l'auteur peut mettre en contraste une fois de plus la foi chrétienne et la foi juive. Il y a aussi une certaine notion symbolique dans le fait que le terme 'juif' est employé par *trois fois* vis-à-vis du juitel. L'auteur avait peut-être l'intention de porter un jugement de valeur en employant le terme *juif*, terme qui qualifie non pas l'individu – l'enfant – mais la foi juive. L'enfant n'est plus dans ce récit ni *juif* ni *l'enfant de juif*, mais simplement *filz* ou *enfans*.[53] A la fin du conte, cet ancien Juif, que Dieu de *son juïsme eslava* (v.678),[54] devient *provoirre* (v.688) et, par

conséquent, *proudons* (v.669), ce qui ne fut pas une mince affaire
pour un Juif converti à une époque d'antisémitisme acharné.

Le personnage du fils est l'enjeu d'une subtile mouvance de
nomenclature, plus claire encore chez son père. Au début du
conte c'est un *juif* (vv.430, 431) *qui voirres fesoit*. Ce n'est que
quand ce personnage 'devient' le père d'un enfant juif déjà connu
du lecteur et méritant son affection – le lecteur sachant déjà que
l'enfant n'aimait que les camarades chrétiens – que l'auteur
fournit plus de détails : d'abord, il est *anciens*[55] (v.436) et violent
(vv.437-8), puis, d'une manière indirecte, un chien :

> entre juïf et crestïen
> s'entrament comme chat et chien.   (vv.439-40)

Alors que l'auteur parle du père il se fourvoye et son récit se
transforme en monologue / sermon contre les juifs, critique
furieuse qui s'attache tout naturellement à ce personnage fictif
du père.[56] *Bien est drois ke nos les haions* (v.441) parce qu'ils ont
tué Jésus *per lor grant fellonie* (v.445); ils ne croient pas aux saints
sacrements et sont donc déjà damnés :

> [...] il gaaignent le juïse
> d'enfer, desoz, en la sentine,
> en l'ordure, en la puantine
> qui toz jors es nez lor purra,
> et en feu ki toz jors durra.
> La sont dampné et la sont vil,
> quar il sont de diable fil.
> Qui les aime et ki les maintient,
> Damedeu por enemi tient...   (vv.450-58)

Il y a donc une mouvance dans la réception / perception
d'un terme neutre : avant ce discours virulent, l'auteur racontait
l'histoire d'*un juif qui voirres fesoit (v.430)*; maintenant, quant il
dit qu'*au fil del juïf m'en revieg (v.463)*, il parle du même personnage
mais avec un courant sous-jacent qui le condamne d'autant plus

fortement. Notons l'ironie dans le fait que le père croit qu'il s'agit d'un complot chrétien (vv.534-7), de même que chez Gautier où il croit que le fils est tombé dans un piège chrétien (v.51). Cette dégradation d'estime continue sur deux plans : celui de l'action – il jette son fils dans le fourneau – et de l'épithète – il est *comme chiens sanz foi, sale et vil* (v.537). Non seulement un *chiens*, le père est *sanz foi*, péché courant dans la *Vie des Pères*, et fils du diable[57] : ainsi répond-il exactement à la description des Juifs qui se trouve dans le discours 'hors texte' de l'auteur. Les paroles du père – il justifie ses actions en défendant *nostre loi* (v.562)[58] – et ses actions violentes – *l'enfant per les temples geta / et de l'estouper ce hasta, / que funs ne chalor n'en issist* (vv.571-3) – sont fidèles, elles aussi, au juif typique déjà présenté : c'est un diable. Le père est au plus bas à ce point, mais, contrairement aux juifs d'Adgar et de Gautier, il ne lui est pas réservé de mort douloureuse. La *Vie des Pères* est un recueil de contes qui illustrent le fait qu'aucun péché – inceste, infanticide, meurtre, reniement de la foi – n'est si grand que Dieu ne veuille le pardonner, pour peu que l'on soit un pénitent vraiment sincère. Il est, donc, tout à fait logique que cette dénonciation véhémente des Juifs soit suivie d'un exemple du pardon d'un Juif-pécheur, et c'est exactement ce qui arrive au père. Quant les voisins lui amènent l'enfant sauvé, le père se repent sur-le-champ. En pleurant – signe de contrition et de foi sincère – il se voue à Dieu avec éloquence, puis reconnaît que son ancien état de Juif ne le menait pas sur la bonne voie :

> Sire, dont vos est ce venu
> que de moi vos est sovenu,
> d'*un larron usurier sanz foi*,
> qui trop a vesu a besloi,
> d'*un ort juif vil et malvais* ?   (vv.635-39, *nos italiques*)

Le père, parlant de lui-même, se distancie de son ancien moi. S'il parle à la troisième personne, c'est parce qu'il se traite de *larron usurier*. Or, au début du conte l'auteur parlait d'un verrier, métier pratiqué par quelques communautés juives

mais qui ne fut pas forcément un 'métier de juifs'. Tout au début
du conte, le père est, comme nous l'avons vu, un personnage assez
neutre.[59] Après les événéments subséquents, il perd cette
neutralité et endosse le rôle d'un Juif infame, dangereux, dia-
bolique. S'il se traite alors d'usurier, c'est pour identifier son
ancien moi à un stéréotype largement répandu. Cette mouvance
des métiers, *verrier* → *usurier*, est le miroir de la réalité, puisque
les Juifs se voyaient interdits des métiers dans la première moitié
du treizième siècle.[60] Son repentir marque un tournant logique,
[61] et il est indirectement responsable de la conversion d'autres
citadins juifs:

> Ensi son affere atorna
> que cel jor se crestïna
>
> c'onques n'i quist delaiement,
> et fist tot son proposement,
> et maint juïf avec lui furent
> que Deu por le miracle crurent.(vv.655-62)

Juitel contient d'autres éléments intéressants qui le distinguent
des deux autres versions traitées ici. La peinture des personnages
est enrichie par la mouvance onomastique, mais l'auteur donne
aussi beaucoup de petits détails qui en eux-mêmes créent des
images claires et humaines. L'enfant juif est chef de la bande
d'enfants (v.473) – détail potentiellement symbolique; il est
triste que ses camarades aillent faire quelque chose sans lui
(vv.482ff); il est tellement excité qu'il n'arrive pas à s'endormir
la veille du jour de Pâques (v.500); il quitte la maison quand ses
parents, très occupés, ne guettaient pas (autre détail symbolique);
à l'église il veut tout voir (vv.516-18); il ne sait pas mentir
(v.551);[62] et il explique le miracle d'après la logique d'un enfant
innocent (*quar cil si est avueques moi | que j'ai hui mengié au mostier*,
vv.606-7). La violence et la cruauté du père sont également très
vives: à l'intérieur du fourneau *li voirres boilloit* (v.570); il prend
l'enfant par les tempes (v.571) et ferme rapidement la porte du
fourneau (vv.572-3); et l'enfant est découvert sain et sauf

entouré de *voirre ki lez lui boilloit* (v.602). Nous remarquons également que le père ne pouvait pas voir l'intérieur du fourneau si la porte était fermée (v.583). L'auteur, lui, est conscient de son art. Il sait, par exemple, qu'il faut revenir au conte (463-4) après son sermon anti-juif, et il crée une ambiance merveilleuse après l'ouverture de la porte du fourneau qui suggère que le miracle continue (vv.610-11). Enfin, notons l'appel à la fin du conte à la croisade contre l'hérésie (vv.683-98) : selon l'auteur, juifs, *Populican* et *Abijoiz* (v.685) sont les mêmes,[63] puisqu'ils professent tous une fausse religion (le conte qui suit *Juitel*, *Sarrasine*, répète cette croyance, tandis que dans *Renieur*, 4ème conte du recueil, il y a un *nigromancier* juif[64]). Les Juifs sont comme tous les autres hérétiques[65]: ces religions ont toutes *bestornees les loiz* (v.686) et leurs pratiquants sont des *faus crestiens* (v.687). La croisade contre les Albigeois, d'actualité à l'époque de la *Vie des Pères*, est sousentendue dans ces vers et apporte au conte encore un détail de la vie actuelle.

Il y a des parallèles assez évidents entre notre légende et l'histoire biblique de Daniel, mais aussi d'autres couches de symbolisme 'acquises' à la création de chaque nouvelle version du récit. Ainsi le fils dans le fourneau symboliserait Jésus dans le tombeau, avant la Résurrection; les flammes et la chaleur du fourneau seraient symboles de l'image médiévale de l'Enfer; le fils est bel et bien *ressuscité*; et, dans *Juitel*, le père, symbole de l'Ancienne Loi – qui est à l'origine du Christianisme – prend conscience de ce nouveau tournant qu'est le Christianisme, comme auraient dû le faire tous les Juifs depuis l'époque de Jésus, et il se convertit.[66] Qui plus est, la mère ne jouerait-elle pas le rôle de la Vierge? et aurait-on tort de souligner la présence d'une sainte trinité (*père, mère, fils*) et d'une transfiguration onomastique du fils (*juif → prêtre*) à la fin du récit? Enfin, n'oublions pas les nombreuses interprétations 'bibliques' qui sont tout à fait possibles.

Nous ne plaidons pas pour une mouvance entre auteurs.[67] Adgar, Gautier et l'auteur de *Juitel* racontaient une légende bien connue et très populaire. (En plus, l'aspect transgressive de la foi juive fut déjà établi à l'ère que nous traitons dans ces lignes.) Il y a de nombreuses différences dans les détails des trois contes – dans *Juitel*, par exemple, il ne s'agit pas d'un miracle de la Vierge et le père n'est pas tué – et, comme l'a remarqué Blumenkranz, la légende allait subir d'autres changements bien après les versions dont il est sujet ici.[68] La mouvance qui nous intéresse est une mouvance d'épithètes, tantôt inconsciente, tantôt volontaire, mais toujours rationnelle, qui élargit le sens d'un conte et qui influence et informe finement le lecteur autrement que le font les commentaires et sermons habituels. *Juitel*, et d'autres contes de la *Vie des Pères* – notamment *Sarrasine, Renieur, Thaïs et Crapaud* -, contiennent des éléments de mouvance des noms souvent voulus et subtils, et témoignent donc d'une finesse largement absente dans les autres versions de la légende. C'est le contexte qui veut que le dénouement de *Juitel* soit différent de celui d'Adgar et de Gautier: ce recueil avait pour but le repentir de son audience.[69] La transgression peut donner lieu au repentir, ce qui mène, lui, au salut. Même les Juifs, coupables de la plus terrible transgression – et ayant besoin, donc, d'accomplir une conversion plus que dramatique – peuvent être sauvés. Ce détail, et l'art de l'auteur – la richesse du détail humain et le désir de montrer la motivation des personnages (l'enfant, le père, Dieu) – font de *Juitel* l'une des versions les plus satisfaisantes d'une légende curieuse et populaire.

University of Hull

1   Pour une édition de 27 de ces textes, datant du 6ème au 18ème siècle et en versions grecque, latine et française nous renvoyons à l'oeuvre de E. Wolter, *Der Judenknabe* (Halle: Max Niemeyer, 1879). Pour les nombreuses versions latines de la légende, voir F.C. Tubach, *Index Exemplorum* (Helsinki: Academia Scientiarum Fennica, 1967), #2041.

2   Adgar, *Le Gracial*, éd. P. Kunstmann (Ottawa: Editions de l'Université d'Ottawa, 1982). *Enfant juif de Bourges* est le Miracle no.14, pp.109-111. Pour une étude du *Gracial*, voir M.D. Legge, *Anglo-Norman Literature and its Background* (Oxford: Clarendon Press, 1963), pp.187-191.

3   Gautier de Coinci, *Les Miracles de Nostre Dame*, éd. V.F. Koenig (Genève: Droz, 1961). *De l'enfant a un giu qui se crestiena* se trouve dans le tome II, pp.95-100. Les études sur Gautier sont très nombreuses: pour une bibliographie récente voir G. Grente, *Dictionnaire des lettres françaises – le Moyen âge*, ouvrage préparé par R. Bossuat, L. Pichard, G. Raynaud de Lage, édition entièrement revue et mise à jour sous la direction de G. Hasenohr & M. Zink (Paris: Fayard, 1992), pp.490-91.

4   *La Vie des Pères*, éd. F. Lecoy (Paris: Société des Anciens Textes Français, I, 1987, II, 1993). *Juitel* est le deuxième conte du recueil et occupe les vers 351-722 (I, pp.14-26). L'étude 'classique' sur la *Vie des Pères* est celle de E. Schwann, 'La Vie des anciens pères', *Romania*, 13 (1884), 233-63, à laquelle on peut rajouter G. Bornäs, *Trois contes de la Vie des Pères* (Lund: Gleerup, 1968) et J. Chaurand, *Fou – Dixième conte de la Vie des Pères* (Genève: Droz, 1971). Pour une bibliographie plus complète, voir notre article, 'The one that got away: The case of the Old French *Vie des Pères*', *French Studies Bulletin*, 55 (1995), 11-15.

5   On a peu étudié le motif du Juif dans la littérature française médiévale. Nous renvoyons à M. Lifschitz-Golden, *Les Juifs dans la littérature française du Moyen Age (Mystères, Miracles, Chroniques)* (New York: Publications of the Institute of French Studies, Columbia University, 1935), dont les pages 103-15 traitent directement cette légende; à G.-B. Depping, *Les Juifs dans le Moyen Age. Essai historique sur leur état civil, commercial et littéraire* (Bruxelles, 1844); et à l'article de G. Dahan, 'Les Juifs dans le théâtre religieux en France du XIIe au XIVe siècles', *Archives Juives*, 13 (1977), 1-10. Voir également B. Blumenkranz, *Les Auteurs chrétiens latins du Moyen Age sur les juifs et le judaïsme* (Paris & La Haye: Mouton & Co, 1963), le compte rendu très détaillé de J.-C. Payen dans *Le Moyen Age*, 72 (1966), 140-44, et M.R. Menocal, *The Arabic Role in Medieval Literary History* (Philadelphia: University of Pennsylvania Press, 1987), pp.139-53.

6   Toutes les citations sont tirées de l'édition de Kunstmann, ed.cit.

6   *Gracial,* pp.13, 14.

8   B. Blumenkranz, *Le Juif médiéval au miroir de l'art chrétien* (Paris: Etudes
Augustiniennes, 1966), p.24. Dans cet excellent livre, plusieurs
reproductions d'enluminures illustrent la légende de l'enfant juif.
Blumenkranz note, à propos d'une miniature anglaise du début du
XIVe siècle, que l'artiste n'a 'pas su différencier les traits du père de
ceux du prêtre catholique' (p.24), suivant l'expulsion des Juifs depuis
la fin du XIIIe siècle.

9   ibid. p.25.

10   Dans son article intitulé 'Les Juifs chez Gautier de Coinci', *Archives
Juives,* 16 (1980), 41-49, G. Dahan pose la question: 'Pourquoi cette
localisation à Bourges? Peut-être faut-il l'expliquer par les récits de
conversions massives de Juifs sous les évêques Félix et Sulpice II, dont
le souvenir devait être resté vivant; d'autre part, on rappellera qu'à la
fin du 12e s. et au 13e la construction d'une nouvelle synagogue à
Bourges a posé un problème dont font état plusieurs lettres de papes'
(p. 43). Notons, par exemple, la lettre du Pape Honoré III, adressée à
Simon de Sully, archévêque de Bourges, en 1221, et éditée par S.
Grayzel dans *The Church and the Jews in the Thirteenth Century*
(Philadelphia: Dropsie College, 1933), p.168: *Pervenit ad audientiam
nostram, quod Judei in tua dioecesi habitantes, synagogas de novo contra
sanciones canonicas construere presumpserint, ideo fraternitati tue per apostolica
scripta mandamus, quatenus, si ita est, synagogas ipsas facias demoliri, fideles
si qui se opposuerint, per censuram ecclesiasticam, appellatione postposita,
compescendo.*

11   Rappellons qu'Adgar écrivait bien avant Latran IV, concile qui voulait
isoler les Juifs d'Europe.

12   Kunstmann, *Vierge et Merveille* (Paris: Bibliothèque médiévale 10/18,
1981), p.21.

13   I. Abrahams, *Jewish Life in the Middle Ages* (London: E. Goldston,
1932), p.423.

14   C. Roth, *A History of the Jews in England* (Oxford: Clarendon Press,
1964), p.10.

15   R.B. Dobson, *The Jews of Medieval York and the Massacre of March 1190*
(York: St Anthony's Press, 1974), p.19.

16   ibid., p.20. Voir également *The Life and Miracles of St William of
Norwich,* éd. A. Jessopp & M.R. James (Cambridge: 1896).

17   Voir J.W.F. Hill, *Medieval Lincoln* (Cambridge: Cambridge University Press, 1948), pp.224-32, et G. Langmuir, *Toward a Definition of Antisemitism* (Berkeley, Los Angeles & London: University of California Press, 1990), pp.237-262.

18   Dobson note que 'the rapid expansion of Jewish activity during the later years of Henry II's reign had begun to evoke a strongly critical reaction', op.cit., p.18.

19   op.cit., p.19. Pour un rapport détaillé de ces événéments, voir R. Chazan, *Medieval Jewry in Northern France : a Political and Social History* (Baltimore: John Hopkins University Press, 1973).

20   Dobson, op.cit., p.25.

21   R. Foreville, *Latran I, II,, III et Latran IV* (Paris: Editions de l'Orante, 1965). Nous renvoyons également à S. Simonsohn, *The Apostolic See and the Jews. Documents: 492-1404* (Toronto: Pontifical Institute of Mediaeval Studies, 1988).

22   Il est important de savoir que l'originalité de Gautier (et surtout de l'auteur de la *Vie des Pères*) se trouve dans le *traitement* du sujet: 'Tous les récits avaient déjà charmé bien des âmes quand Gautier de Coinci les mit en vers', E. Mâle, *L'Art religieux du 13ème siècle en France* (Paris: Armand Colin, 1948), p.347.

23   Dahan note la différence entre Adgar, *Od els sout aprendre letteure / Latin, ebreu...* (vv.15-16) – qu'il trouve 'tout à fait invraisemblable' – et Gautier, *sovent aloit à lor escole* (v.11), version atténuée, art.cit. (1980), p.43.

24   Toutes les citations sont tirées de l'édition de Koenig, ed.cit.

25   L'édition classique de *l'Itinéraire* est celle de M.N. Adler (London, 1907), avec texte hébreu et traduction anglaise. Nous n'avons pu consulter cette édition, mais celle de T. Wright, qui occupe les pages 63-126 de *Early Travels in Palestine* (London: Bohn, 1848). Notons que dans notre légende ce n'est pas toujours un fourneau de verrier dans lequel l'enfant juif se fait jeter; Blumenkranz note que 'par la suite, à mesure que d'une part les Juifs sont éloignés des métiers, et que d'autre part le nombre des prescriptions rabbiniques augmente, il est question d'un chauffe-bain: apparemment, il y a désormais moins de vitriers juifs...', op.cit. (1966), p.22.

26   Grayzel, op.cit., p.34.

27   Dahan note qu' 'à l'inverse de ce que l'on constate dans d'autres

miracles, les épithètes injurieuses à l'égard du Juif sont relativement
rares; il n'est pas présenté comme un monstre de méchanceté mais
comme un père qui peut se montrer affectueux envers son enfant'
(art.cit. (1980), p.44). Nous sommes, au contraire, de l'avis que c'est
justement cette image d'un père capable d'affection qui rend son crime
– et donc son caractère – d'autant plus odieux.

28   Le dépouillement, incomplet, de l'emploi du terme Juif dans les
Chansons de Geste (A. Moisan, *Répertoire des noms propres de personnages
et de lieux cités dans les Chansons de Geste françaises et les oeuvres étrangères
dérivées* (Genève: Droz, 1986), p.632), indique que *Juif mesdisant /
mescreant* fut peut-être une épithète habituelle au Moyen Age (cf.
Bertrand de Bar-sur-Aube, *Girart de Vienne*, éd. W. van Emden (Paris:
Société des Anciens Textes Français, 1977), v.170, et *Florence de Rome*,
éd. A. Wallensköld (Paris, Société des Anciens Textes Français, 1909),
v.4695.

29   La justification / explication théologique du sentiment anti-juif se
trouve dans la Bible. Leur supposée responsabilité collective dans la
crucifixion est suggérée par Matthieu: 'Et tout le peuple dit : "Que son
sang soit sur nous et sur nos enfants !"' (27 : 25); et leur exclusion du
ciel par Jean: 'Heureux ceux qui lavent leurs robes, afin d'avoir droit à
l'arbre de la vie, et afin d'entrer dans la ville par les portes! Dehors les
chiens, les magiciens, les impudiques, les meurtriers, les idolâtres, et
quiconque aime le mensonge et s'y adonne!' (Apocalypse, 22 : 14-15).
Citations extraites de *La Sainte Bible*, (Paris : Desclée et Co., 1923).

30   Car des chiens m'environnent,
      une troupe de scélérats rôde autour de moi;
      ils ont percé mes pieds et mes mains   (Psaume 22 : 17-18)

   Délivre mon âme de l'épée,
      ma vie du pouvoir du chien!   (Psaume 22 : 21)

   Prenez garde à ces chiens, prenez garde à ces mauvais ouvriers...
   (Epître aux Philippiens 3 : 2)

31   Edition du *Bestiaire* de Pierre de Beauvais établie par E. Lindsey (à
partir du ms. BN ff 834) qui se trouve dans l'appendice de *Medieval
French Bestiaries* (Hull [G.B.]: Thèse de 3e cycle, 1976). Plus facilement
accessible est la traduction de G. Bianciotto dans *Bestiaires du Moyen
Age* (Paris: Stock, 1980), pp.17-64. Voir également F. McCulloch,
Mediaeval Latin and French Bestiaries (Chapel Hill: University of
California Press, 1962), pp.110-111.

32   E.C. Block, 'Judaic imagery on medieval choir stalls', *Reinardus*, 8
(1995), 25-47 (p.37).

33 J. Voisenet, *Bestiaire chrétien : l'imagerie animale des auteurs du haut Moyen Age* (Toulouse: P.U. du Mirail, 1994), pp.236-7. Voisenet note également que, selon Hubert de Maastricht, le diable 'pousse un cri d'une voix de bête sauvage' (p.237).

34 Citations empruntées de l'excellente étude de H. Flanders Dunbar, *Symbolism in Medieval Thought and its Consummation in the Divine Comedy* (New Haven: Yale University Press, 1961). L'auteur note que 'throughout the *Divina Commedia* dogs, foxes and wolves, representing wicked men or principles of wickedness, manifest the root of all sin, cupidity, direct opposition to love as cold to heat' (pp.163-4).

35 éd. Lindsey, op.cit; Bianciotto p.39. Une étude récente de la comparaison accablante hyène-Juif est celle de D. Hassig, *Medieval Bestiaries – Text, Image, Ideology* (Cambridge: University Press, 1995), pp.145-55.

36 *Le Roman de Perceval ou le Conte du Graal*, ed. by W. Roach (Genève: Droz, 1956).

37 Rappellons ici les paroles de Schaff, citées par S. Grayzel en 1933 (op.cit., p.3), qui mettent en contexte l'antisémitisme de l'époque: 'The thirteenth century began for the Jews the most unfortunate period of their history...'.

38 J. Simon, 'Histoire des juifs de Nîmes au Moyen Age', *Neumaussa*, 2 (1884-5), 10-18, 94-124, cité par J. Shatzmiller, *Recherches sur la communauté juive de Manosque au Moyen Age 1241-1329* (Paris & La Haye: Mouton & Co, 1973), p.20.

39 ibid., p.21

40 Grayzel, op.cit., p.85.

41 Dahan croit que la version la plus connue de la *Vie des Pères,* qui se trouve dans le ms. BN fr. 1546, 'semble s'inspirer de Gautier' (art.cit. (1980), p.43), mais il ne développe pas cette hypothèse. En fait, il nous semble qu'il s'agissait plutôt d'une source commune que d'une influence directe.

42 La plus récente étude de la structure du recueil est la thèse non-publiée de P.D. Spencer-Ellis, *La Vie des Pères: A Reappraisal of Manuscript Branches and their Contents* (Hull [G.B.] : M.Phil Thesis, 1986).

43 C'est dans le prologue que l'auteur cite sa source, *ensi Salemons le nos dist / afferme per son escrit* (vv.367-8) et nous dit qu'il faut que les enfants apprennent la discipline : nous sommes tous les enfants de Dieu et il nous teste. Il faut se repentir avant la fin de sa vie puisque

L'Escriture dit sanz mentir / qu'a Deu ne puet riches venir / ne ke li chameulz puet entrer / el chaz d'une aguille et passer (vv.412-16). Dans l'épilogue, l'auteur prêche la grandeur de Dieu. Comme on le voit ailleurs dans la *Vie des Pères*, il n'était pas nécessaire d'y avoir une cohérence concrète entre le prologue, l'épilogue et le récit lui-même.

44   Pour l'auteur de la *Vie des Pères*, ce comportement est admirable, même si Latran IV avait découragé les rapports amicaux entre Juifs et Chrétiens. Grayzel a noté que, 'from very early times the Church had [...] sought to prevent the cordial relationships between Christians and their Jewish neighbours. In this they were for a long time unsuccessful. Cordial relations existed in the thirteenth century, so that we still find a Christian girl hiding from her enemies in the home of a Jew, Christians partaking of a Jewish meal, and even synagogues built by the side of a church. Jews mixed with Christians on more or less equal terms socially, they wore the same clothes, and surely spoke the same language,' op.cit., p.59.

45   Toutes les citations sont tirées de l'édition de Lecoy, ed.cit.

46   Pour la valeur symbolique des chiffres, voir J. Ribard, *Le Moyen Age : littérature et symbolisme* (Paris: Champion, 1984).

47   Lettre d'Innocent IV au roi de Navarre, publiée par Grayzel, op.cit., p.260.

48   Cité par Grayzel, ibid., p.14 (note.12).

49   Ce sont souvent les coupables et les damnés livrés au désespoir qui baissent la tête dans l'iconographie médiévale; c'est également un geste volontaire d'abaissement. La Synagogue, ayant perdu son influence, baisse la tête et perd sa couronne, et ce geste peut aussi signifier la tristesse. Pour une excellente étude des gestes dans l'art médiéval nous renvoyons à F. Garnier, *Le Langage de l'image au Moyen Age – signification et symbolique* (Paris: Le Léopard d'Or, 1982).

50   Dans *Renieur*, 4ème conte de la *Vie des Pères* (I, vv. 1195-1708), les paroles positives d'un personnage juif envers le protagoniste chrétien ont un effet négatif : Un Chrétien est désireux de sa voisine, récemment veuve, mais ce sentiment n'est pas réciproque. L'homme se rend alors chez un nécromancien Juif et se dit prêt à renier sa foi pour que la magie noire marche. Le Juif appelle le Chrétien *beaz amis*, mais quand celui-ci ne tient pas sa promesse – il ne veut pas renier la Vierge – il perd le respect du Juif qui change du *vos* au *tu*. La femme, qui avant cette scène n'employait aucun terme honorifique envers son voisin, l'appelle maintenant *amis*...

51   Dans *Girart de Vienne*, la chanson de geste de Bertrand de Bar-sur-

Aube (ed.cit.), nous rencontrons un personnage juif, Joachin, que l'auteur désigne, à trois reprises, comme *li bons juïs* (vv. 4917, 5529, 5572).

52   Pour le motif de la responsabilité directe des Juifs dans la crucifixion en ce qui concerne le théâtre religieux, voir Dahan, art.cit (1977), p.6.

53   Notons quand même que le mot *enfant* n'est pas toujours neutre dans la littérature médiévale. Dans *Le Couronnement de Louis*, éd. E. Langlois (Paris: Classiques Français du Moyen Age, 1888), le terme est péjoratif et désigne le jeune Louis comme indigne / ingrat quand il ne s'avance pas pour prendre la couronne (v.87).

54   Etre juif veut dire être sale: l'auteur de la *Vie des Pères* emploie le verbe *eslaver* dans les prologues de deux autres contes pour exprimer la nécessité de 'laver ses péchés' :

Si lou, tant com loisir avons
que de nos mals nos eslavons.   (*Sarrasine*, vv.781-81)

Si lou ke del fiem vos lavoiz
et ke vos armes eslavoiz
des pechiez dont tuit estes plein
ainz ke mort en vos mete mein.   (*Thaïs*, vv.2219-22)

55   Dans les fabliaux, genre voisin du conte pieux, ce sont souvent les personnages âgés qui se font duper ou qui sont les cibles des blagues (ex. *La vieille qui oint la palme au chevalier, La vieille truande...*), et dans d'autres oeuvres le fait d'être âgé est souvent négatif (ex. le roi dans *Les deus amanz* de Marie de France). Dans *Crapaud*, autre conte de la *Vie des Pères*, le vieux père se fait duper par son fils égoïste mais c'est à lui que revient le dernier mot.

56   Dans l'ensemble, l'auteur de la *Vie des Pères* évite les sermons, mais (à force d'écrire des contes *pieux*) ses narratifs sont tout de même assez souvent ponctués de commentaires de ce genre, qui sont, d'habitude, moins longs que cet exemple. C'est dans les prologues et les épilogues que l'enseignement a lieu. L'action des contes n'est qu'assez rarement interrompue, ce qui veut dire que la lecture de ces contes pieux n'est pas très éloignée de celle des fabliaux.

57   Pour l'identfication des juifs aux pouvoirs du mal, voir Isaïe 56:10 *Les gardiens d'Israël sont tous aveugles, / ils ne savent rien; / ce sont tous des chiens muets....* et aussi Jean 8 : 30-51, surtout le verset 44 : *Le père dont vous êtes issus , c'est le Diable, et vous voulez accomplir les désirs de votre père...* Dahan (art.cit., 1977) renvoie ses lecteurs à une oeuvre de J. Trachtenberg, *The Devil and the Jew* (Baltimore, 1944), que nous n'avons pu consulter.

58   cf. vv.521-24 où l'enfant communie:

> Avant ce trest, un en reçut,
> dont sa loi bleça et descrut
> conme nices ki ne savoit
> se sen ou folie fesoit.

59   Dans ce contexte un Juif ne pourrait pas, peut-être, jouer un rôle entièrement neutre, mais la critique virulente de l'auteur n'avait pas encore commencé.

60   Voir Baron (op.cit) et Abrahams (op.cit), et aussi L. Poliakov, *Histoire de l'Antisémitisme* (Paris: Calmann-Lévy, 1961).

61   C'est peut-être tout à son honneur que dans cette version du conte le père n'interdit pas à son fils de jouer avec les chrétiens, même s'il craint qu'il lui arrive un tel 'malheur' (v.535).

62   Cette vertu l'entraîne presqu' au martyre: Nous y voyons un parallèle avec les anciens pères de l'Eglise: convertis d'une religion non-chrétienne, ils furent souvent mis à morts pour leur nouvelle foi. Ainsi, le père du juitel représenterait l'ancienne loi.

63   M. Camille a noté que dans le *Jeu de Saint Nicolas* le terme *mahommerie* s'applique aussi à la synagogue. (*The Gothic Idol – Ideology and Image-Making in Medieval Art* [Cambridge: University Press, 1989], pp.129-35). Nous avons aussi remarqué cette appellation dans *La Chanson de Roland*:

> Li emperere ad Sarraguce prise,
> A mil Franceis funt ben cercer la vile,
> Les sinagoges e les mahumeries.... (vv.3660-62) ed. by F. Whitehead, (Oxford: Blackwell, 1980).

64   Les Juifs co-opéraient avec le diable et furent donc diaboliques eux-mêmes. L'imaginaire populaire, qui avait son origine dans l'ignorance de la foi juive, donnait au Juif des croyances aberrantes, dont l'adoration des démons. M. Camille constate que 'few Christians would have any notion of Jewish religious rites, or even of the furnishings of a synagogue' (ibid., p.172).

65   Camille note que les Juifs jouaient un rôle ambivalent dans la typologie médiévale, 'on the one hand, as believers in Christ through the Old Testament prophets, and on the other hand, as unredeemed sinners', et il parle d'une 'continual battle of the Church triumphant against the unrepentant Jew' (ibid., p.166).

66 L'Eglise retirait un certain prestige des apostats du Judaïsme; par exemple, Nicole Donin qui, en 1240, s'opposa à Yehiel ben Joseph à l'occasion du *disputatio* de Paris; voir Grayzel, op.cit., pp.278-79, et J. Cohen, *The Friars and the Jews* (Ithaca & Londres: Cornell University Press, 1982), pp.69-74.

67 Il est toujours difficile, et parfois dangereux, de soutenir une thèse de mouvance entre textes, auteurs et époques. Pour un très bon exemple de la présentation précise et claire d'une telle hypothèse (dans une tradition voisine), voir L. Light, 'French Bibles c.1200-30: a new look at the origin of the Paris Bible', in *The Early Medieval Bible*, éd. R. Gameson (Cambridge : University Press, 1994), pp.155-76.

68 voir Blumenkranz, op.cit. (1966), pp.22-25.

69 Depuis Latran IV, la confession est préalable à la communion, et donc au salut éternel.

The Martyr-Figure as Transgressor in Seventeenth-Century French Theatre

Paul Scott

At first glance, the martyr-figure may seem a fairly unlikely exponent of transgression; he or she occupies the pinnacle of sainthood, an example to be admired and venerated. However, the martyr's tale involves disobedience at the highest level, that of a subject to his or her (God-given) ruler, and it this clash with authority that merits the martyr's claim to transgress. This transgression cuts away at the very fabric of the social hierarchy, the subject judges the sovereign, defies him, and implicitly or sometimes explicitly refuses the earthly ruler's jurisdiction. Serge Doubrovsky has noted that the martyr 'renverse l'ordre et la hiérarchie', and that Polyeucte's revolt against the gods 'est aussi rébellion contre la source légitime du pouvoir'.[1] The seventeenth century in France was an age in which speculative thought was questioning the very nature of things hitherto taken for granted, especially the form and substance of authority. During the troubles of the Frondes (1648-53), the king and royal family found themselves exiled from the capital, and the threat to the monarchical system during this period was real.[2] In 1648 while the *parlement* of Paris was taking a prominent part in the uprisings, its English 'counterpart' was dispensing itself from allegiance to its king and in 1649, the second year of the disturbances in the French capital, Charles I of England – Louis's uncle through marriage – was tried and executed. In this essay, I will consider the martyr-figure from this historical context and then I will go on to consider the sociological aspects of the martyr's transgression.

During this period, that is to say from 1596 to 1675, there is a sizeable number of martyr plays, around ninety in all, and this figure does not include reprints – to take just one example, an anonymous play about St Catherine first published in 1649 at Lyon (see appendix) underwent three more editions at Caen and at Paris. The genre[3] reaches its zenith, in terms of production numbers and popularity during the decade 1645-55, that is to say during the time of the greatest internal unrest and moreover at a time when dramatic production in Paris stood at two-thirds of the pre-Frondes total.[4] It seems conceivable then, that the martyr-play strikes a chord with an audience disenchanted with contemporary modes of authority. R.A. Sayce has noted that: 'the subject, martyrdom, forms one of the preoccupations of the time',[5] and it is possible to view some of these contemporary plays as a literary version of the Frondes – therein one has a rebel hero, who though crushed by a tyrant still comes out triumphant at the end.

What rather tends to support the contention that the plays at the time of civil trouble can be viewed as a radical assertion of the accountability of those in power is the observation that the output of the martyr-play diminishes as the monarchy becomes more stable. The genre gradually and noticeably disappears as Louis XIV consolidates his position. If we take the decade from 1645 to 1655, there are 17 plays published on the theme, 13 of these in Paris. Now if we take the decade 1661 to 1671 (1661 being a watershed year for Louis XIV – the start of his personal rule) this has diminished to 11, two of which are annual devotional plays at Autun to celebrate the local patron St Reine. In the next decade after 1671 there is only *one* play on the topic. One would have expected them to linger on in the provinces but this does not seem to have been the case. Even the *Confrérie de la Passion*, which had survived into the seventeenth century, performing mystery-plays – some of which treated martyrs – reached its term in 1676 when it was officially abolished by Louis XIV.[6]

Also noticeable in the post-Frondes period is the observation that these plays seem to avoid dealing with martyrs who defy the Roman emperor directly, such as St Catherine and St Genesius who had earlier been a popular choice. From the beginning of his reign, Louis XIV was associated with the Roman emperor, especially in iconography. Many portraits of Louis depict him in Roman dress with an laurel wreath typified by that of Pierre Mignard of

1673,[7] and equestrian statues usually showed him in the style and pose of the statue of Marcus Aurelius on the Capitol. Significantly, a marble statue of 1654 by Gilles Guérin to celebrate the restoration of order under the king, *Louis Terrassant la Fronde*, has the king 'habillé en César victorieux avec un manteau à la romaine', and this was prominently erected in the courtyard of the Hôtel de Ville.[8] Louis himself encouraged and fostered this cultus, which had begun under the reign of Henry IV. His father had purposefully cultivated this allegory,[9] and it extended to all branches of the arts for it was a 'literary commonplace that Louis was a new Augustus'.[10] His court was the court of Apollo, fostering another link with ancient Rome, and Louis vested and danced as Apollo on at least nine occasions in the 1660s. At the *carrousel* which took place at the Louvre in 1662, Louis actually dressed as a Roman emperor, while details of ceremonial in his court were closely modelled on Rome, such as the *entrée triomphante*, the arrival of the king in a city of the realm and which took the form of a Roman triumph.[11] Several of these took place during his reign, beginning with the proto-entry into Paris in 1643. If Louis was so evidently linked to the Roman emperor in the public imagination,[12] martyr-plays raise an obvious difficulty – here we have plays based on true accounts which reveal the emperors as tyrannical, godless and moreover erroneous. It is unsurprising then that the genre declined during the personal rule of Louis.

Faced with this dichotomy, the playwrights deal with the martyrs' transgression in differing ways. The setting of Corneille's *Polyeucte* (1642) is in the far-flung corner of Armenia, therefore one has immediately been distanced from Rome. The protagonist tells us that:

> Je dois ma vie au peuple, au prince, à sa couronne,
> Mais je la dois bien plus encore au Dieu qui me la donne
> (ll. 1211-12).

Here, the martyr is lacking the rebellion that is present in the original legend. He does not dispense himself from the loyalty due to his sovereign, but rather sees a higher good, and removes the impediments to the God he is eager to join. Corneille has seemingly diluted Polyeucte's transgression, which is reduced to following his conscience rather than judging his monarch. The transgression of disobedience to the highest earthly authority has become an indirect consequence of following the dictates of conscience, rather than at the heart of the martyr's struggle. In fact, the emperor Decius remains a remote, almost benevolent figure during the play. His visible representative, Sévère, comes across as noble and philosophical, the epitome of a seventeenth-century conception of nobility. He is also the emperor's friend as well as his servant, and while he explicitly disagrees with his master's persecution of Christians, which causes him 'trop d'outrage' (V.6), he nevertheless still exhorts the newly-converted governor Félix to:

> Servez bien votre Dieu, servez notre monarque(V. 6).

In other words – your ruler is wrong but you are still bound to obey him. Clearly, the transgressive element has been diminished, ostensibly to support a certain type of political theory which was steadily spreading its roots, that of the divine right of kings.[13] It is perhaps worth adding at this juncture that we know that Louis XIV himself enjoyed a performance of the play.[14] Bossuet was later to echo Sévère's words: 'Le service de Dieu et le respect pour les rois sont choses unies'.[15] Corneille had shown himself preoccupied with the question of authority in the three plays preceding this martyr-play: *Le Cid*, *Horace* and *Cinna*, and one can see *Polyeucte* as a continuation of this theme, dealing with the problem of a polarized clash of interests and duty to two causes.

One can find a similar sanitization of the element of transgression in a play heavily influenced by *Polyeucte*'s success, Jean Rotrou's *Le véritable Saint Genest* (1645). The most celebrated actor of the day, Genêt, is asked to perform before the emperor Diocletian a play parodying Christians, during the course of which Genêt actually becomes a Christian as the result of a celestial vision. In the original version as reported in the *Martyrologium Romanum*,[16] the martyr defies the emperor saying: 'Non est Rex præter Christum',[17] with which he transgresses the entire social order, for he will not accept the jurisdiction of *any* earthly kingship. In Rotrou's rendering however, the emphasis is somewhat different. The martyr *after* his conversion reminds the spectators of the duty we owe to our kings:

> Nos vœux, nos passions, nos vielles et nos peines,
> Et tout le sang enfin qui coule dans nos veines,
> Sont pour eux [rulers] des tributs de *devoir* et d'amour
> Où le ciel *nous oblige* en nous donnant le jour
>
> (V.2, my emphasis).

This speech is highlighted by its position towards the end of the play, just prior to the actual martyrdom, the essential action of the entire tragedy. The martyr is about to shed his blood for Christ, yet tells us that his blood is owed to the sovereign. By speaking in terms of the universal first person 'nous', and by referring to monarchs as 'eux', it seems that the spectator is being drawn into this speech and that Rotrou is not referring to this particular monarch Diocletian, but to all kings, especially the spectator's king. This is a radical alteration of the spirit of the source account.

If one can extract a political interpretation in Rotrou's play, again it is tacit sympathy for an absolutist governmental system. One can see this in his other plays. In his *Antigone* (1638), Créon imparts:

> Dans les desseins d'un roi, comme dans ceux de dieux
> De fidèles sujets *doivent* fermer les yeux
>
> (IV.5, my emphasis).

Again this is in general terms, as if to invite the audience to make an application. To take one more example, in *Bélisaire* (unfinished), Théodora tells herself that:

> Les devoirs qu'on rend à des fronts couronnés
> *Doivent* s'éxécuter sans être examinés
>
> (II.9, my emphasis).

The doctrine of divine right expanded rapidly in seventeenth-century political theory.[18] Under the reign of Louis XIII, the royalist Bishop of Chartres spearheaded a controversy in 1625 over the publication of his *Sententia* which insisted that kings shared in God's divine nature in a special way.[19] What was then to cause debate, would later become the received norm – Bossuet summed up contemporary political thought a few decades later when he wrote that kings 'sont des dieux et participent [...] à la nature divine',[20] which makes the comparison to the emperors of Rome more complete, since Louis has seemingly achieved apotheosis. Indicative of the rise of absolutism is the fact that the word 'tyran', used in many of the earlier plays, almost completely disappears after the Frondes. In Montauban's *Indégonde*, published and performed in Paris the year following the Frondes, 1654 (the year of Louis XIV's coronation), the persecuting king in the play actually displays contrition after executing the Christians, a fundamental alteration from the traditional legend, where the king is brutally inhuman. Baro's *Le Martyre de S. Eustache* has a total dissociation between contemporary monarchy and the tyrant ruler of the play, for in his preface dedicating the play to Henriette-Marie, Louis XIV's aunt and Charles I's widow, the late Charles I is compared to the martyr, being like him 'entre les mains des bourreaux'.

That Corneille and Rotrou, the two best known dramatists of their day, would temper the 'subversive' elements in their interpretation of this subject-matter, is in itself unsurprising.[21] A contemporary play about St Genesius by a lesser known author, Nicholas Desfontaines, also published in 1645 has an

altogether different tone. In his *Illustre Comédien ou le martyre de
S. Genest*, the martyr defies Diocletian, telling him that because
he has refused to heed his, Genesius's, message:

On te traitte en esclave et non en Souverain   (V, 5) [22]

This is the ultimate social transgression – the saint not only
judges the sovereign, but also dispenses himself from his civil
duty owed to his emperor. Moreover, the hierarchical pyramid
has been overturned- the subject does not even treat the
emperor as an equal, but as an inferior, as a slave. Indeed the
crown, metonym for kingship itself is attacked as 'un petit
bandeau'. In his earlier martyr-play, *Le martyre de S. Eustache*,
when the emperor Trajan encourages the martyr to consider his
position and abandon his religion, he is told:

Mais vous même Seigneur, sortez de cette erreur   (V, 5).

This is consonant with the spirit of the original, yet can be seen
as an indirect critique of the growing tendency in political and
religious thought to view the king above any judge but God.
Bossuet was later to express what had been long held by many:
'Il n'y a que Dieu qui puisse juger de leurs jugemens et de leur
personnes'.[23] The conventions or *bienséances* forbade any direct
representation of the king on stage, presumably out of fear of
lèse-majesté. However, as Jean-Marie Apostolidès has noted, this
did not preclude: 'leur présence sous un autre mode'.[24] I believe
that the French king does indeed sometimes appear 'sous le
masque'[25] of the rulers in these plays, and that the transgression
therein is toned down or highlighted according to the persuasion
of the author. For example, the celebrated comment of Ronsard
to Charles IX: 'Souvenez-vous de Dieu dont vous êtes l'image'[26]
is echoed in one martyr-play: 'C'est le destin de Dieux dont vous
êtes l'image'.[27]

As I have remarked, these plays can be seen as a visible
reminder of the fallibility of those in power. Later in the century,

Bossuet spends a great deal of time dwelling on the example of the martyrs in his *Avertissemens aux Protestans*, in particular insisting on the fact that they were, despite appearances, loyal to their monarch. The early martyrs 'nous en fait voir qu'ils étaient fidèles à leur patrie quoiqu'ingrate, et aux empereurs quoiqu'impies et persécuteurs'.[28] In fact, if they were accused of lacking loyalty to their ruler they would view it as a crime and a sacrilege: 'où la majesté de Dieu est violée en la personne de son lieutenant'.[29] Bossuet tones down the seditious nature of the martyrs' example, to counter any political applications dangerous to the State. He insists that armed struggle, such as that of the Machabees 'était extraordinaire' and 'manifestement divin'. This is pertinent for there was a copious quantity of martyr-plays, some treating the Machabees, several of which enjoyed commercial success in Paris and the provinces. The plays peak earlier than Bossuet was writing, but it is clear that he is steering clear of a certain type of politico-religious theory, that of tyrannicide. This had been formulated by the most respected source for Catholic moralists, St Thomas Aquinas, who taught that: 'he who kills a tyrant to free his country is to be praised and rewarded'.[30] Theories of tyrannicide were taught not only by Catholics, especially the Jesuits,[31] but had also been sanctioned by Protestant leaders such as Zwingli and Calvin. There was a marked shift away from this teaching in early modern political theory, something which the martyr-plays reflect. Bossuet quotes extensively from patristic sources (he could hardly use more recent sources which had formulated tyrannicidal solutions) and notably quotes St Ambrose who states: 'Je ne puis pas obéir à des ordres impies, mais je ne dois pas combattre'.[32]

There was a real danger to the life of the French king throughout the seventeenth century. Not only had Henry III and Henry IV been assassinated, in 1589 and 1610 respectively – the latter on the twenty-fourth attempt – but their deaths were viewed by some, including the assassins themselves, as justified tyrannicide.[33] Apart from the danger from those who viewed the Bourbons as usurpers and even, in the case of Louis

XIII, the threat from immediate family, there was the perceived danger from Protestants, who in France were mainly Calvinist, and rose up in armed rebellion in La Rochelle during the 1620s.[34] During the internal upheaval of the Frondes, one of the main speakers of dissent against the government was Cardinal de Retz, who said at the time: 'Il forma dans la plus légitime des monarchies la plus scandaleuse et la plus dangereuse *tyrannie* qui ait jamais peut-être asservi un état',[35] and it is evident why some would see Louis XIV or his government as displaying tyrannical traits. I suggest that the danger of tyrannicide is a major factor in the decline of the genre of the martyr-play and the reason behind the diluting of the transgression element present in the original hagiographies.

The transgression of the martyr-figure is mutated from open rebellion to that of *lèse-majesté*. In Desfontaines's *Illustre Comédien*, Diocletian's response to Genesius's declaration of Christianity and mocking of the 'faux dieux' is to be affronted for his own dignity:

> On me traitte en César, en Empereur Romain   (III. 2).

Similarly, later in the same play there is similar indignation at the conversion of another character:

> Quoi? loin de nous servir on se moque de nous?
> On nous joue, on nous brave...   (IV. 4)

It is the slight given to him which causes offence, the lack of respect to his orders, not any abandonment of traditional religion. Put another way, it is the form not the matter of the transgression which infuriates the emperor so. In Desfontaines's *Tragédie de S. Eustache*, after the protagonist has mocked 'ces Dieux impuissants' Hadrian suggests he goes home to repent at his leisure. However, when Eustache tells him that he is wrong and that *he* should repent, the emperor's tolerance evaporates and Hadrian gives a simple ultimatum, succinctly demonstrating his displeasure:

Si faut-il toutefois ou changer ou périr (V. 5)

The royal person has been attacked, the crime must be punished. This is a presentation of martyrdom which does deviate to some degree from traditional hagiographical accounts of early Roman martyrs, where martyrs were usually killed primarily for their refusal to do honour to the gods. Needless to say, since in the seventeenth century, the French king enjoyed a quasi-sacerdotal status,[36] rebellion against his authority integrally and implicitly was impiety as well. Bossuet would sum this up thus: 'la personne des rois est *sacré*, et qu'attenter sur eux c'est un *sacrilége*'.[37]

I will now move on to more general considerations about the sociological nature of the martyr. The martyr transgresses not only the social order but also the perceived natural order, for he or she defies the two immediate imperatives of human existence – the urges to survive and to reproduce. Unlike the conventional dramatic hero who bravely endures death, the martyr voluntarily embraces death. Although half a century later than the historical Polyeucte, the Council of Illiberis in 303 decreed that anyone being executed for having willfully destroyed idols would not be enrolled in the canon of martyrs, a sort of posthumous excommunication.[38] A seventeenth-century audience might assume that the prohibition occurred earlier and therefore Polyeucte would appear more to be a non conformist martyr. Polyeucte chooses to attend a sacrifice and smash up pagan idols when he could very well have missed the ceremony. When his Christian friend Néarque warns of the consequences of such a course, he asks:

Vous voulez donc mourir?

Polyeucte replies:

Vous aimez donc à vivre?   (II. 6)

He then goes on to enumerate reasons to die – he will be an example to other Christians, he will die in a state of grace and thus be assured of Heaven. These reasons seem closer to the seeking of personal *gloire* than the *gloire de Dieu* and death is sought as a means to bring about this.[39] This desire to die, to see death as a positive not a destructive force is a common factor in any martyr's life and this sets the martyr apart as defying the universal fear of death. When Polyeucte accuses his friend of displaying a certain 'froideur', Néarque sharply retorts that:

> Dieu même a craint la mort   (II. 6)

implying that this fear is absent from Polyeucte and hints at Néarque's incredulous incomprehension. Troterel's St Agnes asked by her inquisitor if she is trembling out of fear of the tortures he has promised her if she will not recant, indignantly replies that it is her body's reaction to the blasphemies he has uttered (Act III).[40] This abnormal reaction to the proximity of extinction makes the martyr a freak, humanly speaking, for he or she transgresses urges that traditionally constitute the essence of humanity – that is if one accepts the premise that 'humanity' can be reduced to any concise notion.

This unnatural craving for self-destruction raises the question of the religious orthodoxy of some marytrs, for is not choosing when and how to die the essential definition of suicide or voluntary euthanasia?[41] In the Christian Church, voluntarily seeking one's own death became prohibited only in the sixth century though Augustine makes a strong case against it, due to the martyr-mania of the Donatist heretics.[42] However, to a seventeenth-century audience, seeking one's own death would probably have appeared a little suspect, perhaps calling to mind duelling, which became a capital offence in 1626. In Baro's *S. Eustache Martyr* (1649), the saint's wife martyrs herself by throwing herself into a burning furnace – without any external constraint to do so – conforming to the original account. Jean-François de Nîmes in his *Ste Cécile couronnée* (1662) has his heroine begging her interrogator to put her to death, even though he is examining her about the location of three Christian corpses. In Pierre Troterel's successful 1615 play, *La tragédie de Ste Agnès*, the saint's mother has to remind her daughter that she should not precipitate herself to her death, for 'Dieu nous deffend par sa loi'.[43] Néarque has to reprimand Polyeucte for rushing into martyrdom pointing out that:

> Il [Dieu] commande point que l'on s'y précipite   (II. 6)

Polyeucte justifies himself by claiming that the more voluntary and willing one goes to death the more merit there is in it, which in theological terms lends itself to misinterpretation at the least. The heroine of Corneille's other martyr-play proposes escaping physical defilement through suicide, believing herself dispensed from the sin attached to it by a special revelation:

> Ma loi me le défend, mais mon Dieu me l'inspire   (III. 3)

Such a proposal is hardly Christian, in fact it appears quite pagan. Plato approved of suicide if it was performed as a form of *anangke* or divine compulsion, which is not far removed from Théodore's philosophy.[44]

Richard Dawkins in *The Selfish Gene* cites the honey bee and other 'social insects' as being natural examples of creatures sacrificing themselves for the good of the larger community – 'apparent altruism'.[45] E. & A. Weiner make the point that 'unlike animals whose capacity for altruistic self sacrifice is genetically linked, human beings can choose to sacrifice themselves for groups'.[46] This begs the question of just how far, in the plays, in violating the most primitive urges to exist, the martyr commits altruistic suicide. Polyeucte does consider the positive aspects of his death as setting an inspiring example for the Christian community, but this is only one reason among several, and revealingly only occurs after he has stated the chief benefit that will come to him through dying fresh from the sacrament of baptism, namely an immortal crown (II. 6: ll.655-671). The martyr usually stands alone, and such a visual presentation tends to stress the individualist nature of martyrdom. In Baro's *S. Eustache*, when the martyr's wife admits she is a Christian thus ensuring her place as a prospective martyr, the stage direction states that: 'dès qu'elle a prononcé ce mot [i.e. chrétienne] ceux qui le suivent l'abandonnent',[47] giving a visually dramatic illustration of the martyr's isolation. The legend of St Catherine, and a tenth of the total plays – eleven – deal with her, depicts the martyr confronting fifty learned men and defeating them in academic debate.[48]

The preoccupation with death is an integral element of the martyr-play, and one can see this as a transgression of the contemporary notion of drama. Instead of a hero being brought down by a tragic flaw, and death often ensuing as a result – the death factor generally being the substance of the drama – the audience is presented with a hero whose death is the essence of their nobility and which instead of losing them their position, in fact their life, gains for them unlimited benefits. The tragic hero dies, and his or her nobility has been proven in their lives – as a warrior or a patriot, the martyr hero dies and death gives them nobility – for one is a martyr only at the moment of death and thereafter. Doubrovsky has noted that in the case of the martyr: 'il ne s'agira plus de *surmonter* la vie, mais de la *supprimer*'.[49] I would suggest that the former is the case of the conventional tragic hero, and the latter is more suitable to apply to the martyr hero. It is not clear whether one can view the martyr as superhuman or inhuman, perhaps a blend of the two is a more apt interpretation.

It is not only the desire to survive that is transgressed, but also the urge to reproduce. A love-interest is an almost universal feature of the martyr-play, even when absent from the original account. This is undoubtedly necessary for the dramatic element, the action of the play since it heightens the emotional conflict. There is something brutal about Polyeucte and Rotrou's Genêt joyfully embracing death and abandoning their spouses – in both the recentness of the marriage is emphasized.[50] Corneille could have set his play at any point in the marriage but chooses to set it two weeks after the couple's nuptials, implicitly suggesting the physical pleasures that the newly-weds are enjoying and are abandoning. Georges Lanson notes that Polyeucte, and this can be applied to many martyrs, 'renonce à tout le bonheur terrestre, même le plus légitime'.[51] Again, the martyr's behaviour appears inhuman, he or she goes beyond what is required of the Christian. Troterel's St Agnes does not reject a present lover, but all prospect of potential happiness. When Simphronie her persecutor and the father of the man who loves her asks her if she is incapable of loving her son, she replies:

> Si j'avais désiré qu'amour fût mon vainqueur,
> J'eusse élue votre fils pour maître de mon cœur (III)

The friends and relations of several martyrs follow (or precede in the case of Polyeucte) the principal martyr to their termination, but it is significant that they do this separately and not together, for nothing must detract from the solitary substance of martyrdom. In some of the plays, the apparent death-wish of the martyr – which begins at their conversion, before any fatal test of their faith – spreads to others. Not only to those close to them, but sometimes even to the persecutor. In Baro's play, the persecting Ormond actually brings the play to a conclusion with the word death:

> Leur example puissant mon âme a convertie,
> Allons publiquement et le dire et *mourir* (V. 6)

In Desfontaines's *Illustre Comédien*, the emperor Trajan closes the play begging his gods to:

> Achevez vos rigeurs et hâtez mon supplice (V. 5)

Likewise in his other marty-play, Desfontaines again gives the emperor the last word:

Je règne et je frémis ; je triomphe et je *meur*(V. 7)

The martyr defies his or her genetic constitution, and influences
others to do the same – the transgression then is of both the
social order, and also the natural order.

It can be said, in some cases at least, that martyrs transgress gender-specific qualities traditionally allocated to their sex.
Some female martyrs display warrior-like aggressiveness.
Troterel's St Agnes, far from being the young girl of the pious
legend, has a very strange desire when she is confronted with the
approaching figure of the Roman governor:

> Que n'ai-je le pouvoir d'être ton homicide
> Pour venger tant de saints . . .(III) [52]

which undoubtedly would have appeared as unfeminine
sentiments to a contemporary audience. Similarly, St Catherine
is an empowered woman who defeats not only the intellectual
élite of Alexandria, but also in some accounts resists the
emperor's attempts to seduce her, his love rendering him
irrational thus depriving him of his 'masculine' stability.[53]
Martian, who is in love with St Agnes (Troterel) sullies his virility
by retreating to his bed in a state of love-sick melancholia:

> Martian étant couché dans son lit, se plaint(II)

This effete behaviour is the antithesis of that displayed by
Agnes. Joan of Arc, who is the subject of at least six plays, wore
male garb to the end of her life, and it has been suggested that
this was inspired by the example of transvestite saints of the
Golden Legend.[54] In one case inverted gender identity is even
applied to the playwright – the publisher of one of the four
female authors of martyr-plays, Mme de Saint-Balmon (the
others being Cosnard, Paschal and de La Chapelle), refers in his
notice to *Les Jumeaux Martyrs* (1650) to the authoress's military
prowess in the Thirty Year's War: 'tous les jours des Croats ou

des Allemands à combattre'. The female martyr assumes active qualities, the male martyr passively submits to death, even when he is a soldier. Such non stereotypical representations of women may be viewed as an attempt to curtail the accusation that actresses would arouse lascivious thoughts in the male section of the audience.[55] Moreover, as Desnain points out in her chapter of the present volume, the exercise of power and the feminine condition are often mutually incompatible in seventeenth-century drama. The female martyr owes her (moral) strength to the emulation of masculinity. The apparent stress that one finds on women in this genre firmly emphasizes their uniqueness – they are seen as strong because they have shed their fundamental 'weakness' – their sex.

In dramatizing the religious theme of the martyr, the authors can be seen as transgressing traditional drama. The *mystère* had declined in the sixteenth century due to pressure from ecclesiastics – the crowds were notoriously rowdy and the content of the plays was often theologically dubious, if not openly heretical.[56] The martyr-play takes up the theme again, and in an age when acclaimed efforts by the Bollandists were providing reliable hagiographies expunged of any superfluous or ridiculous accounts, in particular the *Acta Sanctorum*,[57] most authors of martyr-plays feel liberty to alter essential details of their subjects' narratives.[58] This reflects the waning power of churchmen to control Theatre, which was regarded with great suspicion by some quarters in the seventeenth century, not least because of the danger that a crowd could pose to public order.[59] The three plays in 1645 about St Genesius, patron of actors, seem to proclaim that the Theatre had come of age and Desfontaines's Genest represents the power of the stage as a social force, for he is described as being capable:

> Au gré de sa voix et ses actions [...] changer nos passions
>
> (I. 1)

A somewhat more elevated aim than the usual *plaire* and *instruire*.

Indeed, ecclesiastical opposition to the Theatre often highlighted the function of the actor as the 'transmitter of harmful passions'.[60]

It would seem safe to assume that the genre of the martyr-play is intimately linked to the crisis of authority in the seventeenth century. Even if aspects of the martyrs' transgression are sometimes transformed to conform with received political theories, it is significant that the theme is still chosen. Corneille moves from the clemency of Augustus in *Cinna* to the tyranny of Decius in *Polyeucte*. The protagonist in De la Serre's *Thomas Morus* tells his wife:

Le Roy a beau le permettre: ma conscience me le deffend

(IV. 4)

and this summarizes the martyr. The spectator in his or her heart surely wishes to be a rebel, to have such principles, to achieve the transgression that they see before them on stage? The martyr says 'non serviam' to the old order, to fear and to any impediment to the absolute liberty for which they yearn.[61] He or she is surely a 'living' illustration of the potency of the individual, though undeniably a rather ambiguous one.

It is worth considering that in seventeenth-century England, martyr narratives served to encourage religious dissenters and created a discourse of martydom for those resisting the authority of the established Church.[62] This was not so in France as these martyr-plays had never served as Catholic propaganda, as might have been expected, probably because of the suspicion in which ecclesiastical authorities held sacred drama or even drama *per se*.[63] However, authors clearly felt free to distort the saints' lives for dramatic purposes. Even Boissin de Galladon in *Le Martyre de S. Vincent* (1618) deviates from details in the *Acta Sanctorum* to which he has been faithful in his pious play, to give the martyr a more violent and gory death – he replaces details of St Vincent's martyrdom with those of St

Lawrence. In the *Examen* to *Polyeucte*, Corneille excuses distortions and additions to the legend as mere 'inventions et des embellissements de théâtre'. He believes these permissible since it is not encroaching on sacred scripture, and he even lists eight prominent additions of his own: 'le reste est de *mon* invention', and this seems to be the standpoint of the other playwrights. However, is this not the greatest transgression of all in connection with the martyr-play? Catholic authors emphasize the Bible and ostensibly treat hagiographies as entertainment that they can mould for their plot, narratives to which one owes simply 'une croyance pieuse'.[64] In feeling the liberty to choose what the Church had codified, it is little wonder that the martyr was such a prevalent choice in the seventeenth century, for the martyr is the utter incarnation of independence.

Appendix

This is the first complete list of the martyr-play that has been compiled for seventeenth-century France. This table is by no means exhaustive – for example, I only include a very small representative selection of performances that would have been printed but are no longer extant. I am particularly indebted to J.S. Street's, *French Sacred Drama from Bèze to Corneille* (Cambridge: CUP, 1983), to K.V. Loubovitch, *L'Évolution de la tragédie religieuse en France* (Paris: Droz, 1933) and to H.C. Lancaster, *A History of French Dramatic Literature in the Seventeenth Century* (London: Rivingtons, 1966) which provided me with a substantial amount of this chronology. I treat Heinsius's *Herodes Infanticida* as a French play since the author was regarded in his lifetime as a French author in exile. Moreover, Lancaster, Street and Loubovitch – amongst others – all consider this a French play and indeed Corneille in the *Examen* to *Polyeucte* acknowledges the work as one of the inspirations for his choice of martyr theme. The three plays of 1660 written by Jésus-Marie, a Carmelite friar, are of doubtful authorship and the place and date of the work are unknown, but this date and author are generally accepted (see Lancaster, op. cit., I, p. 403). The only contentious contenders for the title of martyr-play are the anonymous work of 1627 about St Norbert, which contains many of the elements common to the martyr-play, namely the saint suffers an unjust and painful demise, and also Joan of Arc, who was popularly accredited with the glory of martyrdom. I have omitted other examples of populist 'canonization' such as Mary Stuart, about whom there are several seventeenth-century tragedies.

Chronology of French martyr-plays published between 1596-1675

Date	Title	Author	Place
1596	S.Jacques	Bardon de Brun	Limoges
	Dioclétian	Laudun d'Aigaliers	Paris
	Le martyre de S. Sébastien	Laudun d'Aigaliers	Paris
	Ste Barbe	Anon	Lyon
1600	Vitae sanctae Catherinae	A. Le Mire	Anvers
1606	Jeanne d'Arques	Heudon	Rouen
	Tragédie de Jeanne d'Arques	Anon	Rouen
	La Céciliade ou martyre sanglant de ste Cécile	N. Soret	Paris
1607	Décollation de S. Jean	Collège de Chabeuil	
1609	S.Blaise	Anon (performance)	Le Puy
1611	Jeanne d'Arques	Brunet	Rouen
1612	S. Eustache	Anon	Barjols
1613	S.Tarentien et son compagnon	Collège de Namur	
1614	Vies de très illustres vierges et martyres stes Catherine et Ursule	Anon	Liège
1615	Tragédie de Sainte Agnès	Pierre Troterel	Rouen
1616	Tragédie du martyr de Cinq Japonais	Collège de Namur	
1617	S. Pierre et S. Paul	Collège d'Annecy	
1618	Ste Catherine	J.Boissin de Gallardon	Lyon
	S. Vincent	J.Boissin de Gallardon	Lyon
	Théâtre sanglant de Ste Catherine martyre	J.Labarde	Paris
1619	Ste Catherine	E. Poytevin	Paris
1620	S. Jean-Baptiste	Anon	Solliès-Pont
	Agnès	Virey	Rouen

1621	*La vie de Ste Justine et de S. Cyprien*	D. Coppée	Liège
1622	*Ste Catherine*	(Performance)	Le Beausset
	S. Eustache	(Performance)	Barjols
1623	*S. Sébastien*	(Performance)	Cotignac
1624	*S. Lambert*	D. Coppée	Liège
1625	*Antioche, tragédie traitant le martyre de sept enfants machabéens*	J-B. Le Franc	Paris
1626	*Jeanne d'Arques*	Anon	Troyes
1627	*Tragédie de S. Norbert*		
	Tragédie du martyre de S. Sébastien	V. Borée	
	Le martyre de S. Gervais	F. Chevreau	Paris
1628	*La Tragédie du Martyre et mort de saintSébastien*	E. Grandjean	Nancy
	S. Sébastien	Collège de Pont-à-Mousson	
1629	*Epithalamium D. Catharinae*	P. Alamay	
1630	*Sanctus Adrianus Martyr*	L. Cellot	La Flèche
1631	*Martyre de S. Etienne*	(Performance)	Solliéres
1632	*Le martyre de S. Eustache*	P. Bello	Liège
	Herodes Infanticida	D. Heinsius	Leyden
1633	*Histoire de Ste Catherine*	(Performance)	Fréjus
1634	*Ste Barbe*	Brunet	Troyes
1635	*S. Sébastien*	Croock	Ghent
	Procopius Martyr	P. Berthelot	Clermont
	Hermengildus	P. Caussin	La Flèche
1638	*La mort d'enfants d'Hérodes*	G. de La Caprenède	Paris
1640	*Thomas Morus*	P. de la Serre	Paris
1641	*Herménigilde*	La Caprenède	Paris
1642	*La Pucelle d'Orléans*	Abbé d'Aubignac	Paris
	Ste Catherine	P. de la Serre	Paris
	Polyeucte	P. Corneille	Paris
1643	*Le martyre de S. Eustache*	N. Desfontaines	Paris
1645	*Théodore, vierge et martyre*	P. Corneille	Paris
	S. Genest	C. Besogne	
	Le Véritable Saint Genest	J. Rotrou	Paris
	L'Illustre comédien ou le martyre de Saint Genest	N. Desfontaines	Paris
1647	*Le fils exilé ou le martyre de S. Clair*	P. Mouffle	Paris
1649	*Le martyre de Ste Catherine*	Compagnon (pub)	Lyon
	La mort de Théandre	Chevillard	Orléans
	S. Eustache martyr, Poëme dramatique	B. Baro	Paris

1650	*Les Chastes Martyrs*	Mlle Cosnard	Paris
	Les Jumeaux Martyrs	Mme de Saint-Balmon	Paris
	Herménigilde	G.Olivier	Auxerre
1651	*Saint Jean-Baptiste*	J. Bisson de la Coudray	Paris
1654	*Indégonde*	Montauban	Paris
	Natalie ou la Generosité Chrestienne	Montgaudier	Paris
	La Forte Romaine	M. Vallée	Paris
1655	*Le Martyre de ste Ursule*	Yvernaud	Poitiers
	Agathonphile martyr	Mlle F. Paschal	Lyon
1656	*Ste Suzanne martyre*	M. Vallée	Paris
	La Pucelle	Chapelain	Paris
1658	*Dorothée ou la victorieuse martire*	Rampale	Lyon
	Saincte Dorothée	N. de Le Ville	Louvain
	Saincte Ursule	N. de Le Ville	Louvain
1660	*Herménigilde*	Anon monk	
	Sur les Martyre des SS. Innocents	I-J. de Jésus-Marie	
	Sur le Martyre de S. Sébastien	I-J. de Jésus-Marie	
	S. Herménégilde	I-J. de Jésus-Marie	
1661	*Ste Reine d'Alise, vierge et martyre*	H. Millotet	Autun
1662	*Le martyre de la glorieuse Ste Reine d'Alise*	C. Ternet	Autun
	Sainte Cécile couronnée comme vierge et martyre	J. de Nîmes	Autun
1663	*L'Illustre Philosophe ou L'Histoire de Ste Catherine d'Alexandrie*	C. de La Chapelle	Autun
1664	*Le Royal Martyr*	Les Isles le Bas	Rouen
1668	*Dipne, infante d'Irlande*	F. d'Avre	Paris
	Le Martyre de Ste Suzanne	Anon	
1669	*Geneviève ou l'innocence reconnue*	Anon	Paris
1670	*Le Martyre de S. Gervais*	F. de Cheffault	Paris
	Geneviève ou l'innocence reconnue	F. d'Avre	Paris
1671	*Sainte-Reine, vierge et martyre*	A. le Grand	Paris
1675	*Les soupirs de Sifroi*	C. Blessebois	Châtillon

University of Durham

1   *Corneille et la dialétique du héros* (Paris: Gallimard, 1963), p. 241.

2   John Lough considers that a major cause of the revolt 'was the inevitable reaction against the progress which the monarchy had made towards absolutism'. *An Introduction to Seventeenth Century France* (London: Longman, 1966), p. 128.

3   I suggest this classification for these plays, something that hitherto has not tended to happen, as they are usually treated as part of sacred drama or with saint-plays, both of which have a wide pool of inspiration. Since a genre can be defined as 'a recognizable and established category of written work employing common conventions' (C. Baldock, *The Concise Oxford Dictionary of Literary Terms* (Oxford: Oxford University Press, 1990)), and since the martyr-play contains elements that are universal, such as the conversion of the protagonist, the revelation of the new faith, a confrontation, then the martyrdom itself, it would not be straining the definition of genre too much in applying it to the martyr-play.

4   Henry Carrington Lancaster, *History of French Dramatic Literature in the Seventeenth Century*, 8 vols. (London: Rivington, 1966), II, Part 2, p. 675.

5   Corneille, *Polyeucte* (Oxford: Oxford University Press, 1990), p. xxvi.

6   The *mystère* is a forerunner of the martyr-play, though the most popular martyr in these plays, Ste Barbe, only features in one martyr-play of the seventeenth century.

7   Pierre Mignard, *Louis at Maastricht*, oil on canvas, 1673. Pinacoteca, Turin. Repr. in Peter Burke, *The Fabrication of Louis XIV* (New Haven: Yale University Press, 1992), p.80 (fig. 28). This however is perpetuating a common error – the Roman emperor usually wore an oak-leaf wreath. While a laurel wreath was the victor's band, any citizen who saved another's life was entitled to wear a wreath of oak-leaves and since the emperor was symbolically *civium salvator* this was what he tended to wear. It is possible that French artists were portraying Louis as victor rather than saviour, but that fails to account for the total absence of the oak-leaf in royal iconographical representations. Burke's work constitutes a detailed study of representations of Louis XIV (especially pp. 187-198) which recall the precedent of ancient Rome.

8   Photograph in Burke, op. cit., p.40 (fig. 14). The description, quoted in C. Maumené & L. D'Harcourt, *Iconographie des Rois de France*, 2 vols (Paris: Colin, 1931), II, 183, is taken from the actual wording of the commission: the *prévôt des marchands* at Paris commissioned the statue hastily, in fact the very day after the end of the Frondes, to curry favour with the king.

9   'In the age of Louis XIII, Guez de Balzac had suggested the imitation of Roman emperor-worship. Ceremonial specialists [...] studied the rituals of ancient Rome'. Burke, op. cit., p. 195.

10   ibid., p. 195.

11   ibid., p.66 (fig. 22).

12   In the period 'monarchs addressed their subjects in progresses, processions and festivals, as well as in speeches and proclamations' (Nicholas Henshall, *The Myth of Absolutism* (London: Longman, 1992), p. 140). It is clear that a primary model for Louis XIV was that of Rome. Indeed, as the seventeenth century progresses the French sovereign increasingly takes this as his model, an implicit rejection of the Holy Roman Emperor's claim to represent the new caesar.

13   Though as Nicholas Henshall points out, divine right was not a new conception to the French monarchy; only coupled with absolutist tendencies and hereditary succession did it become novel. See Henshall, op. cit., pp. 141-143.

14   John B. Wolf, *Louis XIV* (London: Gollancz, 1968), p. 27.

15   *Politique tireé de l'Écriture sainte*, Livre III, article II. I have used the *Œuvres complètes de Bossuet*, 30 vols (Paris: Louis Vives, 1864), XXIII, 536.

16   A Catholic liturgical calendar providing a brief life of martyrs and other saints. A revised edition had been promulgated by Gregory XIII in 1584. The account of St Genesius occurs in the entry for August 25th.

17   I refer to a modern edition, *Martyrologium Romanum, editio typica* (Rome: Typis Polyglottis Vaticanis, 1923), p. 203. However, the account of Genesius's martyrdom has not altered from the first edition.

18   For a full consideration of absolutism and the theories on kingship, see W.J. Stankiewicz, *Politics and Religion in Seventeenth Century France* (Berkeley: University of California Press, 1960), in particular pp. 92-215.

19   A particularly relevant part is worth quoting: 'Reges a Deo esse [...] Apostoli confirmant, Martyres confitentur, neque tantum a Deo, sed etiam Deos', quoted in *Le Mercure Jésuite* (Geneva, 1631), I, 794.

20   Bossuet, op. cit., XXIII, 538.

21 Antoine Adam considers Jean Rotrou, 'pendant cette période, le plus important de nos auteurs dramatiques après Corneille'. *Histoire de la littérature française au XVIIe siècle*, 4 vols (Paris: Montchrestien, 1948), II, 334.

22 This contrasts fundamentally with Bossuet's reflections on the early martyrs who, according to him, 'demeuraient *assujettis* au roi temporel pour l'amour du Roi éternel'. Bossuet, op. cit., p. 407.

23 ibid., XXIII, 538.

24 Jean-Marie Apostolidès, *Le Prince Sacrifié* (Paris: Minuit, 1985), p. 29.

25 ibid., p. 29.

26 *Institution royale de Charles IX*, 1562.

27 B. Baro, *Sainct Eustache martyr, poëme dramatique* (Paris: Sommaville, 1649), BL 164.c.29.

28 Bossuet, op. cit., XV, 394.

29 ibid., p. 395.

30 Thomas Aquinas, *In 2 sent*, 44.2.2.5 (*Scriptum super Libros Sententiarum*, ed. R.P. Mandonnet (Paris: Lethielleux, 1929), p. 1118) – the English is my translation: 'Qui ad liberationem patriae tyrannum occidit, laudatur et præmium accipit.' Also in the *Summa Theologica* (IIa IIae, 42, art. 3), Aquinas justifies the overthrowing of a tyrannical government: 'ideo pertubatio huius regimins non habet rationem seditionem'.

31 'One of the most influential tracts was the Jesuit Mariana's *De Rege et Regis Institutione* published in 1599 which defended the rights of individuals to kill tyrants'. David Parker, *The Making of French Absolutism* (London: Arnold, 1983), p. 48. The Jesuits were attached to the theory mainly due to the fact it was expounded by celebrated Jesuit theologians such as Suàrez and Bellarmine, who went further than Aquinas and enumerated more circumstances of permissible regicide.

32 Bossuet, op. cit., p. 407.

33 See Roland Mousnier, *The Assassination of Henry IV*, trans. by Joan Spencer (London: Faber, 1973) pp.39-60 and pp. 86-105. Mariana in his *De Rege* of 1599 actually considers the case of Henry III's regicide and concludes that it was clearly tyrannicide.

34 The revolt of the 1620s stemmed from Protestant grievances at the withdrawal of concessions granted to them by the edict of Nantes, not against the king's authority *per se*. Indeed, the Protestants were almost entirely loyal to the Crown during the Frondes.

35 Retz, *Œuvres*, 11 vols (Paris: Feillet, 1870-1920), I, 275

36 The French king alone of Christian kings was anointed with chrism, usually reserved for the conferral of the sacrament of orders, derived from a miraculously self-replenishing source given by an angel at Clovis's baptism. He also received communion under both kinds like a priest and could act as deacon at High Mass. Interestingly enough, Louis XIV was often represented as St Louis, Louis IX, his predecessor (see Peter Burke, op. cit., p. 28).

37 Bossuet, op. cit., XXIII, p. 534.

38 R.A. Sayce, op. cit., p. xiii.

39 'En mourant pour son Dieu, Polyeucte meurt donc exclusivement pour lui-même.' Doubrovsky, op.cit., p.251.

40 Curiously, Lancaster interprets Simphronie's remarks about her ('Vous êtes toute émue et vos sens sont troublés') as evidence of her human frailty, a natural reaction to his threats, seemingly ignoring Agnes's justification of her emotional distress. Lancaster, op. cit., I, 104.

41 This can be countered by St Paul's assertion: 'For to me to live is Christ; and to die is gain [...] and what *I shall choose* I know not' (Philippians 1. 21-22, Douay version, 1963).

42 A.R. Droge & J.D. Tabor, *A Noble Death* (San Francisco: Harper, 1992), p. 5. This work is a helpful study of the sociological aspects of martyrdom.

43 At the beginning of Act III – the Acts are not divided into scenes. I have used a reprint (Paris: Librarie de Bibliophiles, 1875), BL 117.b.2.

44 *Laws*, Book 9 (873cd). See also Droge & Tabor, op. cit., p. 20.

45 Richard Dawkins, *The Selfish Gene* (Oxford: Oxford University Press, 1989), pp. 171-72.

46 E. and A. Weiner, *The Martyr's Conviction- A Sociological Analysis* (Atlanta: Scholars Press, 1990), p. 53.

47 Baro, op. cit., V. 2.

48 In the plays that I have examined, the fifty is reduced to a token few; otherwise, we see Catherine debating with one at a time.

49 Doubrovsky, op. cit., p. 251. The emphasis is mine.

50 In fact in almost identical terms: 'A-t-elle vu flamber les torches d'Hymenée' (Rotrou: II. 6) and 'Les flambeau de l'hymen viennent de s'allumer' (Corneille: I. 1). Rotrou's work owed a debt to Corneille; see, for example, E.T. Dubois, *Le véritable Saint Genest* (Geneva: Droz, 1972), pp. 20-21.

51 Georges Lanson, *Corneille* (Paris: Hachette, 1962), p. 110.

52 Clearly a heterodox religious view. St Peter states: 'Let none of you suffer as a murderer [...] but as a Christian' (I Peter, 4: 15-16).

53 In E. Poytevin's *Ste Catherine* (1619), the emperor has his wife beheaded in order to offer Catherine her crown and his hand, a somewhat unconventional alternative to divorce.

54 N.Z. Davies, *Society and Culture in Early Modern France* (Stanford: Stanford University Press, 1975), pp.144-145.

55 'The focus of the Church's suspicions of the public theatre often fell [...] on actresses who were held to demean the status of their sex and deliberately to arouse lubricious feelings in their male audience.' Henry Phillips, 'Italy and France in the Seventeenth-Century Stage Controversy', *The Seventeenth Century*, 11. 2 (1996), 187-207 (p. 187).

56 The *parlement* of Paris banned religious drama by an *arrêt* of 1548, which kept religious drama off the Parisian public stage until the very end of the sixteenth century. See J.S. Street, *French Sacred Drama from Bèze to Corneille* (Cambridge: Cambridge University Press, 1983), pp. 19-22.

57 The Bollandists were a body of Jesuits fouded by Heribert Rosweyde (1569-1629). By 1681 they had published 21 volumes of the *Acta Sanctorum*, and it was largely agreed that 'the new publication surpassed anything of the kind known at the time', *The Catholic Encyclopedia* , 17 vols. (Baltimore: Encyclopedia Press Inc., 1913), I, 263.

58 The *Golden Legend*, an account of various popular saints and martyrs was the one book likely to be owned by the lower échelons of the laity, therefore the audience would recognize deviations from standard narratives. See N.Z. Davies, op. cit., p. 211.

59   Henry Phillips, *The Theatre and its Critics in Seventeenth-Century France*
      (Oxford: Oxford University Press, 1983), p. 9.

60   Henry Phillips, 'Italy and France in the Seventeenth-Century Stage
      Controversy', loc. cit., p. 187.

61   For the martyr it is a case of reaching: 'la liberté absolue, de détruire
      chez l'homme tout ce qui est esclavage'. Doubrovsky, op. cit., p. 247.

62   See John R. Knott, *Discourses of Martyrdom in English Literature, 1563-
      1694* (Cambridge: Cambridge University Press, 1994).

63   Charles Borromeo, archbishop of Milan (and Pope Pius IV's nephew)
      led a campaign against the theatre which spread over Europe. Church
      councils at Rouen in 1581, Reims, Bordeaux and Tours in 1584 and
      Aix in 1585 all censured the stage. Borromeo's canonization in 1610
      reinforced oppostion to the Theatre.

64   From the *Examen* to *Polyeucte*. Corneille uses as authorities the
      Protestants Heinsius and Buchanan, but after naming precedents to
      the performance of religious drama, he admits that: 'je me suis donné
      des licences qu'ils n'ont pas prises, de *changer l'histoire* en quelque
      chose, et d'y mêler des *épisodes d'invention*' (my emphasis).

L'audace d'une femme :
Gender and Transgression in Racine's Athalie

Véronique Desnain

Racine's last tragedy, *Athalie*, presents us with an unusual character in that she may at first appear to possess no redeeming features, hence contradicting the Aristotelian principle, fully endorsed by the playwright, that a truly tragic character should be neither totally good nor totally bad, but rather 'the sort of man who is not conspicuous for virtue and justice, and whose fall into misery is not due to vice and depravity, but rather to some error'.[1] Athalie, however, is portrayed as criminal and guilty.[2] This is in part due to the fact that our initial view of the character is based on information given by her 'enemies' and therefore necessarily biased. Athalie herself does not appear on stage until II, 3 : 'The Athalie we hear about, then, belongs to myth [...] Athalie's first appearance on stage is striking precisely because it is so little like what we have been led to expect.'[3] Nonetheless there are some details that are undeniable and weigh heavily against her regardless of the impression made by the character's words or behaviour on stage: she is a female ruler in a society where women are subordinate to men and do not normally exert overt power, and therefore a usurper; she is a polytheist in the context of a biblical story; and finally she has killed her grand-children, a crime whose horror is highlighted by constant references to her as Eliacin's potential mother, rather than grand-mother.

Yet a closer look reveals that these apparently multiple transgressions are in fact based on a single detail : Athalie's gender in a predominantly patriarchal belief system. Obviously, transgression can only exist in the context of a specific ideology whose rules can be broken. In Althusser's terms, Athalie is, as any other human being, a social construction and it could therefore be argued that her 'crimes' are merely consequences of the prevalent order. If we accept the structuralist view that there is no 'natural' behaviour then the notion of Athalie as an 'unnatural' woman collapses and we can begin to see how the play's depiction of the character attempts to make sense of, and perhaps justify, the discrepancy between genders on which patriarchy is based.[4] This of course suggest a feminist approach to the text insofar as it highlights the notion of sexual difference rather than excludes it as is so often the case with critics who posit the 'universal' qualities of tragedy. I would claim, as does E. Berg that

> In fact the move of appealing to a transcendence of sexuality serves only to repress the question of sexual difference. This erasure of difference amounts to an erasure of the woman insofar as she becomes a neuter which is rapidly assimilated to a masculine ideal... This move of reducing the difference between [...] characters, and thereby assimilating the woman to a masculine standard, is probably the most frequent strategy of male writers.[5]

This study will therefore emphasise the sexual difference by concentrating on Athalie as a women rather than a genderless character, keeping in mind that 'implicit in this type of analysis is, first and foremost, the idea that women be considered as a separate cultural group'.[6] From this perspective it would seems that Athalie's only real transgression (her failure to act in a way suitable for a woman) is overshadowed, we could almost say disguised, by other, fallacious accusations. As we will see, her deeds are not necessarily transgressive in themselves, by which I mean that they would not be perceived as such if committed by men, and the assumption of guilt rests on the inherent misogyny of the author, his audience and his time, as well as a misunderstanding, or misrepresentation of the character's own society and position. Yet we are sometimes given clues within the text of the play which enable us to perceive the fallacy and it is these, combined with a reassessment of Athalie's so-called crimes in the context of her own society, which I will use to demonstrate both that her gender is the only basis for her transgression and that it is this which renders her character truly tragic.

I will first address the two clear accusations levelled at Athalie by her enemies: that she is [*une*] *impie et meurtrière* (747).[7] Because 'on Racine's stage, the events that can be assimilated to prevailing ideological structures are sanctioned, while exceptional behaviour is condemned as irrational',[8] it is important to recognise that the ideological structures within which the characters move are vastly different from the one recognised and accepted by both Racine's contemporary public and the modern reader. When Joad brands the queen 'une impie' two thousand years of a society based on Judaeo-Christian teachings prompt us to agree. Yet for Athalie, who lives in a polytheist society, the virulence and aggression displayed by the followers of this singular god are incomprehensible. Although she wishes to defend her faith against what she sees as the new cult, she fails to grasp the extent of the devotion of Joad and his followers and still perceives the conflict to be mostly political. She, as the ruler, must stop the wave of sedition which threatens to start up unrest.

> Te voilà, séducteur,
> De ligues, de complots pernicieux auteur,
> Qui dans le trouble seul as mis tes espérances. (1705-7)

She does however genuinely worship her own idol and is not without spirituality. When troubled by dreams she seeks comfort in religion:

> J'allais prier Baal de veiller sur ma vie
> Et chercher du repos au pied de ses autels. (524-5)

She even contemplates a gesture of appeasement towards the god of the Jews:

> Dans le temple des Juifs un instinct m'a poussée,
> Et d'apaiser leur Dieu j'ai conçu la pensée. (527-8)

But the horrified reaction of the worshippers promptly discourages her, before the sight of Joas completes her confusion and prompts her to leave. Yet even without the extraordinary apparition and Athalie's retreat, it is obvious that Joad would not welcome a reconciliation, and his discourse, which insists on her unworthiness as a woman, would no doubt be enough to reignite the anger of a queen who is used to be given respect for her position. Even Abner, who is in her service, does not mention her title, but reduces her in the temple to an appendage:

> Hé quoi ? vous de nos rois et la femme et la mère,
> Etes-vous à ce point parmi nous étrangère ?   (447-8)

Despite this brutal rejection, Athalie shows herself to be a liberal ruler. Although irritated by what she sees as Joad's political agitation, she gives her subjects freedom of worship, even, significantly in Abner's case, to those close to her. When she meets Joas and wishes to adopt him, she makes it clear that religious conversion is not a condition:

> J'ai mon Dieu que je sers, vous servirez le vôtre ;
> Ce sont deux puissants dieux. (684-5)

This god which Athalie serves is in fact one of the predominant deities of her time :

> Les documents historiques révèlent que, au cours de la période
> en question, on peut constater une persistance et même une
> recrudescence des rites cananéens, du respect des hauts lieux,
> des cultes des Baals et des Astratés.[9]

It is therefore Athalie who is in line with the religious practices of the society she lives in, and the monotheists who appear as members of a new, seditious sect, but she clearly fails to understand, used as she is to living in a pluri-religious society, that the only god of the Jew cannot co-exist with any others. She persists in seeing the Jews' struggle mainly as a political one and seeks compromise when the first premise of the establishment of the monotheist faith of the Old Testament is the eradication of all others and of those who oppose it :

> ...la volonté ou le destin du dieu des Juifs est de se présenter comme le seul Dieu et d'éliminer tous les autres; c'est là le sujet même d'*Athalie* : il s'agit pour le Dieu des Juifs de se faire reconnaître comme le Dieu unique. [10]

The ruthlessness demonstrated by the God of the Jews and his followers in this mission has been amply demonstrated by the fate of Athalie's own parents but it should be pointed out at this stage that the horrific manner of Jezebel's death (which Athalie refers to in her dream[11]) is in fact linked to her status as wife of Achab rather than, as Racine would have us believe, her own actions: Elijah's curse to her husband (1 Kings 21.24) affects *her* manner of death (2 Kings 9.35), not Achab's. Nevertheless, it is understood that the curse has been fulfilled, for Jezebel, in death as well as in life, is considered an appendage to her husband.[12] The misogyny inherent in this hardly needs to be highlighted and is typical of the Old Testament system of belief which is based on a strictly patriarchal hierarchy in which God is 'le Père', a loving but authoritarian parent not given to squeamishness when it comes to punishing those who have rebelled against him.

This brings us to the second charge against Athalie: she has killed and, what is more, she has killed children. We instinctively perceive this to be the worst possible transgression. Yet the Bible is full of murders committed in the name of God the Father and in at least two instances (Abraham and Jephthah[13]) he orders the sacrifice of children.[14] But characteristically he chooses men to carry out those orders. This serves to highlight the duality of the standards by which Athalie is judged. The play is ridden with gruesome descriptions of massacres in which the amount of blood poured either highlights the saintliness of the perpetrator, if it is a man, or her barbarity, if it is a woman. Joad revels in a description of the destruction of Athalie's parents :

> L'impie Achab détruit, et de son sang trempé
> Le champ que par le meurtre il avait usurpé ;
> Près de ce champ fatal Jézabel immolée,
> Sous les pieds des chevaux cette reine foulée,
> De son sang inhumain les chiens désaltérés,
> Et de son corps hideux les membres déchirés. (113-8)

To him this scene symbolises *des prodiges fameux* (110), acts inspired and supported by God, and if he later expresses doubts about Jehu, the perpetrator of these brutal murders, it is because he feels betrayed by the fact that Jehu has now abandoned his vengeful crusade and renounced his vendetta against Athalie :

> Jéhu laisse d'Achab l'affreuse fille en paix. (1086)

Although he is presented as a holy man, Joad certainly seems closer to the religious fanatic than to the forgiving Christian and displays a singularly unpleasant penchant for bloodbaths: *Dans l'infidèle sang baignez-vous sans horreur* (1360). Yet in dramatic terms Joad is presented as the positive answer to Athalie's negative role-model because it is assumed that the Christian audience will implicitly accept the righteousness of his struggle :

> Il dupe les Juifs, puisqu'il leur fait croire qu'Athalie veut tuer l'enfant-roi - ce qui est absolument contraire à la vérité [...] Ce prêtre sans scrupule s'enivre parfois de visions sanglantes [...] Le machiavélisme impitoyable de Joad est ainsi motivé et excusé par son ardeur religieuse.[15]

The double standard is clear. There is no doubt that Athalie's murders are repugnant but this infanticide allows her enemies to describe her as monstrous, which is hypocritical for at least two distinct reasons. First her accusers would have had a rather different attitude to such deeds from that of a modern, or even seventeenth-century reader:

The execution of relatives was not uncommon in the case of a newly ordained monarch who wanted to secure their rule, especially when circumstances were difficult; thus king Salomon kills his half-brother Adonijah (1 Kings 2.13-25). The narrator goes to great lengths to justify the act. Athaliah's cruel actions were probably necessary, particularly because no direct male heir existed.[16]

In this case the complexity of blood-ties gives rise to a bitterly ironic situation :

> Selon la logique qui demandait qu'après un changement de dynastie tous les descendants du roi précédant fussent massacrés, Athalie et ses petits-enfants auraient dû subir le même sort de la main de Jéhu. Mais il se trouve que la descendance de Jézabel et d'Achab est aussi la descendance de David. C'est ainsi qu'Athalie, selon la même logique, pour se venger et se protéger, se trouve dans la nécessité d'éliminer toute la descendance royale de Juda, héritière spirituelle du prophète et de son instrument Jéhu, c'est-à-dire ses propres petits-enfants.[17]

We can easily speculate that had Athalie's descent not been linked to David, the very same infanticide would have been Jéhu's doing and he would have been praised for it. Yet Athalie is described as monstrous by her enemies and we suspect that it is not because she killed children but because by doing so she acted in contradiction with the most basic characteristic ascribed to women: they are givers of life, and the taking of life, if it must occur is, as we will see, reserved for men. By overstepping this boundary, Athalie has rejected the qualities which supposedly define her as a woman and has renounced her human status. Furthermore, when Athalie herself describes her actions in II, 7, her words insist on both her pride and the fact that her motivation was revenge. She fails to display any remorse:

> Oui, ma juste fureur, et j'en fais vanité,
>
> A vengé mes parents sur ma postérité. (709-710)

Athalie's own description of events is also important because:

> Dans la scène 7 de l'acte 2, nous apprenons par Athalie le lieu
> causal qui existe entre ses propres crimes et ceux de Jéhu; lien
> auquel les juifs de la pièce ne font pas allusion [...] En somme
> Athalie, et c'est elle-même qui le dit, n'a fait qu'obéir à la loi
> juive du talion: 'Rendre meurtre pour meurtre, outrage pour
> outrage'.[18]

The decision by Racine to keep political motives silent or to suggest
the acceptability of such actions in a biblical context may well
stem from a desire to spare his audience's sensibilities (would
they have found murderous anger more palatable than cold-
blooded assassination?). It is in fact more than likely that there
is a political element beyond the religious one even for Joad:
Jerusalem will be in the hands of whoever emerges victorious
from this 'holy battle'.

> La simple comparaison entre le contexte général d'*Athalie* et
> ses sources scripturaires permet immédiatement de constater
> que Racine attribue aux événements une importance que la
> Bible est loin de leur accorder. Dans le Livre des Rois (ch. 11)
> et les Chroniques (ch. 22, 9-12; ch. 23), il s'agit d'une
> révolution de palais soigneusement orchestrée par la caste
> sacerdotale ou bien par l'armée.[19]

Although Racine himself does not suggest this, he does admit,
in his *Préface,* that he based his tragedy on the most religious
version of events.

> Il est important aussi de noter que Racine choisit la version
> du chroniste en ce qui concerne la conjuration des juifs
> contre Athalie. Dans les *Chroniques*, les cariens et les
> coureurs, c'est-à-dire les mercenaires, sont remplacés par des

lévis et des centeniers aux noms authentiquement israélites.
Le chroniste cherche à mettre en valeur le caractère religieux
et dynastique de la conjuration pour la légitimer aux dépens
de la lutte proprement politique.[20]

To privilege the religious motivations of the characters undoubtedly
serves to put Athalie at a disadvantage (she is after all the *impie*
and therefore has no higher motive for her killings) and to stress
the highly emotional nature of the character as opposed to her
stature as a ruler. Indeed, it redeems and damns her at the same
time. Secondly Joad himself sees the murder of family members
as not only justified but holy when committed by men:

> Ne descendez-vous pas de ces fameux lévites
> [qui ...]
> De leurs plus chers parents saintement homicides,
> Consacrèrent leurs mains dans le sang des perfides, (1362-6)

and this includes infanticide when it is committed by believers
in the service of God :

> N'êtes-vous pas ici sur la montagne sainte
> Où le père des Juifs sur son fils innocent
> Leva sans murmurer un bras obéissant,
> Et mit sur un bûcher ce fruit de sa vieillesse,
> Laissant à Dieu le soin d'accomplir sa promesse,
> Et lui sacrifiant, avec ce fils aimé,
> Tout l'espoir de sa race en lui seul renfermé ? (1438-1444)

Racine clarifies this biblical reference in his *Préface*:

> La montagne sur laquelle le temple fut bâti était la même
> montagne où Abraham avait autrefois offert en sacrifice son
> fils Isaac. [21]

Another look at feminist critics of the Bible itself shows that
such a sacrifice was not only necessary but in fact desirable:

> The institution of sacrifice serves as a mean for men in patrilineal descent groups to affirm their kinship bonds [...] Sacrifice, by socially and religiously establishing lines of descent reckoned solely through males, enables males to transcend their dependence on women's reproductive powers.[22]

Even in a non-biblical context, infanticide is presented as far less taboo when committed by men. Racine's own plays, *Iphigénie* and *Phèdre*, present us with two examples of this. In *Iphigénie* Agamemnon is seen as a tragic, if somewhat spineless character as he debates whether to offer his daughter up for sacrifice, not only to the gods but also to his own ambition. A refusal to obey Calchas' demand would seriously threaten his position as leader of the Greek army :

> Cette soif de régner, que rien ne peut éteindre,
> L'orgueil de voir vingt rois vous servir et vous craindre,
> Tous les droits de l'empire en vos mains confiés,
> Cruel, c'est à ces dieux que vous sacrifiez,
> Et loin de repousser le coup qu'on vous prépare,
> Vous voulez vous en faire un mérite barbare. (1285-1290)

The accusation might seem biassed, coming as it does from Iphigénie's mother, were it not later confirmed by Agamemnon himself :

> Ma gloire intéressée emporte la balance. (1426)

That Iphigénie is saved *in extremis* by a twist of fate does not detract from the fact that Agamemnon had decided in favour of infanticide by proxy, yet D. Clarke's comment on Hardy's *Scédase* could, to a certain extent, be applied to Racine's *Iphigénie*: 'Offering a startling insight into the gender priorities of early seventeenth-century France, the play shows how the hapless father suffered with Stoic fortitude his daughter's misfortune.'[23] Agamemnon is not punished for his decision to offer his daughter as a sacrificial victim, despite the fact that he plays no part in her rescue. On the contrary, his willingness to let his daughter be killed is seen by his allies as proof of his stature as a king: he has risen from the personal to a higher level, one which implies a greater loyalty to society and to patriarchy than to one's own blood, one of the major tenets of *gloire*.

In *Phèdre*, infanticide does take place, although once again it is committed on the orders of the father rather than by his own hand. Having heard the accusation of attempted rape levelled at his son, Thésée promptly asks Neptune to avenge him, not, it must be pointed out, because of the injury done to Phèdre, but because raping her would be an insult to Thésée himself : [24]

> Ah! Qu'est-ce-que j'entends ? Un traître, un téméraire,
> Préparait cet outrage à l'honneur de son père ? (1001-2)

Admittedly, Thésée does not specifically ask for his son's death but he does state *tu cours à ta perte infaillible* (1157) and washes his hands of Hippolyte's fate. In his rush to restore his good name, he is prepared to sacrifice his son without further deliberation, yet : 'Quand il a causé la mort de son fils, Thésée souffre, s'accuse et accuse les dieux, mais il ne meurt pas de honte: la seule tentation amoureuse est perçue comme plus grave que le légéreté criminelle du juge.'[25] Despite the part they play in the death or potential sacrifice of their children, both Agamemnon and Thésée escape the opprobrium faced by Athalie. However they, unlike the queen, have acted within parameters which are perceived as consistent with those of both Greek and seventeenth-century societies : Agamemnon to demonstrate his attachment to army and country and Thésée to redeem his honour and ensure that his wife, but most importantly his bloodline, remain untainted.

It therefore becomes clear that Athalie's crimes lie not simply in her actions *per se* but in the fact that she has abandoned her position as a woman in committing these actions and has persisted in refusing to return to the fold by becoming a powerful monarch. This last aspect would perhaps, for a seventeenth-century audience, appear even more heretical than her deeds:

> Les écrivains politiques n'évoquent pas sans un soupçon d'horreur l'éventualité d'une femme sur le trône de France. Les lois saliques, lois fondamentales du royaume, l'interdisent expressément, mais cet interdit se trouve redoublé par une multitude de rationalisations qui empruntent leurs arguments au domaine psychologique.[26]

The religious setting of the play compounds this. In most of Racine's tragedies womanhood becomes a negative attribute when linked to certain acts or behaviours. In *Athalie*, being a woman can, in itself, be a violation of the law. According to Helen Bates MacDermott, this is the very basis of the tragedy :

> The action of Athalie is presented as a confrontation between opposing members of a duality determined by sexual difference: the battle is between Athalie as female and God as male. The play is thematically arranged around polar opposites which continually reinforce this sex dualism, so that the opposition 'fils de David/fille de Jézabel' carries over into oppositions such as spirituality/corporeality, light/dark, fertility/sterility, cleanliness/corruption, law/transgression and temple/palace.[27]

Most of these oppositions are intertwined in complex and inseparable ways but the last is perhaps the most obvious as it revolves around the legality of Athalie's presence and, by extension, of her very existence as a female ruler. This is most clearly stated when Athalie enters the temple. Zacharie, who has come to explain the commotion to his mother, can hardly find the words to express his outrage. His youth makes him unable to articulate his emotion but one word sums up its cause :

> Une femme... Peut-on la nommer sans blasphème ?
> Une femme. C'était Athalie elle-même. (395-6)

He goes on to describe the confrontation between the queen and Joad :

> Dans un des parvis, aux hommes réservés
> Cette femme superbe entre, le front levé,
> Et se préparait encore à passer les limites... (397-9)

It is obvious that in his mouth *superbe* and *front levé*, which would normally suggest admiration, are unforgivable flaws on a woman's character. He then quotes Joad who again stresses both Athalie's gender and her apparent impiety:

> Reine, sors, a-t-il dit, de ce lieu redoutable,
> D'où te bannit ton sexe et ton impiété. (404-5)

By virtue of her gender, Athalie has become a transgressor and it is her presence in the temple, more than any past sins, which precipitates the events that will lead to her destruction:

> Son intrusion dans l'enceinte sacrée a le caractère d'une profanation religieuse qui la désigne à la vindicte de ses habitants.[28]

By putting *sexe* and *impiété* on a par, Joad makes it clear that even a pious woman is irredeemably tainted by her gender. The very word *femme* becomes negative when uttered amongst the faithful as shown by the fact that it is never used in its generic sense to describe 'the good woman' of the play, Josabet. She is *princesse, illustre Josabet, mère* but never simply *femme*, giving the impression that she has risen above her loathsome condition by taking on more worthy roles. It is also interesting to examine two lines which appear in Ii and seem to find no echo or justification in the rest of the play:

> Du mérite éclatant cette reine jalouse
> Hait surtout Josabet, votre fidèle épouse. (31-2)

We are left to wonder about the usefulness of these lines: nowhere does Athalie herself express hatred for Josabet. Her anger at the time of her defeat is clearly directed at God, Joad and, to an extent, Joas. Consequently one set of possible explanations emerges which has strongly misogynist undertones: that Athalie's jealousy positions her as clearly human and more specifically female; that this jealousy is caused, not only by Josabet's own qualities, but also by her position *as a wife*; that Athalie, despite her power as queen and the apparent serenity about this role she later displays, somehow longs to possess and be loved for the womanly attributes which are at the root of Josabet's *mérite* and perhaps even envies her for being Joad's spouse. This constitutes rather a lot of speculation for two short lines but given the lack of other justification for them we are simply left with the stereotypical image of a strong, independent woman secretly envious of the 'good wife' which the modern reader will be aware still exists in contemporary society in a form somewhat similar to that exemplified by the two biblical characters.

Although Josabet is clearly the embodiment of 'proper' womanhood, it is in relation to Athalie that the most blatantly sexist assumptions about the nature of women are made. Fittingly, this occurs in relation to Athalie's 'weakness', that is to say her reluctance to continue the vendetta and her attempts to find a compromise rather than destroy Joas and those who protect him. Mathan highlights at the same time Athalie's qualities and her difference:

> Ce n'est plus cette reine éclairée, intrépide,
> Elevée au-dessus de son sexe timide. (871-2)

This comes after Athalie's confusion at seeing Eliacin, when a feeling she does not recognise impairs her judgement. Mathan's frustration and his explanation:

> Elle flotte, elle hésite, en un mot : elle est femme (876)

make it clear that womanhood and the exercise of power are strictly incompatible and therefore hints both at Athalie's sin and the dichotomy between authority and females which we are asked to accept :

> Athalie est, selon Racine, le modèle de femme à ne surtout pas imiter parce qu'elle rejette la loi monothéiste et patriarcale. Son crime est en fait d'avoir pris le rôle de l'homme, de s'être fait 'roi' en succédant à son fils et d'avoir incarné l'Ordre et l'Autorité... ce succès temporel de la reine, le dramaturge l'explique à demi-mots : c'est parce qu'elle est sortie de son sexe...tant qu'Athalie était 'homme', dominant prétendument ses passions par le contrôle de la raison, elle pouvait gouverner; 'redevenue femme' (et désormais soi-disant assujettie aux sentiments), elle ne peut plus faire appliquer la loi royale. Sa perte est dès lors consommée.[29]

It is also interesting to note that in order to praise Athalie's qualities as a queen, she must be separated from other women. In short, what may appear as a compliment to the individual woman could just as easily be interpreted as an insult to all women. These overt examples of prejudice should perhaps alert us to the more covert message of the play, for if *Athalie*'s denouement sees the triumph of Yahweh over Baal, this triumph cannot be separated from that of patriarchy over the rebellious woman:

> L'histoire des religions nous apprend de même que ce qui est désigné dans la Bible par le culte de Baal (Hauts Lieux ou Astarté), était attaché au culte de la fertilité et au principe féminin et portait des réminiscences du culte de la déesse-mère. Bien que le texte racinien ne fasse pas allusion au principe féminin inhérent au culte de Baal, il parvient néanmoins à faire surgir du texte biblique tous les mythes attachés à la femme par une tradition judéo-chrétienne.[30]

By doing this Racine does however endow his 'anti-heroine' with a tragic quality: although her 'crimes' are used to justify her fate there is little doubt that the combination of her status and her gender marks her as the necessary victim which will enable patriarchal authority to reassert itself :

> Les modifications effectuées par Racine sur les données bibliques confèrent une dimension typiquement mythique à l'histoire, et [...] les éléments rituels de la performance théâtrale la préparent à culminer dans un geste dramatique où mise à mort et sacrifice ne font qu'un.[31]

The notion of sacrifice is ever-present in the play and is a feature of the Old Testament. In the temple itself the ritual slaughtering of animals is understood to be a fairly regular occurrence :

> Déja, selon la loi, le grand prêtre mon père,
> Après avoir au Dieu qui nourrit les humains
> De la moisson nouvelle offert les premiers pains,
> Lui présentait encore entre ses mains sanglantes
> Des victimes de la paix les entrailles fumantes. (384-8)

> Rentrons, et qu'un sang pur, par mes mains épanché,
> Lave jusques au marbre où ses pas ont touché. (749-50)

These last two lines already link Athalie's presence with the necessity of shedding blood and is fairly ominous since, although it refers here to animal blood, 'the shedding also of *human* blood can be an expiatory rite.'[32] It could be argued that it is a drastic step from one to the other were it not for the fact that human sacrifice has already been hinted at by Joad earlier in the play as God speaks through him:

> Ai-je besoin du sang des boucs et des génisses?
> Le sang de vos rois crie et n'est point écouté.
> Rompez, rompez tout pacte avec l'impiété;
> Du milieu de mon peuple exterminez lez crimes,
> Et vous viendrez alors m'immoler des victimes. (88-92)

'Racine has already made Joad's God a vengeful God who appears to scorn the sacrifice of animals, because He wants more.'[33] Joad knows that *rompre tout pacte avec l'impiété* may involve the shedding of human blood. He later urges his troops to do so by providing them with a historical example : *...ces fameux lévites {qui}...consacrèrent leurs mains dans le sang des perfides* (1362/1366).

We know therefore that a human sacrifice must take place and that, despite Joas' own fears (*Est-ce qu'en holocauste aujourd'hui presenté,/Je dois comme autrefois la fille de Jephté,/Du seigneur, par ma mort, apaiser la colère?* [1259-61]), *bienséance* will not allow the murder of an innocent child. Athalie on the other hand is reviled for her crimes and, by entering the male domain of the temple, she has both placed herself on the scene of the sacrifice to come and confirmed her status as a transgressor. Thus her very first (reported) action within the play hints at her tragic doom. This endows her with a tragic quality: she is the protagonist who forges ahead, whose fate is already sealed, despite her attempts at finding a solution which will re-establish the equilibrium (reconciliation with the god of the Jews, adoption of Joas). Athalie must die for the line of David, and through it the patriarchal order, to prevail:

> Les foi et loi juives, quant à elles, ne triomphent dans les pièces que grâce au sacrifice (sacrifice volontaire ou forcé) des femmes, femmes que l'ordre patriarcal monothéiste immole afin de sauver la communauté juive des fautes commises par les pères.[34]

There is however a major difference between Esther and Athalie. Esther is willing to be sacrificed, she accepts her role as victim and lives, unlike Athalie who refuses to yield to patriarchy, who fights it to and beyond (with her curse on Joas) death. Esther's 'happy ending', when compared to Athalie's tragic one, seems to suggest that the only way for women to survive within the patriarchal system is to collude with their oppressors, that they must display their willingness to die in order to be allowed to live. Furthermore the woman does not die to protect her people (as the plot of *Esther* would have us believe but *Athalie* strongly contradicts) but to seal an alliance between a phallocentric society and its male god:

> L'être féminin doit s'offrir en victime expiatoire pour racheter les fautes d'un ordre social régi par l'homme. Parce que les "pères" ont péché contre le Père, la femme doit être immolée pour racheter l'ordre patriarcal autant que pour sceller la réconciliation entre les "pères" et le Père.[35]

In other words, the woman must be made the scapegoat, the symbol of past disorders which must be atoned for, and this can best be achieved by stressing the difference between the sexes:

> Il s'agit de la lutte entre hénothéisme et monothéisme, lutte entre les sexes, lutte entre matriarcat et patriarcat, entre le permis et le réprouvé, la tolérance et le totalitarisme, la Déesse-mère et le Dieu-père : luttes à l'issue desquelles le monothéisme patriarcal triomphant fera assumer aux femmes le rôle de l'abomination assumé auparavant par le "faux" dieu Baal.[36]

In the biblical context Athalie symbolises the crimes of the chosen people which Esther described as a faithless woman :

> La nation chérie a violé sa foi;
> Elle a répudié son époux et son père,
> Pour rendre à d'autres dieux un honneur adultère.
> (*Esther*, 256-8)

A parallel can be drawn between the description of the guilty 'nation' as a woman and Girard's observations on *The Bacchae* :

> We may therefore wonder if the preponderance of women does not constitute a secondary mythological displacement,

an effort to exonerate from the accusation of violence, not mankind as a whole, but adult males, who have the greatest need to forget their role in the crisis...[37]

In *Athalie*, the queen may be seen as a living embodiement of the chosen people's faithlessness as well as an example of the loss of sexual differentiation also mentioned by Girard. The crisis is symbolised by role reversal (in this case Athalie is taking the male role as ruler) and its resolution shunts the burden of responsibility onto the woman.

Athalie takes the role of the Pharmakos described by Derrida: at once poison and remedy, her presence is reviled yet strictly necessary and her demise is a highly symbolic way to restore order. Unlike the 'martyr', as described in Paul Scott's chapter, Athalie does not choose to die for a higher purpose, '[to] die in a state of grace and thus be assured of heaven', but on the contrary struggles to the very last as an individual and a queen and it is her role as queen which her executioners use to defend their actions :

> Jerusalem, longtemps en proie à ses fureurs,
> De son joug odieux à la fin soulagée,
> Avec joie en son sang la regarde plongée. (1810-12)

This assessment of her reign is contradicted by previous accounts which leads us back to the notion that it is Athalie's gender, linked to her position[38], which marks her as the ideal scapegoat. The victim of the sacrifice must be a woman in order to enable the men to assuage their guilt, align themselves with their divinity and become the embodiment of their god and the guardians of the 'truth' which will justify social constructs. The fact that the woman they sacrifise holds the highest social position only serves to emphasise the androcentric messsage. It could be argued that, by sacrificing the woman, they create a God in their own image : 'L'homme peut exister parce que Dieu l'aide à définir son *genre,* à se situer comme fini par rapport à l'infini. La recrudescence du religieux peut d'ailleurs s'interpréter comme rempart de l'homme en tant qu'homme'.[39] What is more, the outcome of the female's sacrifice is a system in which female spirituality is denied and women are necessarily defined in relation to, and inevitably subordinate to men. 'Pour devenir, il est nécessaire d'avoir un genre ou une essence (dès lors sexuée) comme *horizon*. Sinon le devenir reste partiel et assujetti.'[40]

Athalie's destruction is necessary because she defines herself as a monarch and the social equal (or in her terms superior) of those who have preceded her. Her attempts at 'cohabitation' are doomed to failure because:

> L'unité monothéiste se soutient d'une séparation radicale des sexes : c'est cette séparation même qui en est la condition. Car, sans cet écart entre les deux sexes [...], il aurait été impossible, sur le plan symbolique, d'isoler le principe d'une Loi-Une, Sublimante, Transcendante, garante de l'intérêt idéal de la communauté.[41]

It may be true, as posited by Bruneau, that

> En soulignant l'assimilation métaphorique et métonymique entre le féminin, le culte de Baal, la déesse-mère et Athalie reine et mère, liens qui restent cachés dans le texte biblique, le texte de Racine nous amène à découvrir la ruse fondamentale, fondatrice de la machine monothéiste patriarcale. Ainsi que le dit Julia Kristeva: "La spécificité inouïe du texte biblique accomplit l'immense coup de force qui consiste à subordonner cette puissance maternelle (historique ou fantasmatique, de nature ou de reproduction) à l'ordre symbolique comme pur ordre logique réglant le jeu social, comme loi divine servie par le Temple."[42]

In the end however, and in terms of the lesson learnt by the audience, Racine's play reinforces the monotheist, patriarchal message. Tragic empathy with Athalie may occur because of her isolation, the hopelessness of her cause and the inevitability of her fate but by using preconceptions of appropriate gender behaviour, Racine creates a character who is nonetheless transgressive in the eye of the audience or reader if not in actual fact. Having done this, closure can only result from the destruction of the character and the restoration of the patriarchal order in a dénouement which compounds the audience's prejudices.

University of Bristol

1   Aristotle, *Classical Literary Criticism*, trans. by T.S. Dorsch
    (Harmondsworth : Penguin, 1965), p. 48.

2   Athalie does also transgress the rule of Aristotelian characterisation
    which states that '...the portrayal should be appropriate. For example,
    a character may possess many qualities, but it is not appropriate that a
    female character should be given manliness or cleverness' (ibid., p. 51).
    Athalie as queen is in total contradiction with this in that she is pre-
    sented as a successful ruler :

> Par moi Jérusalem goûte un calme profond,
> Le Jourdain ne voit plus l'Arabe vagabond
> Ni l'altier Philipin, par d'éternels ravages,
> Comme au temps de vos rois, désoler nos rivages.
> Le Syrien me traite et de reine et de soeur.
> Enfin de ma maison le perfide oppresseur,
> Qui devait jusqu'à moi pousser sa barbarie,
> Jéhu, le fier Jéhu, tremble dans Samarie.   (473-480)

(Racine, *Oeuvres Complètes*, ed. J. Morel & A. Viala (Paris: Garnier,
1980)).
In fact, *comme au temps de vos rois* suggests that she has surpassed her
male predecessors in terms of military exploits and achieved what they
had failed to do: namely, to provide peace for her people.

3   H. Bates McDermott, 'Matricide and Filicide in Racine's *Athalie*',
    Symposium, 38 (1984-5), 56-69 (p. 57.)

4   See L. Althusser, 'Ideology and the state', *Essays on ideology* (London :
    Verso, 1984).

5   E. Berg, 'Impossible representation : a reading of *Phèdre*', *The Romanic
    Review*, 73 (1982), 421-437 (p.422)

6   J.A. Schmidt, *If There Are No More Heroes, There Are Heroines* (Lanham :
    University Press of America: 1987), p.5

7   Racine, *Oeuvres Complètes*, ed. J. Morel & A. Viala (Paris: Garnier,
    1980). All line numbers and 'préface' quotations refer to this edition.

8   H. Stone, 'Beyond the promise : Racine's *Andromaque*', *Symposium*, 43
    (1989-90), 284-303 (p. 285).

9   M. F. Bruneau, '*Athalie*, l'unique tragédie pure de Racine', *Romanic
    Review*, 76 (1985), 374-388, (p. 376).

10 M. Butor, *Répertoire* (Paris: Les Editions de Minuit, 1960), p. 57.

11 ··· un horrrible mélange
    D'os et de chairs meurtris et traînés dans la fange,
    Des lambeaux pleins de sang et des membres affreux
    Que des chiens dévorants se disputaient entre eux. (503-6)

12 A. Brenner, *The Israelite Woman : Social role and literary type in biblical narrative* (Sheffield : JSOT, 1985), p. 21. Despite the fact that Elijah states in I Kings 21.19 : *...In the place where dogs licked up Naboth's blood, dogs will lick up your blood - yes, yours!* (*Holy Bible*, London: Hodder and Stoughton, 1988), Ahab is in fact killed in battle at a different location.

13 See Genesis 22 . 9-12 and Judges 11. 29-40.

14 Whether those sacrifices are actually carried out may appear important but could, in a non-religious context, be regarded as a moot point : the willingness of a parent to commit infanticide is damning, regardless of the motives.

15 A. Niderst, *Racine et la tragédie classique* (Paris: Presses Universitaires de France, 1978), p. 73.

16 A. Brenner, p. 29.

17 M.F. Bruneau, p. 377.

18 ibid., p. 382.

19 J.-J. Lépine, 'La barbarie à visage divin', *French Review*, 64. 1 (Oct. 1990), 19-31 (p. 20).

20 M.F. Bruneau, p. 378.

21 ed. cit., p. 693.

22 J. C. Exum, *Fragmented Women. Feminist (Sub)versions of Biblical narratives* (Sheffield : JSOT, 1993), p. 118.

23 D. Clarke, '*User des droits d'un souverain pouvoir*: sexual violence on the tragic stage (1635-40)', *Seventeenth-Century French Studies*, 18 (1996), 103-120 (p. 103).

24 See also E. Forman, '*En un mot, elle est femme* : Racine and feminist criticism', in *Racine: Appraisal and Reappraisal* , ed. by E. Forman (Bristol: University of Bristol, 1991), pp.95-112 (pp. 97-98).

25 J. Pineau, 'Sur la culpabilité de la *Phèdre* de Racine : augustinisme et

poésie', *La Licorne*, 20 (1991), 41-50 (p.45).

26 J.-M. Apostolidès, *Le prince sacrifié : Théâtre et politique au temps de Louis XIV* (Paris: Les Editions de minuit, 1985), p. 105.

27 Bates McDermott, op. cit., p. 56.

28 J.-J. Lépine, p. 28.

29 V. Grégoire, 'La femme et la loi dans la perspective des pièces bibliques raciniennes représentées à St-Cyr', *Dix-septième Siècle*, 179. 2 (avril-juin 1993), 323-336 (p. 333).

30 M.F. Bruneau, p. 384.

31 J.-J. Lépine, p. 20.

32 J. Trethewey, 'Anti-judaism in *Athalie*', *Seventeenth Century French Studies,* 18 (1996), 167-175 (p. 169).

33 ibid., p. 169.

34 V. Grégoire, p. 323.

35 ibid., p. 329.

36 M.F. Bruneau, p. 377.

37 R. Girard, *'Violence and the Sacred'* (London: The John Hopkins University Press, 1977), p. 139.

38 In the biblical context it would appear that a female ruler is necessarily a bad ruler. See Isaiah (3 : 12) : 'Youths oppress my people, women rule over them.'

39 L. Irigaray, 'Femmes divines', *Sexes et parentés* (Paris: Les Editions de Minuit, 1987), p. 73.

40 ibid., p. 73.

41 J. Kristeva, *Des Chinoises* (Paris: Editions des femmes, 1974), p. 23.

42 M.F. Bruneau, pp. 385-6.

'Peindre sa voix pour soutenir son rôle': The Use of écriteaux in Lesage's Théâtre de la Foire, and the Transgressionary Nature of the Aesthetic.

Mark Darlow

This essay has two aims. First, to show how the material conditions of theatrical performance have affected the development of the dramaturgy of *opéra-comique*, and to investigate the use of *écriteaux* in the origins of the Foire theatres;[1] second, to show how theories of transgression, elaborated by Foucault and Bataille, can fruitfully be applied to the social and dramaturgical contexts of theatrical performance. To describe the history of the *Théâtre de la Foire* necessitates investigation of a series of battles between the established Parisian theatres and those considered inferior, to question the perceived hierarchy in French theatrical production, and to ask how these questions relate to the development of a genre, during a period when rivalry for audiences was a constant phenomenon.

This study will attempt to show that the ingenuity of writers for the Foire in avoiding, and flouting, various concrete rules established under Louis XIV, and enforced by the Opéra and the Comédie Française, led not only to a material change in the conditions of theatrical performance, but also to an aesthetic development which was to affect the course of the evolution of *opéra-comique*. That an attempt to close down the Foire theatres actually led to an increase in their popularity, may be considered a historical irony. But the analysis of Foucault and Bataille's theories of transgression will allow us to show that the spirit of transgression – as a social act common to audiences as well as actors – was a fundamental characteristic of the age, and that what we may see as historical irony, is clearly no accident. Studies of the Foire have tended to neglect the *écriteaux* plays. Passing references in histories of the Foire, and of eighteenth-century comedy in general, speak rightly of the important part played by *écriteaux* in the introduction of vaudevilles into *opéra-comique*, but the *écriteaux*, to my knowledge, have never been the object of any separate systematic study. The first part of this essay, based upon Jules Bonnassies's historical study of the Foires,[2] will explain the history of the development of *opéra-comique*, from its origins in 1697, through the use of *écriteaux* in 1710, to the reintroduction of dialogue in 1724, with especial reference to the prohibitions imposed by the Opéra and the Comédie Française. A second section will explore the question of *écriteaux*: their use, their popularity and above all their historical importance, by analysing three *écriteaux* plays written by Lesage in 1713, published in volume 1 of the *Théâtre de la Foire* collection. The third section will be concerned with the philosophical and social basis of transgression and the particular dramaturgical problems posed by *écriteaux* and the vaudevilles which supplemented and finally superseded them, to show that the early *opéra-comique* is a typically transgressionary medium in the theatre.

Historical development of the *Théâtre de la Foire*

A. Background (1697-1709)

Rivalry for audiences was a common feature of Parisian theatrical life in the seventeenth and eighteenth centuries. Any starting-point in a history of *opéra-comique* will necessarily seem arbitrary, but the exile in 1697 of Mezzetin's troupe of Comédiens Italiens, due to an imagined slight against Mme. de Maintenon in their play, *La Fausse Prude*, left a ready audience which the Foires were eager to serve, and we shall take this event, after which the *danseurs de corde* began to establish theatres, as our early limit. The two principal fairs in Paris were that of Saint-Germain and Saint-Laurent. The Foire Saint-Germain ran from 3 February to passion Sunday (two weeks before Easter Sunday): that is, for approximately five weeks. The other, at Saint-Laurent, ran from the end of June to the end of September, and was situated at the site of the present *Gare de l'Est*. In 1698, two troupes were established. The first was run by the Alard brothers and the widow Mauritz von der Beek (known as veuve Maurice). The other consisted of the Bertrand brothers, Dolet and Delaplace.

From the beginning, the monopoly held by the Comédie Française, 'faisant défenses à tous autres comédiens français de s'établir dans Paris et faubourgs'[3] since 21 October 1680, meant that it was forbidden for the Foire to perform 'comedies', meaning regular plays of five or three acts, and farces. Dialogues and individual scenes were, however, still allowed.

The period between 1699 and 1707 consists of a series of complaints from the Comédie Française, anxious not to lose its audiences, against the Foire, of prohibitions of certain types of spectacle, and of the Foire's ignoring of these rulings, as Bonnassies shows. On 16 February 1700, for example, the *Forains* were forbidden to sing or dance in their plays. This, although clearly not constituting a complete ban, was still a serious constraint for a theatrically primitive troupe, formed by *danseurs de corde*, and drawing heavily upon italianate *lazzi*. The documents studied by Bonnassies, and published also by Campardon,[4] led to the conclusion that the Foire's response to such prohibitions must have been to ignore them, since a series of fines were levied during the course of 1702.

A far more serious prohibition levied against Maurice, Bertrand, Selle and Tiquet on 19 February 1706, forbade the use of dialogue in Foire plays. A fine of 300 *livres* was levied, and demolition of the theatres was threatened for non-payment (a further fine of 6000 *livres* was charged on 5 March 1706). After unsuccessful attempts to appeal, notably to Jacob du Frénoy, of the Abbey of Saint-Germain, who owned the land on which the *Forains* performed, the *Forains* decided to comply, but to resist closure by avoiding the prohibition, and elaborating on the monologue, itself not prohibited. In scenes involving more than one character, either each character was allowed to emerge from the wings just to deliver his own lines, and then to retreat off-stage, or else one character would speak, and others would either whisper or mime their answers, which this principal character would then voice for them. A *procès-verbal* of 30 August 1707 by commissaires Dubois and Cailly describes the scene:

> Ayant pris place dans une loge, nous avons observé qu'après
> que les Marionnettes ont été jouées sur le théâtre, il a paru un
> *Scaramouche* et plusieurs acteurs, au nombre de sept, qui ont
> représenté une comédie en trois actes, ayant pour titre:
> *Scaramouche pédant scrupuleux*; que, presque à toutes les scènes,
> l'acteur qui avait parlé se retirait dans la coulisse et revenait
> dans l'instant sur le théâtre, où l'acteur qui était resté parlait
> à son tour et formait par là une espèce de dialogue; que les
> mêmes acteurs se parlaient et répondaient dans les coulisses,
> et que, d'autrefois, l'acteur répétait tout haut ce que son
> camarade lui avait dit tout bas.[5]

Thus a will to force closure of the Foire theatres through seemingly unsurmountable material prohibitions, was resisted by the elaboration of a primitive form, and material transgression had consequences for dramaturgy. After a renewed attempt to close the Foire, and appeals to the Parlement of Paris, the Comédie Française again used its privilege in order to ban the use of monologue. All that was left for the *Forains* was pantomime and strings of sound which could not be considered as language. Attempting to avoid these new restrictions, they wrote 'jargon plays', which combined mute pantomime with jargon Alexandrines, a kind of twelve-syllable nonsense line, which rhymed and scanned correctly. This form allowed not only for the Foire to continue its productions, but actually led to increased popularity (shown by contemporary reports), as it mocked the diction of *grande comédie*. The increase in popularity should be noted, for studies of the Foire and contemporary memoirs insist upon the material difficulty in which the *Forains* were placed, and the restriction of expression which resulted. If we conclude that the literary quality of such works must have suffered, another factor must have entered into the popularity of this genre, as I shall later suggest.

The final development in this history stems from the Foire's wish to redevelop the musical aspect of their performances. Guyenet, Lully's successor as director of the Opéra, contrived to solve the Opéra's recent financial difficulty by selling Maurice and the Alards a 'permission tacite [de] changements de décorations, de chanteurs, [et] de danseurs' in 1708.[6] He was not allowed to do this, as it contravened the Comédie Française's own privilege, and a complaint from the latter on 17 April 1709 forbade the Opéra 'de donner la permission aux danseurs de corde et autres gens publics dans Paris de chanter des pièces de musique entières, ni autrement, de faire aucun ballet, ni danses, d'avoir des machines, même des décorations, même de se servir de plus de deux violons'.[7] All media except for pantomime were henceforth prohibited. The resulting situation is expressed by the following stanza, quoted by Bernardin:

> Air: *Ne m'entendez-vous pas?*
> Je n'ai pu que tout bas
> Vous faire ma harangue;
> On m'a lié la langue,
> Et Rome ne veut pas
> Ne m'entendez-vous pas?[8]

B. The use of *écriteaux*

The only remaining medium available to the *Forains* after this last prohibition was that of mute gesture, and though Goodden's study shows that bodily eloquence is a theatrical medium in its own right,[9] this was clearly insufficient, especially given the prohibition of dance, to sustain interest throughout an entire play. Transgression of the constraints imposed took the form of *écriteaux*, most likely introduced at the Foire Saint-Germain of 1710, according to the *Mémoires* of the Parfaict brothers:

> Alard, à qui le sieur Guyenet avait fait signifier qu'il n'eût plus à se servir de la permission qu'il lui avait donnée de faire chanter et danser dans son théâtre, ouvrit son spectacle par une pièce à la muette. Mais comme le public s'était plaint, à

la précédente foire [Saint-Laurent, 1709], de l'obscurité de beaucoup d'endroits de ses pièces, causée par l'impossibilité où les acteurs étaient d'exprimer par des gestes des choses qui n'en étaient point susceptibles, on imagina l'usage des cartons sur lesquels on imprima en gros caractères et en prose très laconique tout ce que le jeu des acteurs ne pouvait rendre. Ces cartons étaient roulés et chaque acteur en avait dans sa poche droite le nombre qui lui était nécessaire pour son rôle; et, à mesure qu'il avait besoin d'un carton, il le tirait et l'exposait aux yeux des spectateurs, et ensuite le mettait dans sa poche gauche. Ces écriteaux en prose ne parurent pas longtemps au théâtre. Quelques personnes imaginèrent de substituer à cette prose des couplets sur des airs déjà connus qu'on nomme vaudevilles, qui, en rendant la même idée, y jetaient un agrément et une gaieté dont l'autre genre n'était point susceptible. Pour faciliter la lecture de ces couplets, l'orchestre en jouait l'air, et des gens gagés par la troupe et placés au parquet et aux amphithéâtres les chantaient, et par ce moyen engageaient les spectateurs à les imiter. Ces derniers y prirent tellement goût que cela forma un chorus général.[10]

The appendix to this essay provides a list of all *écriteaux* plays which I have been able to trace between their introduction in 1710 and the adoption of *pièces en vaudevilles*, when speech was reallowed in 1724, using works by Brenner, Barberet, Parfaict and Carmody, and the Bibliothèque Nationale and British Library catalogues of printed books and manuscript sources.[11] Brenner provides an accurate and apparently complete list of such plays, but his terminology, following published copies of plays, where such exist, and annals of theatre where not, is inconsistent: some *écriteaux* plays are not designated as such on his list, whereas other sources and the year of their performance, suggest that they should be treated as such. Carmody's excellent study sometimes omits the fact of plays being written *en écriteaux*, and, as with Brenner, I have had to use the dates which he provides, and the more convincing assertions of other sources, as indications of genre. Barberet's work is naturally restricted to works by Lesage, and provides minimal information about other writers of écriteaux plays. Finally the *Mémoires* of the Parfaict brothers, which provide an annual description of the actors, writers and productions of the Foire, and provide useful information on the repertory, though distinguishing between *écriteaux* plays and others, have been shown to be both incomplete and, in some cases, inaccurate:

> Les frères Parfaict ont exclu systématiquement de leurs *Mémoires* l'étude critique des pièces. [...] un sentiment de réserve leur interdit les longues appréciations. En d'autres termes, ils lisent les affiches, pénètrent quelquefois dans les coulisses; mais ils assistent rarement à la représentation: ils se contentent d'écouter du dehors le bruit des applaudissements ou des sifflets.[12]

Whether the reticence of the Parfaict brothers to speak of the Foire is due more to a true lack of personal experience than to the widespread awareness of a need for discretion, due to the place of the Foire in the theatrical hierarchy, is a matter of speculation. Isherwood's study of popular entertainment in eighteenth-century Paris has shown how the Foire was far from attracting an exclusively plebeian audience,[13] and it is likely that writers such as the Parfaict brothers, whose *Dictionnaire des Théâtres de Paris*, completed by Claude Parfaict alone after the death of his brother François on 25 October 1753, frequently speaks of the literary inferiority of the Foire, and whose references to their plays are often grudging at best,[14] would have been reluctant to admit to attending these performances. Besides, as it is conceived more as an interesting work of reference than as an exhaustive historical study,[15] the *Dictionnaire* cannot be relied upon to provide a complete list of Foire plays. Clearly many of the *écriteaux* plays, produced at a primitive moment in the genre's development, were never published: indeed, many have not even survived in manuscript. The establishment of any such list must therefore be dependent upon such references in memoirs and histories as are available.

Clearly more work needs to be undertaken on this early period of the Foire, and many works are doubtless still unknown.

In 1709, the troupes of the Foire Saint-Laurent, fearing reprisals and demolition of their *loges*, as Holtz suffered at the Foire Saint-Germain on 2 March 1709, opened with plays *à la muette*, thus respecting the prohibitions of speech and song. Most historical surveys suggest that *écriteaux* were introduced at the Foire Saint-Germain of 1710. But a reference by Brenner to two plays by Faroard, perfomed 'en écriteaux', suggests that *écriteaux* may have been introduced as early as 1709.[16] Whether this reference is correct can never be verified, as the plays have not survived. But it is clear that in 1710, mute play had become unpopular, and that plays were henceforth performed, either *en écriteaux*, or, where troupes could secure the necessary rights, using dialogue and song. As is shown by the procès-verbal of Dubois and Cailly, in 1712, *écriteaux* were suspended from the fly rather than carried by actors, to allow a greater freedom of movement. The troupes also began to distribute printed copies of the *couplets* used, and introduced a small orchestra, placing their own men in the audience to encourage the audience to sing the lines.[17] We must distinguish between those plays where the public was singing the lines shown by the *écriteaux*, and those where the actors were themselves allowed to sing. It appears that at the end of December 1714 the Opéra sold the right to song to the troupe of Saint-Edme, who could then write plays consisting of sung dialogue, and dispense with the *écriteaux*, charge 1 *écu* per seat (approximately the same price as charged by the Comédie Française), and describe their plays as *opéras-comiques*. Saint-Edme had an alliance with the Dame de Beaulne, and both troupes shared this *privilège*, until it expired, on 8 December 1715. It was then agreed verbally that whoever managed to secure a new *privilège*, would share it with the other troupe as before. But when the Dame de Beaulne bought the privilege for 25000 *livres* on 6 January 1716, she refused to share with Saint-Edme as agreed, until the latter agreed to pay a supplement. This supplement was paid, but their arrangement was again broken in 1717 when the Dame de Beaulne sought exclusive permission *for opéra-comique* at both Foires for a period of 15 years and 2 months. This selective granting of monopoly rights to use song and dialogue between 1714 and 1718 explains numerous references to some plays *en écriteaux*, performed by those troupes who did not have such rights, and to *opéras-comiques*, performed by those who did. Our appendix lists only those plays performed *en écriteaux*.

At the end of the Foire Saint-Laurent of 1718, all Foire theatres were closed after complaints from the Comédie Française, and plays were henceforth performed using prose, jargon, monologues, and did not use song. No *écriteaux* plays are known until 1724, when speech was temporarily reallowed. When the *privilège* passed to Honoré at the Foire Saint-Laurent of 1724, he had little success, and on 25 May 1724 decided to use this *privilège*, to force the competing troupes to abandon performance. These competing troupes resisted and performed until the end of the Foire Saint-Laurent of 1724 with *écriteaux*. The appendix is therefore divided into three sections: from 1709 to 1714; from 1714 to 1718, and from 1719 to 1724.

Lesage and D'Orneval's published collection of works from the Foire contains three of the better *écriteaux* plays, performed in 1713, the year when all plays at the Foire which I have been able to trace, used *écriteaux*: *Arlequin roi de Sérendib*, *Arlequin Thétis*, and *Arlequin invisible*.[18] The second section of this essay takes these three as an example of the genre.

II Dramaturgical analysis of the genre

A. *Arlequin, Roi de Sérendib, Arlequin invisible, Arlequin Thétis*

Lesage's principal contribution to the Foire was to elevate the subject matter and the expression of *opéra-comique*. One important change which he effectuated was to continue to write plays in one act, as it often proved difficult to sustain the audience's interest throughout three acts, but to group related plays, in order to form a more coherent and balanced whole.[19] Often, two plays of one act each would be linked by the use of a short prologue, which often took the form of a *parade*. One of the one-act plays would then be essentially a *pièce à intrigue*, while the other would develop *caractères*, often taking the form of a *pièce à tiroirs*. *Arlequin, Roi de Sérendib*, in three acts, is a notable exception to this practice, but still shows Lesage's concern for continuity and coherence. As such, it is undoubtedly the most successful of the *écriteaux* plays. Bernardin sees the play as 'une parodie mal suivie et très libre, de l'opéra *Iphigénie en Tauride* par Duché et Danchet'.[20] He rightly notes the slight incoherence of the play, but Barberet shows how the work represents a considerable advance on previous attempts by other writers for the Foire, though perhaps overstating the point:

> On y voyait que l'art pouvait entrer même dans une pièce foraine, ce que les auteurs n'avaient point paru croire jusque là. Après *Arlequin baron Allemand*, *Arlequin, roi de Sérendib* était une révélation, et on put croire que la foire avait enfin trouvé son Molière.[21]

Similarly, Lintilhac suggests that the play already shows dramaturgical and thematic features which were later to be characteristic of Lesage's style:

> [Il a pu] remédier à la monotonie des scènes à tiroirs par le piquant d'une intrigue légère et appropriée au genre. Il transporte d'ailleurs en Orient tout le personnel de la Comédie Italienne, à grand renfort de gais couplets, et de vives satires, de parodies et de lazzi, le tout amalgamé avec une limpidité et une prestesse qui seront désormais sa marque. Cette turquerie ayant eu un succès, que renouvelle bientôt *Arlequin invisible*, il puisera souvent, et toujours avec adresse, dans ces recueils de contes arabes et persans, nouvellement traduits, et dont il avait revu le style, ce qui lui donnait au moins le droit d'y prendre son bien.[22]

Important characteristics of these three plays, which we shall examine in order are: the use of variety, in order to sustain the audience's interest; the controlled use of song, which allows for the 'training' of the audience; and thematic continuity with the former Théâtre Italien, which assured popularity.

Variety is assured in *Arlequin, Roi de Sérendib* by the setting of the play, which demonstrates the taste, common to early Foire plays, for exoticism, and which is also seen in *Arlequin invisible chez le roi de Chine*. This exoticism naturally allows for the avoidance of the prohibition of speech through the use of imaginary language, as jargon and nonsense words cannot be defined as dialogue, but can resemble foreign words, or the intonation of a foreign language (see I.i; I.vi; III.iv). To permit comprehension, these nonsense words must be interspersed with *lazzi*, as in III.iv. The use of these *lazzi* is essential for the introduction of music into the plays, because the audience would be unable to sing continuously throughout a play. The whole of act I uses mute scenes interspersed with small units of dialogue expressed by *écriteaux*, such as the following:

> *L'homme pose son turban à terre, fait signe à Arlequin de jetter de l'argent dedans, & le couche en joue, en criant:* Gnaff, Gnaff. *Arlequin effrayé jette plusieurs piéces dans le turban. Le Voleur se retire, & dans le moment il en paroît un autre qui a le bras gauche en écharpe, une jambe de bois & un large coutelas au côté. Celui-ci fait aussi des révérences à Arlequin, qui dit toûjours à part:*

> AIR 2 (*Quand je tiens de ce jus d'Octobre.*)
> Quel autre homme s'offre à ma vûe?
> Il est manchot! Oui, justement,
> C'est un fripon, il me salue;
> C'est du *gnaff, gnaff,* assurément.

This technique progressively encourages the spectators to sing, as towards the end of the play, more music, and less mute pantomime is used, and allows for the audience progressively to learn the music.[23] As Connon and Evans state, such a technique is not possible in the shorter Foire plays.[24]

Continuity is assured by the use of the characters of the Théâtre Italien, with their traditional characteristics. Thus, in *Arlequin, Roi de Sérendib*, Arlequin shows his sexuality (II.iv), and his greed:

> Puisque sur le trône | Vous m'avez placé, | Vîte, je l'ordonne, | Le buffet dressé. (I.v)

This is essential in the early *opéra-comique*, as the Foires are competing for the audiences who are used to the plays performed until 1697 by Mezzetin's Italian troupe. The simplicity of the action of each play is clear. *Arlequin invisible chez le roi de Chine* is set in the palace of the King of China. A note on the title page tells the reader that this play is a sequel to another, where Arlequin saves Asmodée, and asks, in return, to be transported to China. The action of the play is as follows. Arlequin and Asmodée, alone in the apartment of the King, attach a feather to Arlequin's hat, which renders him invisible (sc. I). This property is then exploited, as Arlequin sings an echo to a slave's song about the Queen, locked up by her jealous husband. The slave is unable to see him, until Arlequin chooses to show himself (sc II). The Queen and her confidante await her lover (sc III), who finally arrives (sc IV). In the scene which follows, Arlequin enters invisible, just before the King. He plays tricks on both the King and Queen, including hiding the King's sword when the lover is threatened. The ensuing confusion, as Arlequin is still invisible, allows the Queen and her confidante to persuade the King that he is mistaken about the lover, and the play ends happily with the King's apology. This plot, though very simple, has the advantage of being more logically constructed than earlier Foire plays, and providing scope for expression in spite of the current material restrictions, as the invisibility of Arlequin naturally allows for mute pantomime.

B. The popularity of the *écriteaux* plays

It was suggested earlier that if the literary quality of these plays suffered from a restriction of means of expression, then another element must explain the popularity of the *écriteaux* plays. Bernardin states that this genre was immediately successful:

> Il est inutile de dire que le public s'amusait follement de cette innovation, qui lui donnait un rôle dans la lutte; et quant à la Comédie Française, elle ne pouvait toujours rien dire, puisqu'il n'y avait pas de dialogue, ni l'Opéra, puisque ce n'étaient pas les acteurs qui chantaient, mais bien les spectateurs.[25]

With the help of Bakhtin's analysis of carnival in *Rabelais et la culture populaire au Moyen-âge et sous la Renaissance*, and secondary criticisms thereof, of the work of Michel Foucault, especially in his 'Préface à la transgression', and of Georges Bataille's *L'Erotisme*, I should like to proceed to an analysis of the resulting dramatic situation in *écriteaux* plays, with reference both to symbolic inversion and to philosophical theories of transgression, in order to suggest that the spirit of transgression itself played an important part in the success of the genre.

Stallybrass and White draw upon Bakhtin's analysis of the carnival in Rabelais's work in order to ground a theory of transgression in a set of literary and social inversions. Having shown that the carnival frequently coincides with social conflicts,[26] they go on to show how the carnival may often act as 'catalyst and *site of actual and symbolic struggle*',[27] and cite Babcock's definition of inversion as 'any act of expressive behaviour which inverts, contradicts, abrogates, or in some fashion presents an alternative to commonly held cultural codes, values and norms be they linguistic, literary or artistic, religious, social and political'.[28] Inversions are fundamental to carnival, as the limit between different domains is repeatedly crossed. Transgression, defined as the breaking, or crossing, of limits, reaffirms each domain in its inversion. It is possible to analyse the dramaturgical basis of the *écriteaux* plays as a network of symbolic inversions, both technical – between action and passivity, speech and writing, individuality and sociability, and thematic – between high and low, male and female.

The article 'Transgression' in the *Encyclopédie* defines the transgressor as (s)he who commits the transgressive act.[29] This definition poses a problem, for the very acts involved in the *écriteaux* plays are based precisely upon the inversion of action and passivity. As well as avoiding the prohibitions imposed, because the actors of the troupe are not actually singing, the use of *écriteaux* transforms the actor into a mute, at times passive figure, while the audience sings. As Bernardin, quoted earlier, claims, 'le public s'amusait follement de cette invention, qui lui donnait un rôle dans la lutte'.[30] It is clearly essential for contemporary audiences to feel involved in the quarrel which involves the Foire actors:

> Dans les démêlés auxquels nous allons assister, les forains – remarquons-le d'avance – auront pour eux les oisifs, les jeunes seigneurs, les *Moncades*, dont de nouveaux spectacles augmentent les distractions, et qui vont joyeusement 's'encanailler' à y entendre des polissonneries et des satires audacieuses; ils auront aussi la faveur du menu peuple, qui, éloigné de la Comédie par une littérature aristocratique, sent déjà le besoin de spectacles plus nombreux et à sa portée.[31]

Similarly, as we shall see, the use of song in the Foire is not neutral, as it unifies the audience through a social act, thus excluding *sensibilité*,[32] and favouring comic effect.

A large proportion of the plays listed in our appendix, as well as of the repertory of the Foire in general, consists of parodies of opera. The term 'parody' has a double definition in *opéra-comique*, as it refers both to the burlesque imitation of another, serious, work (the definition most commonly used today), but also the setting to pre-existing music of a new text, which is inspired from a previous model. Barberet rightly states that '[le théâtre de la foire] a causé tant de soucis et d'ennuis aux Comédies française et italienne, il a rendu de tels services à l'Opéra, qu'il fait partie de leur histoire'.[33] Similarly, the works of the Foire are inspired precisely in relation to the models which they parody. That is, they find their place in the theatrical hierarchy, in opposition to the hegemony of the Opéra.[34]

Lesage's parodies usually take the form of an *opéra-comique en vaudevilles*, as Barberet states, as this allows both the parody (in both senses of the term) of the text, and the burlesque imitation of the music. Barberet insists upon the novelty of *Arlequin Thétis*, stating that '[c']est le premier ouvrage régulier de ce genre qui ait paru au Théâtre Français, et Lesage peut être regardé comme le créateur de la parodie musicale; car on ne peut donner ce nom aux essais incohérents par lesquels ses prédécesseurs avaient prétendu critiquer l'Opéra'.[35] Many of the works which are not designated as parodies still contain passing references to the Opéra, as in *Arlequin, Roi de Sérendib*, which mocks the poor success of *L'Irrésolu* of Destouches-Campra (II.vi, and footnote), *Callirhoé* of Destouches (II.vi; III.v), *Sancho Pança* of Philidor (II.vii), and which ends with an extensive parody of the dénouement of *Iphigénie en Tauride* of Duché de Vancy and Danchet, set to music by Desmarets and Campra (see from III.vii, and note, to end).

In *Arlequin Thétis*, parody of *Thétis et Pelée*, recognisable characters from the Théâtre Italien are disguised as characters from *Thétis et Pélée*. A burlesque comic effect is assured by the inversion of male and female characters: Arlequin is disguised as Thétis, and declares his love for Pelée (Léandre), and complains of being loved by Jupiter (Mezzetin):

> Neptune m'aime, hélas! | Que mon âme est troublée! | Son grand valet Pelée | A pour moi plus d'apas. | Ne m'entendez-vous pas? (I.i)

But the question of inversion is more complex than a simple breaking of rules. Roger Caillois shows how the *fête*, which he describes as a 'monde d'exception', reaffirms rules and prohibitions in their rupture:

> Les interdits habituels sont renforcés, des prohibitions nouvelles sont imposées [...] le sacré dans la vie ordinaire, on l'a vu, se manifeste presque exclusivement par des interdits. [...] Il apparaît donc essentiellement comme *négatif*. [...] Ainsi s'explique que les seules manifestations du sacré soient des interdictions, des protections contre tout ce qui pourrait menacer la régularité cosmique ou des expiations, des réparations de tout ce qui a pu la troubler.'[36]

Similarly, Bataille develops a dialectal analysis of transgression and limits, stating that transgression 'lève l'interdit sans le supprimer'.[37] His analysis is, I think, superseded by Foucault's 'Préface à la transgression', which speaks of passing limits, rather than of breaking them.[38] Passing a limit does not necessarily imply breaking that limit, as the limit closes up again after transgression. Transgression is to be seen more as a complex spiral of inversions, as the rule imposed can never truly be broken. Hence the Théâtre de la Foire and the material prohibitions imposed stand in a relationship of 'non-positive affirmation', to borrow from the words of Blanchot and Foucault.[39] That is, the prohibitions are negatively asserted in being transgressed, while the theatres find their *raison d'être*, at least in the eyes of contemporary audiences, by their transgressionary spirit. This spirit is exemplified by the use of the vaudeville which can, by definition, carry pre-existing satirical or political meaning through the force of melody, and thus create subjacent meaning and comic effect. Isherwood shows that political songs abounded under the Ancien Régime, precisely because the song was the most efficient, and safest, means of expressing unorthodox views.[40] As the melody of a song needs only to be heard for the original meaning of the words to be remembered, transformations of the words of a song do not entirely erase the original meaning. But it is likely that the replacement of political words in several seventeenth-century songs with more banal, or *grivois* lyrics, represents a deliberate attempt on the part of the Paris authorities, who are known to have employed song-writers, to suppress the opinions which the songs in question represent. The use of such songs in the theatre is therefore not neutral, as singing is a vital part, not only of social life, and of the culture of the *fête*, but also of the transgressionary spirit which, as we have seen, proved so popular to contemporary audiences.

Some critics imply that the use of vaudevilles in comic theatre dates from the Foire plays. But Lintilhac rightly points out that the use of music is already clear in the Théâtre Italien prior to 1697, and cites seven plays published in Gherardi's collection:

> Mais c'est dans les comédies du recueil de Gherardi, avec des couplets sur des timbres populaires ou sur des airs de Gillier et d'autres, qu'il faut chercher les véritables origines de cette *comédie en vaudevilles* et de cette *comédie en ariettes* qui constitueront le soi-disant opéra comique concurremment, du moins, jusqu'à la date des représentations mémorables de *la Servante Maîtresse* [1752].[41]

The interest of the vaudeville within the context of the Foire is, however, different. Philip Robinson distinguishes two separate definitions of the vaudeville: the terminal vaudeville which consists of a song composed for the end of a play, or of one act of a play, and that which is sung to a pre-existing melody, known by its *timbre*, often mixing new verses (*couplets*) with the *timbre*'s characteristic chorus (*refrain*).[42] Terminal vaudevilles are more commonly used in Gherardi, but pre-existing *timbres* constitute the more common use of music in the early decades of the Foire. The interest of verses newly set to *timbres* is both that they allow audiences to sing, as the melodies chosen are well-known; second, that they can carry a pre-existing meaning through the force of melody: it suffices to hear the melody in order to remember the old meaning of the song in question. The more talented writers of *opéra-comique* use the relation between the pre-existing meaning of a timbre and the new text set, in order to create subjacent meaning, or comic effects. The analysis of the use of two such timbres in *Arlequin, Roi de Sérendib* to emphasise differences of social status, will serve as an example.

The history of the development of the timbre 'Or écoutez, petits et grands'during the seventeenth century until the development of *opéra-comique* in the 1760s, has been studied by Philip Robinson.[43] He cites 17 songs from the reign of Louis XIV and the Regency which use this timbre, explaining that by the beginning of the eighteenth century the timbre is 'riche [...] d'un trésor de connotations traditionnelles'.[44] The most common use of the song is to satirise authority, as in 'La Mort de Mazarin', 'Les Rochellois', 'Les adieux de Louis XIV'.[45] Later in the century, the timbre is used in the theatre to satirize the authority of the pedagogue.

In *Arlequin, Roi de Sérendib*, the timbre is used to signify social status, as Arlequin is about to be sacrificed. This question of status is carried by the earlier words of the song, which deals with a person's authority, and is fundamental to the play, as the comic situation is principally created through the disproportion between Arlequin's traditional role, and his elevation to the rank of King of Sérendib:

Arlequin: **Air: *Or écoutez, petits et grands***

C'est donc pour répandre mon sang
Qu'on m'a mis dans un si haut rang!
Le sort me gardait pour victime,
C'était son dernier coup de lime.
Mes pleurs, puiqu'on va m'immoler,
Coulez, hâtez-vous de couler. (III.v)

Similarly, the timbre 'Je ne suis né ni Roi ni Prince' appears in a satirical song celebrating the death of cardinal Richelieu in 1642,[46] and is used throughout the century to signify, first, the joy at the death of an oppressor, and later a vaguer nuance of social rank, which is shown by the new title 'Je ne suis né ni Roi ni Prince'. The timbre is used in act III of *Arlequin, roi de Sérendib*, when the chief Eunuch presents the Greek slave-girl to Arlequin:

Chef des Eunuques: Air: *Faire l'amour la nuit et le jour*
                     La loi n'est pas contraire;
                     A plus de beauté,
                     Seigneur, vous pouvez faire
                     L'amour
                     La nuit et le jour.
                     Air: *Je ne suis né ni Roy ni Prince*
                     Mais il faut que je vous présente
                     Une Grecque toute charmante
                     Que jamais Vénus n'égala.
       Arlequin: La peste! Ce portrait me touche!
                     Tu me gardais donc celle-là,
                     Vieux coquin, pour la bonne bouche? (III.i)

These two examples show that song can carry original meaning through the force of its melody, and that it can be used in the theatre to create meaning and comic effect. It should be noted that it is the social nature of song which allows this effect; that sensibility, which Bergson sees as individual, is not suited to the vaudeville.[47]

It is clear that the early *opéra-comique* is a simple, often primitive form, whose popularity is due to various factors. Not least, the spirit of transgression unifies the performances, both materially and technically (in the process of symbolic inversions), and also socially. The use of the vaudeville retains the transgressive spirit of the *chansonniers* of the Pont-Neuf, whereas the transgression of material constraints in the Foire is essential to the course of the development of *opéra-comique*, as it acts as a catalyst for the introduction of pre-existing vaudevilles into comedy, which will be one of the distinctive features of the genre until the preference for newly-composed *ariettes* during the course of the 1750s. I hope to have shown that the material restrictions placed upon the Forains at the beginning of the eighteenth century were to play a role in the development of *opéra-comique*. In this way, we may conclude, following Gide, that 'l'art naît de contrainte, vit de lutte, meurt de liberté.'[48]

Appendix: *Ecriteaux* plays at the Foires, 1709-1724[49]

I. 1709 – 1713

1709 – Foire Saint-Laurent

Faroard, *Atrée et Thyeste*, parodie pantomime en jargon. 1 acte, en écriteaux. Parodie d'*Atrée et Thyeste*, de P.J. de Crébillon. [Représenté en juillet; troupe de Selles]{non imprimée}Attribuée aussi à Lenoble.

Faroard, *Les Poussins de Léda*, parodie en monologues et en vers, en écriteaux. Parodie des *Tyndarides*, de Danchet. [Troupe de Dolet-Laplace] {non imprimée} Attribuée aussi à Lenoble.

1710 – Foire Saint-Germain

Dominique [Pierre François Biancolelli, dit], *Arlequin Atys*, 3 actes, en écriteaux [?]. 'Parodie de l'ouvrage de Quinault avec musique de l'opéra.' [Parfaict] [Représenté le 3.2.1710 'avec des agréments de chants et de danses' [Parfaict]].

– Foire Saint-Laurent

Lenoble, *Arlequin aux Champs Elisées*, 3 actes, en écriteaux [Représenté le 25.7.1710; troupe de Dolet-Laplace] {BN f.f.9295; 'Imprimée dans un recueil à Amsterdam' [Parfaict]}.

Dominique, *La Foire Galante, ou le Mariage d'Arlequin*, parodie, 3 actes, en écriteaux [?]. Divertissement du ballet de l'*Europe Galante* [par Lamotte]. [Représenté le 26.6.1710].

1711 – Foire Saint-Germain

Raguenet [?],[50] *Les Aventures comiques d'Arlequin, ou Le Triomphe de Bacchus & de Venus* (par un acteur muet), 3 actes, en écriteaux. [Représenté le 3.2.1711; troupe de Dolet-Laplace-

Bertrand] {Paris, [s.pub.], 1711, 12o}.

Raguenet, *Apollon à la Foire*, divertissement muet, 3 actes, avec prologue et vaudevilles, en écriteaux. [Représenté le 1.3.1711; troupe d'Alard et de Lalauze: Jeu de Paume] {Paris, [s.n.] ,1711, 12o} Attribué aussi à Fuselier.

– Foire Saint-Laurent

Pellegrin, Simon-Joseph, *Arlequin à la guinguette*, divertissement, 3 entrées, avec prologue et vaudevilles, en écriteaux. [Représenté le 25.7.1711; troupe de Bel-Air] { Ms. B.N. f.f.25476; Paris, M. Rebuffé, 1711; 31pp., 12o}.

[anonyme], *La Femme juge et partie*, divertissement muet, 3 actes, avec prologue et vaudevilles, en écriteaux. [Représenté le 6.8.1711] {Paris, J. Josse, 1711 12o}.

– Fuzelier, Louis, *Les Amours de Mars et de Vénus*, divertissement, 1 acte, avec pantomime et couplets, en écriteaux.

Raguenet, *Le Mariage d'Arlequin*, divertissement muet, 3 actes, avec prologue, en écriteaux. [Représenté le 16.7.1711; troupe de Dolet-Laplace].

Fuselier, *Arlequin (ou Orphée) aux Enfers*, en écriteaux. [Représenté le 12.9.1711].

—, *Arlequin Enée, ou La Prise de Troyes*, pièce, 3 actes, avec prologue, en écriteaux. [Représenté le 25.7.1711; troupe d'Alard].

—, *Arlequin et Scaramouche vendangeurs*, en écriteaux.

1712 – Foire Saint-Germain

Fatouville [?], *Arlequin empereur de {dans?} la lune*, pièce, 3 actes, en écriteaux. [Représenté le 3.2.1712; troupe d'Alard-

Octave]. Mis en couplets 'avec beaucoup de nouvelles scènes' [Parfaict] par Rémy-Chaillot.

[anonyme], *Les Plaideurs*, pièce, 3 actes, en écriteaux. [Représenté le 3.2.1712; troupe de Dolet-Laplace]. {Ms. BN f.f.25476; Paris, [s.n.], 1712 12o}.

Fuselier, *Arlequin, baron allemand, ou Le Triomphe de la folie*, pièce, 3 actes, en vaudevilles, en écriteaux. [Représenté le 12.2.1712; Troupe de la Dame Baron] {Paris, G. Valleyre, 1712; in-12o}. Collaboration de Lesage et D'Orneval.

Prologue: *Le Retour d'Arlequin à la foire*, divertisement à la muette.

– Foire Saint-Laurent[51]

Fuzelier, Louis, *Arlequin rival du docteur pédant et scrupuleux*, pièce, 2 actes, avec prologue, en écriteaux. [Représenté le 29.7.1712].

[anonyme], *L'Ecole des jaloux*, divertissement, 3 actes, en écriteaux. {Ms. B.N. f.f.9271; Paris, G. Valleyre, 1713, 12o}.

Lesage, *Les Petits-Maîtres*, pièce, 5 actes en vaudevilles, en écriteaux. [Représenté le 19.9.1712; troupe de Bel-Air, théâtre de la dame Baron]. {Ms. B.N. f.f.9314} Performed anonymously.

Lesage, *Arlequin et Mezzetin morts par amour*, pièce, 1 acte, avec des vaudevilles, en écriteaux. [Représenté le 19.9.1712; théâtre de la dame Baron]. {Ms. B.N. f.f.9314} Performed anonymously.

1713 – Foire Saint-Germain

Dominique, *Arlequin prince et paysan*, opéra-comique, 3 actes, avec vaudevilles, en écriteaux. [Représenté le 3.2.1713; troupe de Saint-Edme] {Mss. BN f.f.9331, 25480} Performed anonymously [Parfaict].

Dominique, *Arlequin grand vizir*, pièce, 3 actes, avec vaudevilles, en écriteaux. [Représenté le 3.2.1713; troupe de Dominique (Saint-Edme)] {Mss. B.N. f.f.9335 (incomplet), 25480}. Complété par Fuselier.

— *Arlequin larron, prévost et juge*, pièce, 3 actes, avec couplets, en écriteaux. [Représenté le 3.2.1713].

Lesage, *Arlequin, roi de Serendib*, pièce, 3 actes, avec vaudevilles, en écriteaux. [Représenté le 3.2.1713; troupe de Baxter et Saurin; théâtre de la dame Baron] {*Théâtre de la Foire*, I (1721)}. Musique de Gilliers.

- Foire Saint-Laurent

Pellegrin, Simon-Joseph, *Arlequin marquis financier*, pièce, 3 actes, avec des couplets, en écriteaux. [Représenté le 25.7.1713].

Lesage, *Arlequin Thétis*, parodie, 1 acte, avec vaudevilles, en écriteaux. Parodie de *Thétis et Pelée*, tragédie lyrique de Fontenelle et Colasse (1689). [Représenté le 25.7.1713; théâtre de la dame Baron] {*Théâtre de la Foire*, I (1721)}. Musique de Gilliers.

Lesage, *Arlequin invisible chez le roi de Chine*, pièce, 1 acte, avec vaudevilles, en écriteaux. [Représenté le 30.7.1713; troupe de Baxter & Saurin. Théâtre de la dame Baron] {*Théâtre de la Foire*, I (1721)}. Musique de Gilliers.

II. 1714 – 1718

1714: Reallowance of dialogue and music: no *écriteaux* plays known until 1718.

1718 – Foire Saint-Germain

Lesage, *Le Château des lutins*, pièce, 1 acte, avec prologue, en écriteaux. [Représenté 3.2.1718; troupe de Saint-Edme].

Lesage, *Arlequin valet de Merlin*, pièce, 1 acte, en écriteaux. [Représenté le 1.3.1718; troupe de Saint-Edme].

Lesage, *Les Filles ennuyées*, prologue en prose, avec vaudevilles, en écriteaux. [Représenté le 3.3.1718].

Lesage, *Arlequin Orphée le cadet*, pièce, 1 acte, en écriteaux. [Représenté le 8.3.1718].

– Foire Saint-Laurent

Pellegrin, Simon-Joseph, *Le Pied de nez*, opéra-comique, 3 actes, en écriteaux.

Charpentier, *Qui dort dîne*, 3 actes. [Représenté par la troupe de Péclavé]. Collaboration de Pellegrin?

—, *La Vache Io, ou Jupiter amoureux d'Io*, 2 actes. [Représenté par la troupe de Péclavé]. Collaboration de Pellegrin?

'A la fin de cette Foire, tous les Spectacles Forains furent totalement supprimés par ordre de la cour. Cette suppression subsista pendant tout le cours de l'année suivante 1719.' [Parfaict]

III. 1719-1724

'En 1720 les Troupes Foraines firent quelques tentatives, & jouèrent par tolérance, sans oser mêler leurs chants à leurs jeux.' {Parfaict}

1724 – Foire Saint-Laurent

Lesage, *La Toison d'or*, pièce, 1 acte en prose, en écriteaux.
[Théâtre de Dolet]. {Ms. B.N. f.f.25471}. Collaboration de
D'Orneval.

Lesage, *Les Captifs d'Alger*, prologue en prose, en écriteaux.
[Théâtre de Dolet]. {Mss. B.N. f.f.9314, 25471}.

Lesage, *L'Oracle muet*, pièce, 1 acte en prose, en écriteaux.
[Théâtre de Dolet]. {Mss. B.N. f.f.9314, 25471}.
Collaboration de D'Orneval.

'Ces pièces étaient en Prose; le succès qu'elles eurent allarma
l'Entrepreneur de l'Opéra-Comique [Honoré] qui dès le
troisième jour, obtint un ordre pour interdire la parole à cette
Troupe; au bout de quelques jours, Dolet et son associé obtin-
rent permission de jouer par écriteaux [les trois pièces précé-
dentes, et les trois suivantes]' [Parfaict, II, p.26].

Lesage, *La Matrone de Charenton*, pièce, 1 acte, en écriteaux.
Parodie de *la Matronne d'Ephèse*, de Fuzelier. [Théâtre de Dolet].
{Mss. B.N. f.f.9314, 25471}. Collaboration de D'Orneval.

Lesage, *La Pudeur à la foire*, prologue, avec vaudevilles, en
écriteaux. [Théâtre de Dolet]. {Mss. B.N. f.f.9314, 25471}.
Collaboration de D'Orneval.

Lesage, *Les Vendanges de la foire*, pièce, 1 acte en prose, en
écriteaux. [Théâtre de Dolet]. {Mss. B.N. f.f.9314, 25471}.
Collaboration de D'Orneval.

University of Kent at Canterbury

1   *Ecriteaux* are defined in a footnote to the published copy of Lesage's *Arlequin, Roi de Sérendib*, as follows: 'Les Ecriteaux étoient une espéce de Cartouche de toile roulée sur un bâton, & dans lequel étoit écrit en gros caractére [sic] le Couplet, avec le nom du Personnage qui auroit dû le chanter. L'Ecriteau descendoit du ceintre, & étoit porté par deux Enfans habillez en Amours, qui le tenoient en support. Les Enfans suspendus en l'air par le moyen des contrepoids, déroulaient l'Ecriteau; l'Orchestre jouoit aussi-tôt l'air du Couplet, & donnoit le ton aux Spectateurs, qui chantoient eux-mêmes ce qu'ils voyaient écrit, pendant que les Acteurs y accommodaient leurs gestes.' Alain-René Lesage et D'Orneval, *Le Théâtre de la Foire: ou L'Opéra Comique. Contenant les meilleures pièces qui ont été représentées aux foires de S. Germain et de S. Laurent*, 10 vols in 2 (Paris: Gandouin, 1737; repr. Geneva: Slatkine Reprints, 1968), I, 19-20. The title of the present essay is taken from the following stanza, describing the appearance of *écriteaux* plays, quoted by Lintilhac:

> Vous croyez régner cette fois
> Héros du Capitole
> Et qu'Arlequin est aux abois
> Privé de la parole
> Mais il a fait peindre sa voix
> Pour soutenir son rôle.

Eugène Lintilhac, *Histoire générale du théâtre en France,* 5 vols (Paris: Flammarion, 1904-11): IV, 'La Comédie au dix-huitième siècle', p.18.

2   Jules Bonnassies, *Les Spectacles forains et la Comédie Française* (Paris: Dentu, 1875). This book also contains the following two articles: 'Le Droit des pauvres avant et après 1789'; 'Les Auteurs dramatiques et la comédie au dix-neuvième siècle, d'après les documents inédits'.

3   Quoted in full by Lintilhac, op. cit.: III, 'La Comédie au dix-septième siècle', p.15.

4   Emile Campardon, *Les Spectacles de la Foire: Documents inédits recueillis aux Archives Nationales*, 2 vols (Paris: Berger-Levrault, 1877).

5   Bonnassies, op. cit.

6   Bernardin, op. cit., p.86

7   ibid., p.87.

8   Napoléon-Maurice Bernardin, *La Comédie Italienne en France, et les Théâtres de la Foire et du Boulevard (1570-1791)* (Paris: Revue Bleue, 1902), p.89. In this instance 'Rome' refers to the Comédie Française, who were known as 'Les Romains'.

9   Angelica Goodden, *Actio and Persuasion: Dramatic Performance in Eighteenth-century France* (Oxford: Clarendon Press, 1986), *passim*.

10 Claude and François Parfaict, *Mémoires pour servir à l'histoire des spectacles de la Foire par un acteur forain*, 2 vols (Paris: Briasson, 1743).

11 Clarence D. Brenner, *A Bibliographical List of Plays in the French Language (1700-1789)* (Berkeley: s.n., 1947; New York: AMS Reprints, 1979); Vincent Barberet, *Lesage et le Théâtre de la Foire* (Nancy, Sordoillet,1887); Claude and François Parfaict, op. cit.; Parfaict, *Dictionnaire des Théâtres de Paris*, 7 vols (Paris: Lambert, 1756); Francis J. Carmody, 'Le Répertoire de l'opéra-comique en vaudevilles de 1708 à 1764', *University of California Publications in Modern Philology* 16.4 (1932-3), pp. 373-438.

12 Barberet, op. cit., p.12.

13 Robert M. Isherwood, *Farce and Fantasy: Popular Entertainment in Eighteenth-Century Paris* (NewYork and Oxford: O.U.P., 1986). See especially chapter 4, 'The Politics of Culture: The Struggle against Privilege', pp. 81-97.

14 Cf. their analysis of *Les Plaideurs*: 'L'impression de cet ouvrage, qui n'a aucun mérite, nous dispense d'en donner l'extrait.' op. cit. II, 154.

15 Cf. préface: 'L'Objet de cet Ouvrage est d'exposer par ordre Alphabétique, tout ce qu'offre d'*intéressant* cette partie de la Littérature Françoise.' (p. iv: emphasis added). We should note also the inherent bias in Parfaict's choice of material, despite the assurance that their presentation of extracts from the plays is made independently of the play's success; Cf. préface, p. v-vi: 'Il a paru important d'en [les pièces manuscrites] faire l'Extrait, & d'en donner l'analyse. Ce seroit ne pas rendre justice à l'Auteur de regarder ce travail comme inutile, sous prétexte que les meilleures Piéces ont été imprimées, & qu'il n'y a que celles qui ont eu peu de succès aux représentations, que leurs Auteurs ont refusé d'exposer à un plus grand jour. Outre que le succès des représentations n'est pas toujoutrs ce qui doit faire juger du mérite d'une piéce, on verra par la maniere dont on a traité cet objet, qu'il est possible de faire un Extrait amusant & instructif d'une Piéce que les défauts ou les circonstances malheureuses ont fait tomber.' Compare with their analysis of, *inter alia*, *Le Jugement d'Appolon et de Pan par Midas* (1721): 'On ne donne aucun extrait de ces ouvrages, qui n'ont point eu de succès.' This bias is also clear from the full title of the work: 'Dictionnaire des théâtres de Paris: Contenant toutes les Pieces qui ont été représentées jusqu'à présent sur les différens *Théâtres François*, & sur celui de l'*Académie Royale de Musique*: les Extraits de celles qui ont été jouées par les *Comédiens Italiens*, depuis leur rétablisse-

ment en 1716, ainsi que des *Opéra Comiques*, & **principaux** Spectacles des Foires *Saint Germain & Saint Laurent* [...]' (title-page; emphasis added).

16   Brener, op. cit., 6153, 6154 (p.64).

17   This is shown by the first footnote in the printed copy of *Arlequin, Roi de Sérendib*, op. cit.

18   Lesage-D'Orneval, op. cit. I, 16-104.

19   See Barberet, op. cit., and especially Chapter 1, 'De l'action et du merveilleux'.

20   Bernardin, op. cit., pp.92-3.

21   Barberet, op. cit., p.65.

22   Lintilhac, op. cit., pp.336-7.

23   We should also note that *lazzi* are always defined in the Italian theatre as short scenes, which break the monotony of performances.

24   Derek Connon and George Evans (eds.), *Anthologie de pièces du Théâtre de la Foire* (Egham: Runnymede, 1996). See their introduction to *Arlequin, Roi de Sérendib*, note 1.

25   Bernardin, op. cit., p.90.

26   Peter Stallybrass and Allon White, *The Politics and Poetics of Transgression* (London: Methuen, 1986): 'The high-low opposition in each of our four symbolic domains – psychic forms, the human body, geographical space and the social order – is a fundamental basis to mechanisms of ordering and sense making in European cultures. [...] [T]ransgressing the rules of hierarchy and order in any one of the domains may have major consequences in the others' (p.3).

27   ibid., p.14.

28   B. Babcock, *The Reversible World: Symbolic Inversion in Art and Society* (Ithaca: Cornell U.P., 1978), p.14 (quoted by Stallybrass and White, op. cit., p.17).

29   'TRANSGRESSER, v. act. (Gram.) enfreindre, outrepasser. Il se dit des commendemens de Dieu & de l'Eglise. Si vous enlevez à un homme son boeuf, sa servante, ou sa femme, vous *transgressez* les commandemens de la loi. On dit aussi, *transgresser* les ordres d'un souverain. On appelle *transgresseur* celui qui commet la faute, & *transgression* la faute

commise.' *L'Encyclopédie: ou Dictionnaire raisonné des sciences, des arts et des métiers* (Paris: Briasson, 1765), XVI, 553.

30   See note 19.

31   Bonnassies, op. cit., pp.11-12.

32   In *Le Rire*, Bergson shows how it is precisely the social element of comedy which excludes *attendrissement*: 'Voilà le troisième fait sur lequel nous désirions attirer l'attention. On ne goûterait pas le comique si l'on se sentait isolé. [...] Notre rire est le rire d'un groupe.' Bergson, *Le Rire: Essai sur la signification du comique* (Paris: P.U.F., collection 'Quadrige', 1940), pp.4-5. We shall see later how the vaudeville itself is hardly suited to the *larmoyant*, but to comic effect, as shown by Philip Robinson.

33   Barberet, op. cit., p.6.

34   'Son [Lesage] style n'a guère que des rapports d'opposition avec celui de l'ouvrage parodié.' ibid., p.115.

35   ibid., p.113.

36   Roger Caillois, *L'Homme et le sacré*, 4th edn (Paris: Gallimard, 1950), pp.130-3.

37   Georges Bataille, *L'Erotisme* (Paris: Minuit, 1957), p.41.

38   'La transgression est un geste qui concerne la limite; c'est là, en cette minceur de la ligne, que se manifeste l'éclair de son passage, mais peut-être aussi sa trajectoire en sa totalité, son origine même. Le trait qu'elle croise pourrait bien être tout son espace. Le jeu des limites et de la transgression semble être régi par une obstination simple: la transgression franchit et ne cesse de recommencer à franchir une ligne qui, derrière elle, aussitôt se referme en une vague de peu de mémoire, reculant ainsi à nouveau jusqu'à l'horizon de l'infranchissable. Mais ce jeu met en jeu bien plus que de tels éléments; il les situe dans une incertitude, dans des certitudes aussitôt inversées où la pensée s'embarrasse vite à vouloir les saisir.
La limite et la transgression se doivent l'une à l'autre la densité de leur être: inexistence d'une limite qui ne pourrait absolument pas être franchie; vanité en retour d'une transgression qui ne franchirait qu'une limite d'illusion ou d'ombre. Mais la limite a-t-elle une existence véritable en dehors du geste qui glorieusement la traverse et la nie? Que serait-elle, après, et que pouvait-elle être, avant?' Michel Foucault, 'Préface à la transgression', *Critique*, 195-196 (1963), 751-769 (pp.754-755).

39   ibid., p.756.

40   Isherwood, op. cit.; see especially chapter 1, 'The Singing Culture of
      the Pont-Neuf', op. cit., pp. 3-21.

41   Evaristo Gherardi, *Le Théâtre Italien: ou Recueil général de toutes les
      comédies et scènes françaises jouées par les comédiens italiens du roy, avec tous les
      airs qu'on y a chantez, gravez, notez et corrigez, avec leur basse continue
      chiffrée à la fin de chaque volume,* 6 vols. (Amsterdam: Charles le Cene,
      1721). These plays are: *l'Opéra de campagne*; *la Baguette de Vulcain*; *Le
      Départ des comédiens*; *Attendez-moi sous l'orme*; *les Promenades de Paris*; *La
      Foire Saint-Germain*; *les Souhaits*.

42   Philip Robinson, 'Les Vaudevilles: Un Médium théâtral', *Dix-huitième
      Siècle,* 28 (1996), 431-447 (pp.432-33).

43   ibid.

44   ibid., p.435.

45   'Mort de Mazarin', in Pierre Barbier et France Vernillat, *Histoire de
      France par les chansons,* 8 vols (Paris: Gallimard, 1956-61), II, pp.55-56;
      'Les Rochellois', ibid., I, p.142; 'Les adieux de Louis XIV' Maurepas,
      *Recueil Clairambault-Maurepas: Chansonnier historique du XVIIIe siècle,
      publié avec introduction et notes par Emile Prammié,* 10 vols (Paris:
      Quantin, 1879-84), I, 17.

46   'La Mort de Richelieu', B.N. ms fr. 12666, quoted in Barbier-
      Vernillat, op. cit., I, 150-1.

47   See also Philip Robinson, 'Vaudevilles et genre comique en France au
      milieu du dix-huitième siècle', *Actes du colloque tenu à Bad-Homburg,
      Septembre 1996* (publication forthcoming).

48   André Gide, 'L'Evolution du théâtre', in *Oeuvres Complètes,* ed. by Louis
      Martin-Chauffier, 15 vols (Paris: NRF, 1932-1939), IV, 199-218
      (p.207).

49   This appendix consists of a list of all *écriteaux* plays which I have been
      able to trace. Likely *écriteaux* plays, not designated as such by certain
      sources, contain the remark 'en écriteaux [?]' Sources of other remarks
      are indicated in square brackets. References to Parfaict are to the
      Mémoires, quoted above. Unsure or doubtful references are followed by
      [?]. References are to author, title, description of the work as provided
      by Brenner, performance details, manuscript or publication details,
      and finally any supplementary observations.

50   'Je crois cette Piéce de Raguenet, Acteur qui parut pour la première fois à cette Foire, & dont je vais parler en peu de mots.' (Parfaict, *Mémoires*, p.125-6).

51   'Octave est arrêté sous lettre de cachet. Les autres Troupes, dont j'ai parlé à la Foire Saint-Germain précédente, continuèrent leurs spectacles à la présente Foire.' (ibid., p.151).

PART TWO

The Nineteenth Century

The 'Superfluous Man' in Nineteenth-Century French Literature

Sue Bedry

Superfluous man (Russian *lishni chelovek*), the name given to an important character type recurrent in nineteenth-century Russian literature. The term denotes a hero who is sensitive to social and ethical problems, but who fails to act, partly because of personal weakness, partly because of political and social restraints on his freedom of action.[1]

The 'superfluous man' is a hero-type of paramount importance in nineteenth-century Russian literature. Endowed with exceptional intelligence and sensibility, socially and politically idealistic, he is, nevertheless, fundamentally impotent; deeply disenchanted with the failure of contemporary society to meet his ideals, he is unable either to resign himself to this failure or to effect change. He is usually noble by heritage, but considers himself superior on the basis of his intelligence, sensibility, and talent rather than rank and is, in fact, deeply alienated from conventional society. With no role in the existing social structure and no constructive outlet for his abilities, he is reduced to futile transgression against social mores. Although he is often a moral, especially sexual, transgressor, his importance lies primarily in his transgression against social and political norms. Despite – and because of – the abortive nature of his rebellion, the superfluous man is of immense significance. As F.D. Reeve notes:

> The superfluous man is not a do-nothing but a man who is morally alienated, who has lived out all the experience his society can offer. He has used up his society but cannot alter it or be reconciled to it. As a channel marker shows the limits of navigable water, so he shows the bounds of the extremes of social behavior. He does not represent his age. He moves against it.[2]

The superfluous man – in his idealism, in his rebellion, and in his impotence – is, above all, a powerful literary indicator of the breakdown of the traditional societal elite of the nobility and the formation of a new elite based, not on rank, but on intelligence, education, and political and social radicalism – an 'intelligentsia'. As Richard Freeborn remarks: 'The history of the Russian intelligentsia was to be written initially in the Russian novel.'[3]

Although the superfluous man is typically considered an exclusively Russian phenomenon, it is my contention that not only does an analogous figure exist in nineteenth-century French literature, but also that he is of similar significance as a symbol of the decline of the traditional societal elite of the nobility and the emergence of an identifiable intellectual elite in nineteenth-century France. By using critical categories commonly used to describe phases in Russian literature, we can illuminate aspects of nineteenth-century French literature from a new and unusual angle.

Indeed, several scholars have come tantalizingly close to the concept of the superfluous man in their analyses of the hero in nineteenth-century French literature. George Ross Ridge, for example, classes the French romantic hero into 'five roles and a pseudo-role', and concludes that the sole aspect which all romantic heroes share is 'self-consciousness':

> The hero has a romantic sensibility which the herdsmen do not possess, and he is self-conscious because he is aware of this fundamental difference. [...] The romantic hero is self-consciously unique; he knows that he is different from and does not belong to the herd, society. He is, in truth, outside society.[4]

In his appraisal of the romantic 'anti-hero' (his 'pseudo-role') especially, Ridge approaches the concept of the superfluous man:

The romantic hero and the anti-hero are both motivated by self-consciousness, i.e., awareness plus the romantic sensibility, though they evince far different traits. The anti-hero, too, is self-conscious and does possess heroic potentiality. He is aware of the forces which mold him and the social forces against which he struggles. But self-consciousness is differently orientated in the anti-hero, since it represents his ironic appraisal of self in the social context. [...] The anti-hero always observes himself and he wryly comments upon his own weakness. He withers under his own debilitating irony, turned within.[5]

Glyn Holmes doubts that any universal definition can be established, and instead attempts to establish a sub-type of romantic hero, based on Constant's *Adolphe*, which he calls the 'Adolphe type'. Here is his description of the crucial traits of this 'type':

All are young men, born into a class of society which protects them from the harsher aspects of life, and who, upon entry into society, have little idea what to do in life, and show virtually no interest in pursuing what the society of their time might regard as a useful career. They subsequently find themselves in opposition to many of the conventions and attitudes adopted by the society of the time, into which they are unable to integrate. They consider themselves superior to the herd and, feeling themselves to be morally isolated from most of their contemporaries, develop a tendency towards introversion and self-analysis. They are also unable to acquire a firm religious faith, and this fact, coupled with their inability to integrate into society, leads them to seek fulfillment in personally conceived ideals. [6]

Like the scholars who link the Russian superfluous man to his historical milieu, Holmes also explicitly identifies his type with the decline of the traditional nobility:

When, within a limited period of time, there is a proliferation of very similar heroes, this phenomenon can in part be explained by the fact that these heroes bear at least some kind of relation to the historical context of the age in which they appeared. [...] These heroes can be seen as more or less obvious reflections of the effects of historical events upon certain sections of French society, particularly the younger intellectuals, during the first half of the nineteenth century. [...] Many French men, particularly the young aristocrats, found themselves caught in a kind of void between past and future. With the destruction of the old values, and no new ones yet firmly established, doubt and confusion seemed the order of the day.[7]

Victor Brombert also comes very close indeed to the concept of a French 'superfluous man' in nineteenth-century society and literature:

The emergence of the intellectual hero, and the key position he occupies in the modern French novel, can no doubt also be attributed to the growing prestige of an intellectual elite which, beginning in the late eighteenth century, saw itself further and further estranged in a society whose culture it inherited, but whose moral and aesthetic criteria it felt compelled to reject. Literature reflects the pride of this new aristocracy of the intellect. Rousseau's Saint-Preux, Stendhal's Julian Sorel, the ambitious young men of Balzac, Vigny's Chatterton and Stello, combine passionate temperaments with a fierce nobility that no longer marks a nobility of the blood or heroic deeds, but a nobility of the mind. The typical Romantic hero – often non-heroic, self-conscious and hyper-nervous – asserts himself less through physical prowess or striking adventures than through the distinction of his spirit. The irremediable clash between his social condition and his spiritual vocation predestines him to tragedy.[8]

It is clear that a literary type similar to the Russian superfluous man does exist in French literature; indeed, George Sand invented the strikingly similar term *homme inutile* to describe her hero Jacques (*Jacques*, 1834). When this question of parallels is discussed, however, it is typically within the context of derivation; in other words, that the Russian superfluous man shares certain qualities with nineteenth-century French literary heroes because of the enormous influence which French literature wielded at the time. Although this is perhaps true up to a point, it smacks of cultural elitism – and does not take into account the vitality of the Russian literary scene which was, by the nineteenth century, blazing a trail independent of Western tradition. This study, therefore, will discount questions of direct influence in favor of an examination of how similar economic, social and political trends produced comparable hero-types.

A.N. Dobrolyubov – who, in 1859, was perhaps the first critic to attempt to codify the connections between various Russian super-fluous men and their social and political milieu – observes that:

> 'Superfluous men' can be found anywhere and everywhere, in all ages, among all nations. [...] There are epochs which especially foster the appearance of the superfluous man – and just such an epoch in Russian social life was the hundred years from the middle of the eighteenth to the middle of the nineteenth century.[9]

It is my contention that the corresponding era in French social life was also 'just such an epoch'. Thus, to establish more than a superficial similarity between these two groups of alienated and world-weary heroes – as well as to fully understand the significance of the superfluous man – it is first necessary to place him within the context of two interlinked historical trends: 1) The decline of the traditional hereditary nobility and the concurrent rise of individualism within the class structure, and 2) The growing prestige and importance of an increasingly independent and critical breed of writers and thinkers.

I. The decline of the nobility and the rise of individualism within the class structure

The decline of the Russian nobility did not begin with the Emancipation of the serfs in 1861; although the Emancipation did a great deal to hasten the economic disintegration of the traditional landowning gentry, the real roots of the decay were as much philosophical and psychological as economic – and must be traced back to the eighteenth century.

Historically, the Russian nobility was based on the concept of service to the state, as Marc Raeff notes:

> [The] Russian nobleman of the eighteenth century quite clearly was exclusively a servant of the state. [...] The stress was on the nobleman's usefulness to the state and to society at large, not his worth as a private individual or his role as a member of a special group. Outside service a Russian noble-man in the eighteenth century had no socially meaningful and acceptable outlet for his talents, energy, and activities.[10]

This emphasis on service meant that a nobleman was wholly dependent on the state for his person, property, and family status; nobility was a state that could be lost, and noblemen who did not serve were considered undeserving of their rank. Another important byproduct of the service mentality was a certain feeling of rootlessness among the service nobility; both military and civil service entailed moving to wherever the state dictated, and thus broke the bonds of the landowning gentry with their family estates. Against this background, Peter the Great's extensive re-organization of the service system assumes paramount importance: in 1722, Peter systematized the service principle by creating the 'Table of Ranks', with fourteen grades of civil servants, based on German titles and equivalent to military ranks. Most significantly, the service system was changed to admit talented commoners, who could then achieve personal or hereditary nobility after a successful service career. This revolutionary

'equalization' was to have huge consequences: new concepts of
merit, hierarchy, and reward entered the psychology of the
nobility, and the function of service was now to prove one's
personal merit and talent, rather than to fulfill a preordained
role for which, by virtue of birth, one was already suited. This
new emphasis amounted to an endorsement of individualism
over class identity, as Raeff notes:

> The merit clause of the Table of Ranks provided both the
> stimulus and the foundation for the development of
> individualism. It was the first time, since the Times of
> Troubles at least, that an individual's worth was given public
> recognition and status in Russia. [...] But at the same time a
> new element of personal insecurity was introduced: no one
> could feel he had a place and role in society (and the state)
> until he had secured it by dint of his own efforts and work.[11]

After the institution of the Table of Ranks, the service role of the
Russian nobility continued to be redefined and diminished. In
1736, compulsory state service for noblemen was limited to a
period of twenty-five years, and in 1762, the nobility was freed
completely from compulsory service and those serving were
allowed to resign. Although the decrees of 1736 and 1762 can
be (and often are) seen as triumphs for the nobility over the
state, the newly optional status of state service signaled, in
effect, the state's autonomy from the nobility and would lead to
the emergence of a burgeoning 'bureaucratic' class. This new
'caste' of bureaucrats and career officials – many of whom, by
the mid-nineteenth century, were non-noble – would usurp the
nobility's traditional role within the state, 'taking over the
positions of prominence and securing rewards, recognition, and
high status, while the nobility was withdrawing from direct
participation in the business of the state.'[12]

During the remainder of the eighteenth century and
throughout the nineteenth, the traditional rights and privileges
of the gentry were to be eroded and their social and political

roles modified,[13] while their viability as an economic class –
tenuous even before the Emancipation – was further diminished.

As in Russia, the decline of the French nobility cannot be
ascribed to one single, catastrophic event, but was instead a
gradual process with its roots in the eighteenth century – and
one that offers intriguing parallels with the situation outlined
above. Although the Russian nobility is often considered as
intrinsically different from those of Western Europe by virtue of
its status as a 'service' nobility, more basis for comparison exists
than typically thought. Firstly, the Russian nobility did, despite
its service status, set great store on heredity rank.[14] And
secondly, not only was service the origin of many French noble
families, but the tradition of ennobling 'servants' of common
birth was well established in France. Historically, the French
nobility was composed of three groups: the *noblesse de parage*,
based on land possession and originating in feudal times; the
noblesse d'épée, ennobled for military service; and the later *noblesse
de robe*, ennobled for high judicial or legal service. (Napoleon was
therefore to follow an established tradition in creating his *noblesse
impériale*.) The concept of service – although never codified, as it
was in Russia – was, historically, of paramount importance to the
psychology of the French nobility, as Michael Confino notes:

> Au milieu du XVe siècle le gentilhomme bourguignon
> Gilbert de Lanoy instruisait ses lecteurs nobles que les
> 'richesses' devaient être acquises 'honorablement', et il
> ajoutait qu'aucune source de richesse n'était plus honorable
> que le service du prince. Un représentant de la noblesse aux
> Etats Généraux de 1588 déclarait qu'il représentait non
> seulement les nobles de son temps, mais aussi toutes les
> générations aristocratiques qui les avaient précédés, et que
> c'était 'l'exemple ancestral de la générosité héritée qui inspirait
> à leurs descendants de servir l'Etat'. Un magistrat de
> province écrivait en 1602 au Chancelier de France 'qu'un
> lingnage distingué obligeait l'homme de servir l'Etat.' Au
> milieu du XVIIIe siècle, Montesquieu disait, comme on sait,

qu'une noblesse héréditaire était essentielle pour maintenir le caractère du régime monarchique; mais il ajoutait aussi que les hommes de naissance distinguée poursuivraient 'naturellement" honneur et prestige au service de leur maître royal. [...] Pour les grands seigneurs, le service représentait une question de prestige et une voie d'accès aux allées de pouvoir. Le 'prolétariat nobiliaire' le considérait comme une nécessité financière et – par voie de mimétisme social – comme un moyen de 'vivre noblement', c'est-à-dire de prétendre que lui aussi participait au genre de vie canonisé par les familles illustres (et riches) de sa classe.[15]

This notion of the role of service continued into the eighteenth century, as G. Chaussinand-Nogaret notes:

> Servir – et c'est là un des principes essentiels de définition de la noblesse au XVIIIe siècle – est l'ambition de tous, ou presque. Si l'on ne sert pas, ce n'est pas, sauf exception, par calcul, par volonté de non-engagement, mais par impossibilité ou par déception: défaut de fortune ou carrière bouchée. Le droit au service est considéré comme un privilège essentiel du statut nobiliaire et explique en partie l'hostilité de la noblesse – hostilité relative et qui comporte bien des nuances – à la roture de service. Servir le roi est à la fois un droit, un devoir, et un honneur, et un gentilhomme ne saurait se soustraire à ces obligations morales. Seules la pauvreté, les limites du recrutement et l'injustice du système maintiennent certains dans l'inactivité.[16]

Thus, service, although never a legal obligation, as in Russia, did indeed play a fundamental role in defining the status – social, political, economic, and psychological – of the French nobility within the state.

Throughout the eighteenth century, although the outward structure of French society remained the same as that of the preceding century, the hereditary nobility was, in fact, in the process of being progressively pushed out of its traditional service roles. The hereditary nobility had already lost a great deal of its economic power to both the *noblesse de robe* and to the rapidly rising bourgeoisie, which had succeeded in consolidating the advantages acquired under Louis XIV. Already alienated from the traditional power bases of their provincial estates by Louis XIV, many impoverished noblemen sold off their estates to the peasantry and became further alienated from the land. As France became ever more commercially and industrially oriented, the hereditary nobility found itself gradually overtaken in the sphere of economic and political influence. The traditional nobility was already in decline by the Revolution of 1789.

Following the Revolution and throughout the nineteenth century, of course, the social upheavals accompanying each of the successive governments of the first Empire, the Restoration, the July Monarchy, the Second Republic, the Second Empire, and the Third Republic meant that the situation of the hereditary nobility was to become ever more precarious and marginalized. Although a significant number of nobles did retain considerable influence and wealth, the nobility *as a class* was fast losing its defining roles – economic, political, and social – in French society.

Thus, both the Russian and the French nobilities found themselves gradually pushed out of their traditional roles, progressively alienated from both the central government and from the provincial power base of their estates, and slowly losing economic viability as a class. In each country, noblemen were gradually beginning to see themselves as part of a cultural elite; and to preserve his status, a nobleman had to carve out a role for himself independent of traditional state service, hereditary rank or land ownership.

The rise of an independent 'class' of writers and thinkers

In his anxiety to modernize (and westernize, for at the time the two terms were considered synonymous) Russia, Peter the

Great laid a great stress on a modern and Western education. Inevitably, a 'modern' education became the hallmark of a highly-placed nobleman and a goal to which not only the poorer gentry, but also the nascent middle class of bureaucrats, professionals, and clergy aspired.[17] This led to a further weakening of the class-based system and altered the very foundations of the traditional system of hierarchy.

By the end of the eighteenth century, the concept of what constituted a nobleman had changed from an narrow, exclusively hereditary notion to a much broader and indefinite image, the primary component of which was a superior education and a modern social and cultural outlook; indeed, by the nineteenth, a commoner who had acquired both the desired level of education and the necessary cultural philosophy was quite easily admitted into the ranks of the nobility both socially and legally.[18] Thus, the primary role of a nobleman was no longer found in government service – although the majority of noblemen continued to serve – but in cultural leadership, as a bringer of social enlightenment and cultural and educational sophistication. An elite based on non-hereditary criteria had begun to form.

Inevitably, the values and goals of this embryonic intelligentsia – who now regarded their rightful role as much broader than simply propping up the state – began to clash with the government. Indeed, following Alexander Radishchev's *A Journey from St Petersburg to Moscow* (1790), the theme of civic criticism in literature, muted in the eighteenth century, would come to the forefront until by the mid-nineteenth century it was seen as the primary purpose of literature. As Joe Andrew notes: 'Both opposition and government viewed literature as a kind of "alternative government", a second voice which was able, if only indirectly, to offer some kind of challenge to established ideas and behavior when more obvious political methods were virtually impossible.'[19]

In France, too, the foundations for an intellectual elite were laid in the eighteenth century, as Theodore Zeldin notes:

The basis for this new role for the intellectuals had been laid in the eighteenth century. Around 1700 the 'man of letters' usually lived in a state of insecurity and constraint, shackled by an arbitrary censorship exercised simultaneously by the king, the *parlement* and the Sorbonne. He often had to use pseudonyms or conceal his identity altogether. Only in the second half of the century did a few of them manage to live by their pens. These successes did a good deal to raise the status of what was becoming almost a profession. The government began employing writers to influence public opinion, 'to prepare the way for legislation', as Moreau described his own function. But it was slow to accept advice from them. [...] The first stage in their ascent was for them to win honor, respect and security. They did not think of power yet. [...] However, as the censorship relaxed, books on politics gave the writers increasing authority. Foreign admirers in particular did much to raise their status. It was the *philosophes*, not the nobles, whom the visitors from abroad came to see. [...] On the eve of the Revolution in 1778, Mercier wrote, 'the influence of writers is such that they can today proclaim their power and no longer disguise the legitimate authority they have over men's minds'.[20]

Thus, by the Revolution of 1789, the establishment of a distinct intellectual elite had already begun. Following the Revolution and throughout the nineteenth century, this nascent elite would become progressively influential – and progressively alienated from the state. 'It was now open to any man to have ideas and publish and propagate them. It is in this way that the intellectual in politics arrived.'[21]

Frank F. Seeley has divided the rise of the Russian intelligentsia into three stages: 'happy growth', 'estrangement', and 'reintegration', at the beginning of which 'the government regards the intelligentsia as an instrument for running the state and maintaining the powers and privileges of the rulers' and at the end of which the intelligentsia has evolved into 'a vanguard of intellectuals and

leaders of the national life' in its own right.[22] As we have seen,
the period of 'happy growth' lasted throughout the latter part of
the eighteenth century, as a distinct class of writers and thinkers
began to form in both Russia and France, while 'reintegration'
may be considered as wholly accomplished by the last few
decades of the nineteenth century.[23] This, then, leaves the bulk
of the nineteenth century to the period of estrangement – 'The
period of uncertainty and comparative inaction marking the
transition of the intelligentsia from its 18th-century function as
an instrument of the autocracy to its 19th-century function as
protagonist of a new order'[24] – in both nations. This transitional
period of 'uncertainty and comparative inaction' is, of course, the
era of the superfluous man.[25]

II.

The evolving nature of the Russian superfluous man has
long been recognized; the idea of types or stages of superfluous
men is widely accepted as both valid and useful. Seeley has
suggested three 'main varieties' of superfluous man in Russian
literature as he evolves under the pressure of historical circumstance:
the 'skeptics and dandies' of the 1820's; the 'demons of revolt' of
the 1830's; and the 'preachers' of the 1840's.[26] I propose four
'generations' of superfluous men in both Russian and French literature,
and term them: 'dandies', 'rebels', 'visionaries', and 'dreamers'. By
studying the progression of these four generations of doomed
transgressors, one can trace the gradual ascendance of the 'intellectual'
over the 'noble' in both literature and society.

The Dandy

> Pouvoir sans savoir est fort dangereux; savoir sans pouvoir est
> inutile est triste.[27]

In Russian literature, Griboyedev's Chatsky (*Woe from Wit*,
1822-4) and Pushkin's Onegin (*Eugene Onegin*, 1823-31) are the
earliest examples of the nineteenth-century superfluous man,

and thus form both the foundation of the type and the template for any comparison. The French 'dandy' emerges slightly earlier than his Russian cousin; I consider Chateaubriand's René (*René*, 1802), Senancour's Obermann (*Obermann*, 1804), and Constant's Adolphe (*Adolphe*, 1816) to mark the debut of the French 'superfluous man'.[28]

The dandy's era is thus roughly the first quarter of the nineteenth century in both Russia and France.[29] Although the histories of the two nations during this time are of course widely divergent, a broadly similar current can be identified: a period of rising hopes which are gradually stifled, leading eventually to a revolutionary movement and ending in a crackdown by the authorities. In Russia, the early portion of the reign of Alexander I was marked for its domestic liberalism; he subdued the secret police, made some attempts to improve the position of the serfs, and began to reform the educational system. However, the latter part of his reign marked a sharp turnaround: national and liberal movements were suppressed, many of his earlier liberal efforts were abrogated, and the infamous military colonies of peasant-soldiers were established. In 1825, of course, came the accession of Nicholas I and the abortive Decembrist Uprising. In France, liberal hopes raised by the advent of Napoleon were disappointed by the First Empire and the Restoration, with their ever-increasing restrictions upon personal and press liberties. In 1830, the 'Trois Glorieuses' led to the July Monarchy of Louis Philippe.

The stage was set for a generation of young noblemen to become frustrated idealists, raised with great expectations but unable to realize them in contemporary society, and it is against this background of pre-revolutionary tension that the dandy must be seen. The aristocracy in each nation was backward-looking, anachronistic, and reactionary; and no viable alternative elite had yet presented itself.

The dandy – direct descendant of the eighteenth-century 'philosophe' and educated and noble 'man of letters' and inspired by the Napoleonic spirit of individualism – is unable to reconcile himself to the values of conventional society. Chatsky, Onegin, René, Obermann, and Adolphe are all endowed with exceptional intelligence and sensibility, and clearly consider themselves superior on the basis of this rather than rank – all are, in fact, deeply alienated from conventional noble society. Significantly, they are all deeply idealistic and disappointed by the failure of contemporary society to meet their ideals. Futile as this is – for by definition, the superfluous man is unable to translate conviction into action – it is nevertheless vital, for it is in this 'civic sense' that the superfluous man most strongly presages the politically radical and socially reformist intellectual.

The dandy's civic sense is somewhat wavering and unsteady; his loudly proclaimed convictions bear little fruit, and are muted at the first sign of opposition. Despite this essentially dilettante nature, however, all of our dandies can be seen as politically or socially subversive: radical, if not revolutionary.

Both Chatsky and Onegin are linked with the Decembrist movement in Russia, and therefore take on a clear political significance. Chatsky is the most explicitly political of our dandies – and is clearly recognized as such by society:[30] he is not only a 'radical' and a 'Carbonarist', but 'a dangerous man to know'. Onegin, in the final version of the novel at least, is much less overtly politicized than Chatsky. However, the deleted portions of *Onegin's Journey* show him to have been, in an earlier conception, at least as politically radical. Not only do the deleted stanzas openly criticize government policy, but both Alexander I and Paul I are mocked.[31] Onegin, if not a Decembrist himself (as Pushkin himself was) was at least a sympathizer.

The final edition of *René* contains little of an explicitly political nature, stressing instead his metaphysical incompatibility with contemporary society. However, as Colin Smethurst notes, both the first edition of *René* and *Les Natchez* show René in a different light:

In *Les Natchez*, for example, rumors are spread in New Orleans that René is the political leader of the Natchez Indians, an anti-colonial fighter: 'Adario, Chactas même, et René surtout, étaient représentés comme les auteurs d'une conspiration permanente, comme des hommes qui... s'opposaient à l'établissement des concessionnaires'. René is brought to trial and, just as Julian Sorel in *Le Rouge et le Noir* at his own trial proudly assumes the political role rumor accuses him of adopting, so René makes a virulent anti-colonial speech denouncing the 'vil ramas d'hommes enlevés à la corruption de l'Europe, [qui] a dépouillé de ses terres une nation indépendante'. René is delighted to be unjustly condemned: 'se sentir innocent et être condamné par la loi, était, dans la nature des idées de René, une espèce de triomphe sur l'ordre social.' [...]These are the buried possibilities of the René figure which have been deliberately toned down in *René*.[32]

That Obermann's rejection of contemporary society is socially and politically motivated is clear: 'retenu par l'ami, accusé par le moraliste, condamné par ma patrie, coupable aux yeux de l'hòmme social',[33] his flight further and further into the wilds of Switzerland – like that of René to the wilds of America – is an overt attempt to escape the social order, and even his consideration of suicide is an explicitly political act:

> Si ce pouvait être un crime d'abandonner la vie, c'est vous [la société] que j'accuserais, vous dont les innovations funestes m'ont conduit à vouloir la mort, que sans vous j'eusse éloignée. [...] Opprimez ma vie, la loi est souvent aussi le droit le plus fort; mais la mort est la borne que je veux poser à votre pouvoir. Ailleurs vous commanderez, ici il faut prouver. [...] Toute société est fondée sur une réunion de facultés un échange de services; mais quand je nuis à la société, ne refuse-t-elle pas de me protéger? Si donc elle ne fait rien pour moi, ou si elle fait beaucoup contre moi, j'ai aussi le doit de refuser de la servir. Notre pacte ne lui

convient plus, elle le rompt; il ne me convient plus, je le romps aussi: je ne me révolte pas, je sors.[34]

Adolphe is the least political of our five dandies; but even he is quite deliberately socially subversive, as his volatile behavior in both Germany and Poland shows. His youthful admiration of the elderly lady had developed in him, we are told: 'une insurmontable aversion pour toutes les maximes communes et pour toutes les formules dogmatiques'.[35] And, of course, his continuing defense of Ellénore in the face of (for him) intolerable pressure from society – and, indeed, his attraction for her in the first place – has a great deal to do with her status as outsider and exile, and can therefore be interpreted as an act of protest, if not revolt.

Despite his superior intelligence and sensibility and his strong ethical and moral underpinning, however, the dandy is wholly unable to translate his ethical convictions into either concrete form or meaningful action; he is forever characterized by 'savoir sans pouvoir'. Thus, Chatsky is splendid in his tirades, but accomplishes nothing except his own exile from both Petersburg and Moscow. Onegin eases his serfs' burden by allowing them to pay quitrent – but would never consider freeing them completely, and indeed, does so more in a spirit of experimentation than of reform. Adolphe rails against the hypocrisy of society even as he surrenders to it. René and Obermann simply flee; the grand courtroom speech of the one, and the virulent suicide note of the other, come to nothing. Fatally lacking in strength of will, the dandy has no 'reserves'; when seriously challenged or threatened, his perilously thin philosophical foundation crumbles. Thus, Chatsky flees Moscow; Onegin murders Lensky; Adolphe sacrifices Ellénore; René escapes to America; Obermann buries himself in the wilds of Switzerland. Adolphe notes at one point that 'Cette société d'ailleurs n'a rien à craindre'.[36] Not yet – but the civic sense of the dandy, unsteady though it is, nevertheless lays the foundation for future generations of superfluous men and the eventual emergence of the intellectual hero. His social and political transgression – futile as it is – is an indicator that the attitude of a portion of the societal elite was already deeply at odds with that of conventional society.

The dandy's reign was to be short-lived. He was simply not robust enough to stand in opposition to society for long, and he did not have the wherewithal to break free of the old order. When the political and social situation in each country reached the crisis point, the dandy was not equipped to deal with it. As Seeley notes:

> The education and outlook of [the dandy's] generation were largely conditioned by the eighteenth century. Not one of our dandies was a revolutionary or radical. Most were progressively conservative or moderately liberal: in other words, enlightened critics of the old order rather than pro-tagonists of a new order. And so when the old order, instead of collapsing [...], gathered itself for a formidable counter-offensive, the dandies had no base of principle from which to oppose it – no purpose of their own, no course, no clear conception even of their relation to society – only an inner conviction of their superiority and a habit of criticism.[37]

Despite his weakness in the face of opposition, however, the dandy leaves an important legacy – a tradition of individualism and independant thought allied to social, political, and moral protest.

The Rebel

With the next generation of superfluous man – the rebel – this weakness in the face of opposition is eliminated; indeed, the rebel's will is his dominant characteristic. For, if the period in which the dandy emerged – the first quarter of the nineteenth century- was characterized by uncertainty and disappointment, then the period of the rebel – the thirties and forties – is one of deep disenchantment and open rebellion. The 1830's were to

mark the collapse of the dandy and the ascendance of the rebel
in both Russia and France. In each nation, hopes for increasing
political and social liberalism would be thwarted, and the dandy's
vague dissatisfaction would be replaced by open rebellion,
brought on in each case by a new and repressive regime:
Nicholas I in Russia, Louis-Philippe in France. Both of these
leaders had been heralded as more progressive, more liberal,
than their predecessors. Each, frightened by revolutionary stirrings,
would become just as repressive. In both countries, the
grandiose hopes of a generation had been betrayed – in 1825 in
Russia, in 1830 in France – and the literary rebel would emerge
to personify the frustration of a second generation of thwarted
idealists. Lermontov's Pechorin (*A Hero of Our Time*, 1840) marks
the advent of this second generation of superfluous man in
Russian literature, while Musset's Lorenzo (*Lorenzaccio*, 1834) is
the best example of this stage in French literature.[38]

The rebel is no longer 'conditioned by the eighteenth
century', but wholly a product of the nineteenth, a member of
the post-Decembrist, post-July Revolution generation, for
whom inaction is no longer satisfactory. He has inherited the
dandy's individualism, and he is no longer hampered from
expressing it. Radical though he might be in his rejection of
societal norms, however, the rebel is no revolutionary; in fact, he
has less of a clearly defined social agenda than the dandy.
Although he discards completely the passivity of the dandy for
action and open rebellion against society, he still has no 'base of
principle', no 'purpose of his own' – and he has rejected as futile
what ethical ballast the dandy retained. The rebel is no longer
characterized by 'savoir sans pouvoir', as was the dandy, but by
'pouvoir sans savoir' – and he is very dangerous indeed. As Janko
Lavrin notes, Pechorin is:

> a new variety of Onegin: a sinister and tragic variety. The
> more so because he is endowed with intelligence, strength,
> and will-power. Before 1825, he probably would have been a
> Decembrist. In the 'thirties, however, he was deprived even

of such an outlet. So he became a rancorous déclassé from above, with all the elements of potential nihilism. [...] Pechorin is here presented as an ironically cold and aloof symbol of frustration; as a suppressed idealist, skeptical of all ideals. Superior to his surroundings by his gifts, his ambitions, his strength of will, he is yet devoid of any positive aim or channel. So his strength turns not only against himself, but also against the people who come into contact with him.[39]

The rebel is the most overtly transgressive of our superfluous men, even if he would seem to lack the dandy's political idealism.[40] Both Pechorin and Lorenzo, like Chatsky, are dangerous men to know – not, however, because of their political radicalism, but simply because they refuse to recognize any social ethos. Not only does the rebel deliberately transgress against the mores of conventional society – he is determined to exact vengeance from society for its betrayal. In this context, the fact that both Pechorin and Lorenzo are murderers is extremely significant. Onegin, René, and Adolphe can all be considered 'killers'; but they kill more or less despite themselves. Pechorin and Lorenzo, in contrast, kill deliberately and in cold blood.

Of course, the rebel's 'vengeance' is futile; he cannot strike at the causes of his unhappiness because, in fact, he has no clear idea of what they really are. As C.J.G. Turner notes: '[Pechorin's] sense of frustration is at least partly due to this lack of definition about the object of his hostility',[41] and Lorenzo's case is strikingly similar. The rebel's lack of any clearly defined goal thus defeats any civic sense that he possesses – and condemns him to superfluity. Pechorin constantly rails against the shallowness and hypocrisy of society, but his victims are wholly inappropriate; Lorenzo admits that his act of murder is not only futile, but also at least as much a form of personal revenge as a revolutionary act:

Je voulais agir seul, sans le secours d'aucune homme. Je travaillais pour l'humanité; mais mon orgueil restait solitaire au milieu de tous mes rêves philanthropiques. Il fallait donc

entamer par la ruse un combat singulier avec mon ennemi. Je
ne voulais pas soulever les masses, ni conquérir la gloire
bavarde d'un paralytique comme Cicéron; je voulais arriver à
l'homme, me prendre corps à corps avec la tyrannie vivante,
la tuer, et après cela porter mon épée sanglante sur la tribune,
et laisser la fumée du sang d'Alexandre monter au nez des
harangueurs, pour réchauffer leur cervelle ampoulée.[42]

Janko Lavrin, above, calls Pechorin a 'suppressed idealist'.
However, the dandy was a 'suppressed idealist' – for the rebel,
'corrupted idealist' is more accurate. We are no longer dealing
with a mere suppression of good impulses, but a wholesale
perversion of them. This is explicitly presented in each work as
a split between idealism and corruption which has reached the
very core of their characters:

> I became a moral cripple. One half of my soul had ceased to
> exist. It had withered and died, so I cut it off and cast it
> away.[43]

> Il est trop tard. Je me suis fait à mon métier. Le vice a été
> pour moi un vêtement; maintenant il est collé à mon peau.[44]

Society has failed to recognize and utilize the strength of the
rebel; the rebel has failed to find a purpose, a role in life – and
thus heal this inner division. As Ronald Grimsley notes:

> A part of his [Lorenzo's] present torment lies in the thought
> that this original purpose has not been fulfilled. The
> depraved life which was first accepted as a means of attaining
> a good end has become an integral part of his personality, a
> mode of existence desired for its own sake. What was once a
> mere mask is now 'collé à son peau', a 'Deianeira's garment'
> from which he cannot tear himself free. 'Je me suis fait à mon
> métier', he admits, '...Je suis vraiment un ruffian.' This, however,
> is not all, for if he were completely identified with this new
> role, some unity – albeit a demonic one – might be given to

his life. His difficulty is that, is spite of its obvious corruption, his present self is still tormented by the memory of its lost innocence.[45]

The rebel marks a huge step away from the dandy. He has succeeded in shaking off the dandy's ineffectual passivity; he is energetic and vital, angry and capable. Although he has the strength of will to accomplish great things, however, his lack of ethical ballast prevents him from finding any purpose in life or role within society; his action is energetic but directionless – and therefore futile. For this reason, the rebel could no more survive or prosper than the dandy.

The rebel's stand against society is thus as short-lived as the dandy's; where the dandy more or less faded away, the rebel self-destructs. Because his rebellion had no focus, it was impossible to maintain. The rebel – to borrow a phrase coined for a very different 'rebel' – lived fast and died young. By the 1840's, he had been replaced in Russian literature by the third 'generation' of superfluous man – the visionary. No other generation of superfluous man, however, would achieve the sheer vitality of the rebel; and this is his legacy.

The Visionary

The visionary is no less a product of his times than the dandy or the rebel: as the hopes of the Revolutionary and Napoleonic eras raised the expectations of the dandy beyond all sense of realism; as the ensuing repression and stagnation both crushed the dandy and resulted in the rebel's splendid but futile rebellion; the stifling atmosphere which surrounded the mid-point of the nineteenth century in both Russia and France produced the visionary, who can see his goal – but is unable to reach it.

In Russia, the era of the visionary roughly encompasses the last decade or so of the reign of Nicholas I (1825-55), and the

first few years of Alexander II (1855-81): the time of immense
transition leading up to the Emancipation. Throughout, this
period was one of diametrically opposing forces: a socially rigid
and economically stagnant time of social and political repression
sandwiched between two periods of reform.[46] It also marked
both the triumph of bureaucracy and the arrival of the
'raznochintsy' – literally, 'men of no rank' – in the respective
spheres of state and culture. In France, this era of turmoil is of
longer duration; incorporating roughly the last few years of the
July Monarchy, the short-lived Second Republic, and the Second
Empire, it is distinguished, of course, by the decisive victory of
the bourgeoisie in all spheres of social, economic, and political
life, and although (for the most part) vibrant economically was
a time of malaise among the young would-be intellectuals.

The visionary is best represented in Russian literature by
Turgenev's Rudin (*Rudin*, 1857).[47] I shall draw upon three
literary heroes from the whole range of the period in France –
Sand's Horace (*Horace*, 1842), Flaubert's Frédéric Moreau
(*L'Education sentimentale*, 1869) and Zola's Lazare (*La Joie de vivre*,
1884) – to represent the French visionary.[48]

The visionary, like all superfluous men, is distinguished by
his extraordinary intelligence and sensibility. Rudin, Horace,
Frédéric, and Lazare all clearly share an almost unwavering belief
in their own potential, and combine the dandy's lofty expectations
with the rebel's ambition. However, unlike either the dandy or
the rebel, the visionary is *dependent* upon his intelligence and
sensibility to distinguish himself from the crowd; for he marks a
turning point in the social status of the superfluous man.
Whereas the dandy and the rebel, however much they transgressed against social norms, were still recognizably a part of
noble society, the visionary – reflecting the breakdown of
traditional class barriers in both nations – is no longer an
integral part of it. Rudin, although of noble origin, is shabby
and poor, economically and socially marginalized. Horace,
Frédéric, and Lazare, of course, are all bourgeois (although both

Frédéric and Lazare are of vaguely noble origin on the maternal side), but unable to accept the 'bourgeois' ideal. The visionary must, therefore, distinguish himself by means of ideas – and in this, he strongly heralds the emergence of the intellectual hero in literature and of the intelligentsia in society.

If the dandy can be summarized as possessing a social conscience without sufficient will to act upon it, and the rebel the will to act without a social conscience, the visionary is the recognizable beginning of a synthesis between the two. Victor Ripp notes that *Rudin* 'repeats one of the most vexing questions of Russian intellectual life: what is the connection between abstract ideals and purposeful activity?'[49] This – the connection between abstract ideals and purposeful activity – is the question at the crux of the struggle of not just Rudin, but also Horace, Frédéric, and Lazare. The visionary has inherited the social and political progressiveness of the dandy; significantly, he at least attempts to translate his idealistic convictions into real actions. Thus, Rudin, while serving as the manager of a large estate, attempts to introduce new principles of social agronomy (which, of course, implies modernizing the system of serfdom); Lazare builds and rebuilds a breakwater to save his provincial village from innundation; both Horace and Frédéric attempt political and careers among numerous other projects.

All of these efforts, of course, prove futile; as with all superfluous men, the visionary's reach exceeds his grasp. The visionary is unaware of – and wholly incapable of – the degree of commitment which successful completion of any one of his projects would require. His grandiose visions are fated to stay just that – visions, rather than realities – because the visionary's engagement is unable to live up to his intentions. Despite his strong ethical and civic sense, the idealistic cerebralism of the visionary fatally hampers him from finding the connection between abstract ideals and purposeful, meaningful action. None of our visionaries are lacking in physical courage – indeed, all four face danger calmly and bravely (Rudin on a revolutionary

barricade; Horace facing down several would-be attackers;
Frédéric in his duel; Lazare in the burning house), and all do
stand up for their ideals (think, for example, of Frédéric in the
Dambreuse salon); but except for Rudin's futile last stand, this
heroic action is either wholly unavoidable or it is the impulse of
a moment. It is when the visionary is faced with a decision, with
considered action which would demonstrate, once and for all,
his commitment to a cause, that he falters. As Horace cries
despairingly: 'Je voudrais, moi aussi, avoir une espérance, une
conviction assez forte pour me faire hacher à coups de sabre
derrière une barricade.'[50]

Thus, the visionary does not flout social norms for effect, as
did the dandy, or for vengeance, as did the rebel. Instead, he
transgresses almost without consciously intending to; in his
quest to find a sphere of action in which he can realize his ideals
and a role in which to utilize his gifts, he tramples over society's
expectations at every turn. Rudin cannot be satisfied with the
role of social hanger-on to which his lack of fortune condemns
him in noble society; he is no more able to fit into the stultified
world of traditional education or the mercenary one of business.
Horace, Frédéric, and Lazare are, of course, defined by their
inability to conform to their bourgeois environment, which
'affords little scope for exploits and passions on the epic or the
romantic scale'[51] – and all three of our bourgeois heroes transgress in a clear attempt to transcend their mediocre background.

From the dandy, the visionary inherited social and political
progressiveness; from the rebel, the ideas and ideals of romantic
heroism. He is endowed, too – like all superfluous men – with
superior intelligence and sensibility. Despite this potent mix,
however, the visionary is wholly unable to bridge the gap
between abstract ideals and meaningful action. His vision,
although inspired, is fatally unrealistic; he 'sees' the ideal rather
than the real – and his efforts are thus misdirected and, ultimately,
futile. Forced, unlike his predecessors, to rely on his intrinsic
abilities to distinguish himself from the crowd, the visionary has

come to rely too much on the power of ideas alone. He is a prophet, rather than a missionary – able to cry in the wilderness but not to conquer it. Rudin, Horace, Frédéric, and Lazare are all fundamentally passive; they are caught up by events and moved by forces outside their control – and often outside their understanding, for their naïve concentration on a future ideal leaves little room for the present reality. The potential of the visionary thus remains – like that of all superfluous men – unfulfilled.

Despite his superfluity, however, the visionary is nevertheless the direct and recognizable predecessor of the modern intellectual in literature and in life. Appearing at a time of unprecedented social change – the emergence in Russia of the raznochintsy as a societal force and the triumph in France of the bourgeoisie – the visionary heralds the formation of a non-class based 'intelligentsia' in both Russia and France. His faith in ideas and ideals and his social and political progressiveness – even his naïve refusal to recognize the sheer inertial power of conventional society – are the recognizable precursors of the socially active and politically radical modern intellectual. The significance of the visionary lies not not in what he achieved – but in what he attempted. Freeborn notes that: 'All Turgenev's heroes embody ideas and aspire to emulate ideals. The degree of success or failure which they experience in their lives is gauged by the extent to which they are able to put their ideas to the service of their chosen ideals,'[52] and all of our visionaries indeed attempt to put their ideas to the service of their chosen ideals. Although the visionary continually falls short of his own ideals, he does succeed in justifying by his personal example the worth of those ideals. Ripp notes about Rudin that:

> Although by the end of the book Rudin stands condemned, his guilt is not absolute. He is no simple poseur; he has at least groped towards an ideal. Those who condemn him, on the other hand, only sit smugly by. [...] In a world of fools and idlers, the man who most energetically tried to integrate value and action is most harshly judged.[53]

and the same can be seen to apply also to Horace, Frédéric, and Lazare.

The visionary stands, as Seeley notes, at a 'parting of the ways'. On the one hand, he is superseded by the intellectual hero, who, inheriting his idealism and social conscience, is radical and progressive – and above all, capable of translating ideals into action: the visionary 'could not take that road, but he looked along it and urged others to follow it.'[54] On the other, however, he is succeeded by the final generation of nineteenth-century superfluous man – the 'dreamer' – who inherits not only his idealism, but his superfluity.

The Dreamer

The 'dreamer', best represented in Russian literature by Goncharov's Oblomov (*Oblomov*, 1859) and in French literature by Huysmans' des Esseintes (*A Rebours*, 1884), is the fourth 'generation' of nineteenth-century superfluous men. Unlike his predecessors, however, he does not exist in the relatively straight progression towards the formation of an intellectual elite, but rather in a sort of shadowy backwater after the fact. He can be considered, in fact, almost the opposite of our earlier superfluous men; Ellen B. Chances goes so far as to call Oblomov 'almost a parody' of his literary ancestors.[55] Despite this, however, the dreamer is indeed a true superfluous man. Like his superfluous predecessors, he is 'both a social and a metaphysical outcast'[56] and like them, he regards himself as different and superior on the basis of his intelligence and sensibility, rather than hereditary rank. Most importantly, he shares their ideological idealism and inability to come to terms with contemporary society – their 'civic sense' – and he consciously transgresses against social mores in a futile attempt at rebellion against society. He is unlike his predecessors in that his rebellion largely involves not overt struggle against society, but withdrawal from society. As George Ross Ridge notes, however, this in itself is a form of rebellion: '[Any] hero-type acts in response to his society. In this case it is an ugly, decadent society. He withdraws from it in disgust, but the very withdrawal, let it be stressed, is assuredly a form of response.'[57]

Although des Esseintes, especially, does transgress in the real world (several of des Esseintes' 'experiments' have socio-political overtones, and his attempt to 'create a murderer' out of the young Auguste Langlois, especially, is an overt attempt at subversion: 'La vérité c'est que je tâche simplement de préparer un assassin. [...] Alors, mon but sera atteint, j'aurai contribué, dans la mesure de mes ressources, à créer un gredin, un ennemi de plus pour cette hideuse société qui nous rançonne.'[58]), the primary form of rebellion of both Oblomov and des Esseintes remains their conscious refusal to engage with the society that disgusts them. Thus, both Oblomov and des Esseintes prefer to inhabit the realm of imagination: Oblomov creates an imaginary 'Oblomovka', loosely based on his real provincial estate, and barely notices his real surroundings; des Esseintes, of course, builds a fantasy world for himself at Fontenay. However, the dreamer's chosen form of transgression also condemns him to total superfluity; in using their considerable intelligence and abilities to escape the demands of the real world both Oblomov and des Esseintes find it difficult, if not impossible, to separate their private fantasies from the world around them – and thus lose any relevance to that world. Ridge notes that:

> The world is too heavy for the decadent. It does not meet his expectations, it disgusts him, it overwhelms him. Nature has a negative not positive value, and reality never meets his wish. Thus the decadent rejects actuality, he retreats into himself, and he creates a more satisfactory world of his own. Hence he becomes a cerebral hero, the ideal man of inaction. For what is the purpose of engaging in idealistic quests in a most imperfect world? To do so is not only useless but even naïve.[59]

and this judgment applies equally well to Oblomov. Fully aware that the world is passing him by, the dreamer is also aware that he is wholly incapable of adapting or of openly fighting – so he chooses to withdraw. In so doing, he is transgressing against the social mores of society no less than the dandy, rebel, and visionary.

The dreamer thus marks the end of the nineteenth-century superfluous man – with a whimper, rather than a bang. He is, more or less, an evolutionary dead end, the intellectual hero being firmly established in both French and Russian literature by the end of the century, although superfluous men did continue to appear. His rejection of contemporary society, however, is both as valid and as revealing, as Ridge notes:

> Perhaps decadence is even noble. [...] Perhaps the decadent, like a true hero, is even willing to die for the benefit of his race: he will commit suicide. [...] The decadent, in short, welcomes destruction at the hands of the barbarians. He knows, ironically, that he has no further purpose and that nature must replace him. He runs to accept nature's verdict. Is it masochism that impels him to seek death under the barbarian sword? Or is it rather nobility – the reasoned thinking that it is best for him to die?[60]

Both Oblomov and des Esseintes understand their superfluity; this is why they choose to dream, rather than to live. Both also understand that their fantasy life will destroy them – and it does. Oblomov perishes of and for his ideal of repose and plenty – he dies of a stroke brought on by overeating and inactivity – and Des Esseintes comes very close indeed to perishing of and for his – he nearly dies of a nervous condition brought on by solitude and experimentation. Oblomov lives and dies his dream; des Esseintes eventually chooses to commit hara-kiri on the 'barbarian sword'.

III.

This study, for reasons of both space and clarity, has examined only a limited number of literary heroes; there are, of course, many, many more who could be profitably included. Nevertheless, it is clear that not only do a significant number of representative French literary heroes share the fundamental characteristics of the Russian superfluous man, but also that a literary 'type' analogous to the Russian superfluous man exists in French nineteenth-century literature – and that this type arises from comparable historical pressures and follows a strikingly similar path of transition. It would seem, then, that the concept of the superfluous man is one which has a great deal of utility in formulating a coherent overview of the transitional period leading to the emergence of the intellectual in French literature and society.

The term 'intelligentsia' only came into common usage in Russia in the 1860's; the noun 'intellectuel' was not used in France until the very end of the nineteenth century.[61] However, as Brombert notes: 'The intellectual type could not possibly have penetrated so fast and so deeply into literature had he not first slowly emerged and become aware of himself as a social reality. The entire nineteenth century felt the need for the word.'[62] Similarly, the term 'superfluous man' only appeared in Russian literature in 1850, when it was invented by Turgenev for the title of his *Diary of a Superfluous Man*; the fact that it was immediately seized upon to describe not only other literary characters stretching back to the 1820's, but also contemporary people, testifies to its significance. The superfluous man – in his self-image based on intelligence and sensibility rather than on rank, in his impotent idealism, in his rampant individualism, and in his futile transgression of contemporary societal norms – personifies the struggle of a nascent intellectual elite to gain social and political significance in both Russia and France.

The theme of the alienated and frustrated outsider, oppressed by a society with which he shares little in terms of values or ethics, is, of course, a theme which neither originated nor ended with the nineteenth-century superfluous man. However, the superfluous man of the nineteenth century is a very specific incarnation which is inextricably linked with his social and political

milieu, and as such, he has a very specific role in the formation
and consolidation of the intellectual elite. From the unformed
idealism of the dandy, through the futile but splendid anarchy of
the rebel and the hopeless struggle of the visionary to combine
'pouvoir' with 'savoir', the rise of the intellectual elite is charted
– and in the inadequacy of the aristocratic dreamer, it is confirmed.
As the pace of social change accelerated, so did the various
'generations' of superfluous man, until the point where the
visionary, dreamer, and intellectual hero emerge more or less
simultaneously.[63] At this point, the 'intelligentsia' has arrived as
a true societal elite.

Brombert sums up the traits of the modern French
intellectual as follows:

> Sensibility modeled on thought; faith in the efficiency of
> ideas as an organizational force in the tangible world; the
> utilization of culture as an instrument for criticizing tradition;
> the unselfish, gratuitous pursuit of truth, but simultaneously
> the pursuit of a humanitarian ideal; the transmission or
> preaching of moral values; the sensation, now proud, now
> humiliating, of existing outside the social framework, and
> yet, on the whole, an obvious sympathy for the laboring
> groups of the country and a consequent attraction to Leftist
> political parties; a feeling of 'not belonging' and of impotence;
> jealously of the man of action; the cult of revolt, sometimes
> even of anarchy; the nearly obsessive fear of being caught on
> the side of injustice; nostalgia for the masses coupled with the
> complexes of a *fils de bourgeois* ashamed of belonging to the
> privileged classes.[64]

He concludes that: 'Our intellectuals and those of 1898 are of
one and the same family. Yet it is also evident that they existed
avant la lettre.'[65] Of course they did – and their origin is revealed
in the person of the superfluous man.[66]

University of Glasgow

1   William E. Harkins, *Dictionary of Russian Literature* (London: Allen & Unwin , 1957), p. 373.

2   F.D. Reeve, *The Russian Novel* (London: Frederick Muller, 1967), p. 55.

3   Richard Freeborn, *The Rise of the Russian Novel* (London: Cambridge University Press, 1973), p. 117.

4   George Ross Ridge, *The Hero in French Romantic Literature* (Athens: University of Georgia Press, 1959), p. 6.

5   Ridge, p. 128.

6   Glyn Holmes, *The 'Adolphe Type' in French Fiction in the First Half of the Nineteenth Century* (Quebec: Editions Naaman,1977).

7   Holmes, pp. 18-19.

8   Victor Brombert, *The Intellectual Hero: Studies in the French Novel 1880-1955* (London: Faber and Faber, 1961), p. 14.

9   A.N. Dobrolyubov, 'What is Oblomovshchina?' in *Selected Philosophical Essays* (Moscow: Foreign Languages Publishing House, 1959), pp. 174-217, (p. 175).

10   Marc Raeff, *Origins of the Russian intelligentsia: the eighteenth-century nobility* (New York: Harcourt, Brace, and World, 1966), p. 120.

11   Raeff, p. 41.

12   Raeff, p. 107.

13   For example, the abolition in 1730 of the law of entail (established by Peter the Great to safeguard the estates of the nobility) restored the tradition that all children of a nobleman shared in his estate and led to the fragmentation and sale of many properties, further reducing the connection of the nobility to the land. After Emancipation, too, this trend continued: for example, in 1863 restrictions on corporal punishment were introduced, followed in 1874 by universal liability to conscription.

14   There was, within the Russian gentry (as within most, if not all nobilities) a clear 'pecking order', with families who could claim descent from Rurik or ancient Lithuanian princely families at the top. Peter never intended to wipe the slate clean with the Table of Ranks: firstly, there was no existing change for existing noble families, who were never seriously threatened with disentitlement; secondly, those

who had reached the eighth rank (and who therefore obtained a
hereditary, rather than personal, title) could unconditionally transmit
that title to their offspring, who were not obliged to work their way
up through the ranks to obtain noble status.

15 Michael Confino, 'A propos de la notion de service dans la noblesse
russe aux XVIIIe et XIXe siècles', *Cahiers du Monde russe et soviétique*,
34.1-2 (1993), 47-58 (pp. 53-4).

16 G. Chaussinand-Nogaret, *La noblesse au XVIIIe siècle: De la féodalité aux
Lumières* (Paris: Hachette,1976), p. 73.

17 Although a shopkeeper and merchant class did exist in Russia, it had
nowhere near the influence (or size) of the French petite bourgeoisie.

18 Although this is not to say that he was equated with the 'grandes
familles' who proudly traced their noble origins back to Rurik.

19 Joe Andrew, *Russian Writers and Society in the Second Half of the
Nineteenth Century* (London: Macmillan Press,1982), p. x.

20 Theodore Zeldin, *France 1848-1945* (Oxford: Clarendon Press, 1973),
pp. 428-9.

21 Zeldin, p. 431.

22 Frank F. Seeley, *From the Heyday of the Superfluous Man to Chekhov. Essays
on 19th-century Russian Literature* (Nottingham: Astra Press, 1994), pp.
3-4.

23 The question of whether or not the French intellectual elite – or,
indeed, any non-Russian intellectual elite – can be considered an
'intelligentsia' is a thorny one, for no real consensus exists on a
definition. Although the term has gained common currency as simply
denoting a class of intellectuals regarded as possessing culture and
political initiative, Russian uses of the word often imply both political
radicalism and 'progressiveness' – which in the context of nineteenth-
century Russia connotes western European influence. It would seem,
therefore, that the French intellectual elite would not qualify for
consideration as an intelligentsia under this criterion. However, French
intellectuals did consistently assume both the role of enlightened
cosmopolitan and the burden of cultural ambassadorship for foreign –
particularly German and British – ideas, although they never
acknowledged the superiority of a foreign culture in its entirety as
happened in Russia. Although any resolution of whether or not the
French intellectual elite is a true 'intelligentsia' falls outside the scope
of this article, it is clear that sufficient parallels exist to make
comparison not only possible, but worthwhile.

24   Seeley, pp. 5-6.

25   Although some literary historians have extended the concept of the superfluous man to Chekhov and even to twentieth-century Soviet literature, we are concerned here with his nineteenth-century function as transitional figure and precursor of a new elite.

26   Seeley, p. 6.

27   *Obermann* (Paris: Charpentier, 1874), p. 402.

28   This raises the question of paternity, for these works are conventionally seen as having influenced subsequent Russian characters. As I have already mentioned, however,, I will not be considering questions of direct or indirect influence for I believe this issue to be of little importance to our focus here. I am not trying to establish influence or paternity. The very point is that Russia does not have a monopoly on the 'superfluous man', just as she does not on the conditions which created him.

29   It is important to note at this point that this first generation of superfluous man should not in any case be confused with the later 'dandyism' of Baudelaire and his contemporaries, nor am I concerned with their sartorial elegance (as the word 'dandy' has come to denote), but with their particular response to their inability to come to terms with their lack of a clear-cut role in a changing society. Thus, categorizing René and Obermann as 'dandies' is not the outright contradiction that it may appear.

30   And, of course, by the censor: *Woe from Wit* was not published in its entirety in Russia until the Academy edition of Griboyedev's complete works in 1911-17 (although it was widely circulated in manuscript form). Several commentators have suggested that he flees from Moscow, not because of his disillusionment with Sofia, but out of fear of arrest; Skalozub's threat to Repetilov (Act IV, p. 153) is very thinly veiled indeed.

31   See Vladimir Nabokov's commentary to *Eugene Onegin*, III, 256-7 and p. 315; and *Eugene Onegin*, Ch. 10, I and XII .

32   Colin Smethurst, *Chateaubriand: Atala and René* (London: Grant & Cutler Ltd., 1995), p. 63.

33   *Obermann*, pp. 160-1.

34   *Obermann*, pp. 166-7.

35   *Adolphe* (Paris: Poche Gallimard, 1958), p.25.

36   *Adolphe*, p. 26.

37   Seeley, p. 13.

38   Although his Octave (*La Confession d'un enfant du siècle*, 1836) and Stendhal's slightly earlier Octave de Malivert (*Armance*, 1827) also exhibit many primary characteristics of the type.

39   Janko Lavrin, *An Introduction to the Russian Novel* (London: Methuen & Co., 1945), p. 21.

40   Seeley, however, postulates that this trait 'may only have been camouflaged in the 1830's' and asserts that 'if he [Pechorin] shows even less political consciousness than Onegin, we can claim with even greater confidence that this was essentially out of consideration for the censorship, since Pechorin was a far more unambiguous self-portrait than Onegin, and we know from Lermontov's poetry that his civic sense was at least as lively as Pushkin's in the 1820's' (p. 16).

41   C. J. G. Turner, *Pechorin: An Essay on Lermontov's A Hero of Our Time* (Birmingham: Dept. of Russian Language and Literature, University of Birmingham, 1988), p. 31.

42   *Lorenzaccio* (Paris: Larousse, 1971), III, 3, pp. 88-89.

43   *A Hero of Our Time*, Trans. by Paul Foote (London: Penguin, 1966), p. 130.

44   *Lorenzaccio*, III, III (p. 93).

45   Ronald Grimsley, 'The Character of Lorenzaccio', *French Studies*, 11 (1957), 16-27 (pp. 17-18 and pp.24-25).

46   Nicholas, in the '30's, limited landlord's powers over their serfs, and built the first Russian railway; Alexander embarked on a program of modernization and reform after the Crimean War (1853-6).

47   Although Herzen's Beltov (*Who is to Blame?*, 1859) is also a good example.

48   At this point in French literature the Russian 'model' would seem to fit less well than in our other three 'generations', due to the overwhelming dominance of the slightly divergent 'bourgeois' hero – a figure which simply did not appear on the Russian literary scene to anything like the same degree due to the lack of a real bourgeoisie in Russia. This does indeed present an obstacle, for the tradition of the Russian

superfluous man is conventionally considered as paralleling the declining fortunes of the nobility – and thus far, the French heroes which we have studied have been compatible with this tradition. The introduction of the bourgeois hero – who, of course, is traditionally seen in the ascending, rather than the declining line – would seem to signal a definitive break between the line of Russian superfluous men and the French. However, in reality, this marks only a divergence between the two lines (which, indeed, come back together for the final generation of superfluous man). Despite some significant differences, there is a subset of the bourgeois hero – similar to what Raymond Giraud calls the 'unheroic hero' – which shares both the primary characteristics of the visionary type, and fulfills the same functions – as both the immediate predecessor of the intellectual hero in French literature, and a clear signal that the dominance of the nobility as societal elite is giving way to a non-class-based intellectual elite.

49   Victor Ripp, *Turgenev's Russia: From* Notes of a Hunter *to* Fathers and Sons (London: Cornell University Press, 1980), p. 128.

50   *Horace* (Paris: Michel Lé vy, 1875), p. 233.

51   Raymond Giraud, *The Unheroic Hero in the Novels of Stendhal, Balzac, and Flaubert* (New Brunswick, NJ: Rutgers University Press, 1957), p. 12.

52   Richard Freeborn, *Turgenev: The Novelist's Novelist* (London: Oxford University Press, 1960), p. 75.

53   Ripp, p. 128.

54   Seeley, p. 19.

55   Ellen B. Chances, *Conformity's Children: An Approach to the Superfluous Man in Russian Literature* (Columbus, Ohio: Slavica, 1978).

56   Ibid.

57   George Ross Ridge, *The Hero in French Decadent Literature* (Athens: University of Georgia Press, 1961), p.105.

58   *A rebours*, pp. 165-6. Richard Shryock interprets *A rebours* as an anarchist novel, with this episode 'the most striking example'. See 'Ce cri rompit le cauchemar qui l'opprimait: Huysmans and the Politics of *A rebours*', *French Review,* Vol. 66, No. 2, December 1992, pp. 243-54.

59   Ridge, *The Hero in French Decadent Literature*, p. 83.

60   Ridge, *The Hero in French Decadent Literature*, p. 23.

61   Louis Bodin, in his *Les intellectuels* (Paris: Presses Universitaires de France, 1962) notes that 'intellectuel' is not found in the *Littré* of 1876, the *Grand Dictionnaire universel de Pierre Larousse* of 1866-78, or in the *Grande Encyclopédie* of 1885-1902.

62   Brombert, p. 35.

63   *Rudin* appeared in 1857, *Oblomov* in 1859, while *La Joie de vivre* was published in the very same year (1884) as *A rebours*.

64   Brombert, p. 34.

65   Brombert, p. 35.

66   A greatly expanded treatment of this argument is to be found in an M.Litt. thesis by the same author, submitted to the University of Glasgow under the same title in June 1997.

Du Dandysme et de la transgression: la règle et la différence

Anne Frémiot

> Le dandysme se joue de la règle et pourtant la respecte
> encore. Il en souffre et s'en venge tout en la subissant; il s'en
> réclame quand il y échappe; il la domine et en est dominé
> tour à tour: double et muable caractère!
> Barbey d'Aurevilly.[1]

> On peut mépriser insolemment la société, la bafouer par le
> dédain et la provocation, la contester par un mode de vie: on
> ne l'étrangle pas avec un noeud de cravate, si artistique soit-il.
> Emilien Carassus.[2]

Au-delà de l'image d'Epinal qui nous reste du dandy, et qui nous
renvoie à la dimension d'une simple élégance vestimentaire, le
dandy a essayé d'élaborer un discours critique dont la mise en
habit n'est que la technique et non le principe. Le dandy pose un
point d'interrogation sur les critères identificateurs du dix-
neuvième siècle et, donc sur la légitimité de ces critères qu'il
tente de transgresser afin de se créer autre. Cependant, la transgression du dandy, son devoir de désobéissance, est paradoxale.
Ce n'est pas une indépendance aveugle et à tout prix, mais
plutôt la traduction d'un désir d'unicité qui ne peut en fait se
définir que grâce et par rapport aux autres. Dans cette étude,
j'analyse comment le dandy 'se joue de la règle' sociale tout en
restant dans les limites de cette règle; comment en fait, il est un
marginal intégré qui, voulant protester contre les normes sociales
sans les renverser, joue en fait leur jeu et contribue à reproduire
le système même qu'il critique.

Un dandy ne peut accepter qu'il n'y ait qu'une règle,
des conventions qui s'adressent à tous dans la nouvelle loi
démocratisante et nivelante de l'après 1789. Au début du
XIXème, la noblesse revient peu à peu de son exil, financièrement

diminuée, et son rôle social a quasiment disparu. Toutefois, comme le note Roland Barthes, 'même vaincu politiquement, le noble détenait encore un prestige puissant, quoique limité à l'art de vivre'.[3] L'époque est désormais à la libre entreprise, à la spéculation; le travail est une valeur en hausse, il n'est plus dégradant, au contraire, il devient synonyme de respectabilité. L'argent et non plus uniquement les lettres de noblesse devient le critère d'élection hiérarchique de cette nouvelle société. La haute bourgeoisie argentée tente de s'associer à l'élite de prestige, l'aristocratie, par le mariage et l'achat de titres.[4] Cet argent permet l'accès à la haute société, aux cercles les plus fermés. Le peuple entier tente, lui aussi, de se reconnaître dans le slogan matérialiste lancé par Guizot, 'enrichissez-vous'. Le dandy, dans son souci d'indépendance refuse de suivre la tendance générale et se manifeste par son anti-utilitarisme, cependant cela ne veut en aucun cas dire qu'il renonce à toute ambition sociale. Simplement, son ascension sociale s'effectuera selon d'autres critères que ceux proposés.

Le dandy reprendra à son compte l'héritage romantique d'individualisme qui s'oppose au conformisme bourgeois et essayera de dresser contre un devenir général de la société un mode de vie dandy. Plutôt que de se lancer à corps perdu dans la poursuite du progrès, il va ériger l'utopie d'une élite alternative basée sur un art de soi. Pour signifier son refus du présent, il cherche à vivre en suspension de l'histoire, dans une évolution qui n'offre pas de changement.

Ce que le dandy en fait nous propose, c'est l'élaboration d'une élite de l'artifice, une accession à un pouvoir absolu et sans partage basé sur cet artifice comme code. Plutôt que de s'élever contre les structures en place, ce qui entraînerait son exclusion de la société au lieu de lui permettre d'en atteindre les plus hautes marches, il préférera utiliser les failles de cette société, exploiter l'espace de possibilités entrouvert par une déchéance de l'aristo-cratie, une ascension de la bourgeoisie et une permanence d'une certaine hiérarchie conjuguées, comme l'annonce Baudelaire:

> Le dandysme apparaît surtout aux époques transitoires où la démocratie n'est pas encore toute puissante, où l'aristocratie n'est que partiellement chancelante et avilie. Dans le trouble de ces époques, quelques hommes déclassés, dégoûtés, désoeuvrés, mais tous riches de force native, peuvent concevoir le projet de fonder une espèce nouvelle d'aristocratie, d'autant plus difficile à rompre qu'elle sera basée sur les facultés les plus précieuses, les plus indestructibles, et sur les dons célestes que le travail et l'argent ne peuvent conférer.[5]

Ces mots de Baudelaire ont l'avantage de situer et de contextualiser le dandysme dans son dix-neuvième siècle, en résumant rapidement le cadre socio-historique de l'époque. Toutefois, Baudelaire reste plus que vague quant aux hommes qui vont composer ou, qui composent déjà le dandysme. Leur nombre? Ils sont 'quelques'. Leurs caractéristiques? L'ennui, l'écoeurement, mais qu'entend Baudelaire par 'déclassés'? Leur but? S'ériger en une élite au-dessus de l'aristocratie mais qui aurait la forme d'une aristocratie. Leur légitimité? Des 'dons célestes', des 'facultés précieuses'; tout cela semble bien mystérieux voire même mystique. La seule chose qui semble sûre et qui s'annonce par une négation par rapport à un système est le refus de la loi du 'travail' et de 'l'argent'. Tout le problème de tenter de définir ce qui fait le dandy, ce qui légitime à ses yeux sa volonté de pouvoir, demeure à peu près entier. Barbey d'Aurevilly est aussi flou que Baudelaire sur ce point quand il note: 'ce qui fait le dandy, c'est l'indépendance. Autrement il y aurait une législation du Dandysme et il n'y en a pas'.[6] Le dandy semble se refuser à toute tentative de définition. Dès lors, son indépendance comment va-t-elle se manifester dans cette société uniforme?

> En France, l'originalité n'a point de patrie: on lui interdit le feu et l'eau; on la hait comme une distinction nobiliaire. Elle soulève les gens médiocres, toujours prêts, contre ceux qui sont *autrement qu'eux*, à une de ces morsures qui ne déchirent pas, mais qui salissent. *Etre comme tout le monde*, est le principe équivalant pour les hommes, au principe dont on bourre la

tête des jeunes filles: 'Sois considérée, il le faut', du *Mariage de Figaro*.[7]

D'Aurevilly réaffirme le besoin de se démarquer de l'opinion publique, de cette nouvelle société qui accumule les interdits contre tout ce qui risque d'échapper à son emprise. Il s'élève contre le règne de l'identique prôné par un pouvoir paranoïaque inquiété par toutes les possibilités d'un contournement ou d'une transgression de l'ordre établi. Il est important de noter que, comme Baudelaire, d'Aurevilly semble associer une idée de la noblesse et du dandysme car, comme une 'distinction nobiliaire', l'originalité qui caractérise le dandy est haïe. Le dandysme s'élèvera contre le 'vulgaire' de la pensée collective, contre 'les gens médiocres'. Le dandysme va donc se manifester à travers l'élaboration d'un discours de la différence dans le siècle de l'uniforme. Cette recherche d'une différence s'axera tout d'abord autour de la 'haine du bourgeois'.

Le dandy cherche à supplanter l'aristocrate dans son mode de vie, la seule sphère sur laquelle il règne encore, et à transgresser les idéaux bourgeois. Le dandy se fabrique de lui-même et pour lui-même par réaction à des situations données. Il fait table rase sur son passé pour deux raisons: la première est qu'il n'existe que pour l'instant présent, la seconde est encore son désir d'altérité. C'est pourquoi il ne veut être strictement enchaîné à aucun groupe, à aucun mouvement collectif qui menaceraient la singularité de son identité (ce qui se passe dans la réalité est un autre problème). Il a besoin de se donner une quasi-totale liberté d'action que l'appartenance à une famille biologique limiterait, d'autant plus que la famille au XIXème devient le terrain d'exercice du pouvoir, incarnant l'utilitarisme et la productivité bourgeois. Le pouvoir ne se limite plus à un pouvoir de mort exercé par les autorités en place sur les individus, quel que soit l'idéal politique auquel obéit ce gouvernement (l'Ancien Régime, la Terreur, les débuts de la République), il se mute et se transforme en un pouvoir sur la vie du peuple tout entier. Foucault dans *La Volonté de Savoir*, le premier volume de son

Histoire de la Sexualité, montre ce changement de tendance et cette mise en place de ce que l'on pourrait appeler une 'bio-politique':

> Ensuite lorsque l'organisation de la famille 'canonique' a paru, autour des années 1830, un instrument de contrôle politique et de régulation économique indispensable à l'assujettissement du prolétariat urbain: une grande campagne pour la 'moralisation des classes pauvres'.[8]

La famille devient un lieu protégé et surveillé, le mariage productif, une utilité nécessaire à l'élargissement de la population et de la force productive de la richesse nationale. Par là, elle devient le terrain privilégié de l'exercice politique. La famille est une unité sociale qui représente une cellule close dans laquelle s'exercent les forces et les pouvoirs à l'intérieur de la société du XIXème: elle est au coeur d'une bio-politique. On peut citer en exemple la création sous Napoléon de la Police des Moeurs, responsable d'un système de régularisation des pratiques sexuelles qui va de l'espionnage au fichage des homosexuels et des prostituées. Notons que cette Police des Moeurs était sous l'égide de la Préfecture de Police dont le nom se changera en 1817 en Sûreté. De Police, du grec **polis**, la ville, l'organisation de la Cité, l'appellation de la Force publique se mue en Sûreté, du latin **securitas** qui signifie promesse, assurance: le contrôle de l'État change de dimension; il n'est plus simple organisation et protection, il s'enrichit d'une promesse de futur et d'avenir. Je pense fortement que ce changement de nom est significatif du dessein bio-politique du pouvoir de cette époque: la sexualité de son peuple devient une affaire de sûreté nationale et doit dès lors être réglementée et contrôlée étroitement.[9] Cette idée de famille en tant que véhicule des valeurs sociales s'énonce de manière similaire en Angleterre avec Lord Shaftesbury:

> There can be no security to society, no honour, no prosperity, no dignity at home, no nobleness of attitude towards foreign nations, unless the strength of the people rests upon the purity and firmness of the domestic system.

> Schools are but auxiliaries. At home the principles of sub-
> ordination are first implanted and the man is trained to be a
> good citizen.[10]

De plus, la famille est le véhicule de codes identitaires, qu'ils
soient biologiques, culturels ou sociaux. Au niveau biologique,
elle rappelle au dandy qu'il n'est que le produit de circonstances
naturelles liées à la reproduction, à la perpétuation d'une espèce
animale, en même temps qu'elle transmet une parenté, des
ressemblances physiques qui l'identifient comme partie d'un
tout, appartenant à autre chose qu'à lui-même. La famille assure
aussi la transmission du nom, des biens, d'un capital social. Elle
est encore la loi dans un microcosme, l'autorité et le pouvoir sur
l'individu. Le dandy pour atteindre une certaine indépendance
doit s'en éloigner, car cette famille met en péril sa liberté d'action
et l'identité qu'il tente de se confectionner. Dès lors, il remet en
cause l'autorité paternelle, et même le concept entier de famille.
La transgression du dandy va s'attaquer au fondement même de
la nouvelle société bourgeoise, la sainte famille. Les personnages
des romans de Barbey d'Aurevilly ont un passé flou et énigmatique,
des foyers brisés au sein desquels le père ou la mère sont absents,
incompétents, obsessionnels (folie de vengeance), où les relations
familiales sont perverties par l'inceste (*Ce qui ne meurt*), minées
par le mensonge et le secret ('Le Dessous de Cartes'), la transgression sexuelle('Le Rideau cramoisi'), la violence et l'adultère
('A un Dîner d'Athées'). Plutôt que d'y voir une transposition
biographique[11] des fantômes de l'auteur, de sa vie, de son
enfance, je préférerai considérer ces problèmes familiaux comme
une manifestation iconoclaste du dandysme, de la haine de la
famille canonique bourgeoise qui interdit mais qui, en générant
l'interdit-même crée toute une gamme de perversions (entre
autre parce qu'elle les nomme). Ainsi la production littéraire de
Barbey d'Aurevilly est-elle paradoxale puisqu'elle reproduit ce
même processus bourgeois qu'elle dénonce.

S'il rejette et foule au pied une famille selon le modèle
bourgeois, le dandy est encore plus enclin à en dénigrer son

institutionnalisation, le sacro-saint mariage. Il refuse de s'identifier à la pratique sociale, légale et religieuse du mariage, à cette institutionnalisation de la sexualité dans des cadres donnés. Michel Foucault écrit à propos de la société bourgeoise du XIXème:

> La sexualité est alors soigneusement renfermée. Elle emménage. La famille conjugale la confisque. Et l'absorbe toute entière dans le sérieux de la fonction de reproduire. Autour du sexe, on se tait. Le couple, légitime et procréateur fait la loi.[12]

Le couple 'procréateur' symbolise les valeurs de la bourgeoisie et son souci économique: le mariage est rentabilité et productivité. Il sert à perpétuer la génération, à transmettre le capital, à s'assurer une forme de postérité, de même qu'il constitue une force de travail, une économie. Le mariage dans cette optique implique une utilité de l'acte amoureux, au détriment de la passion, telle que la refuse le couple du 'Bonheur dans le Crime':[13]

> - Et ils n'ont jamais eu d'enfants, docteur? - lui dis-je.
> - Ah! - fit le docteur Torty, - vous croyez que c'est là la fêlure, la revanche du Sort, et ce que vous appelez la vengeance ou la justice de Dieu? Non, ils n'ont jamais eu d'enfants. Souvenez-vous! Une fois, j'avais eu l'idée qu'ils n'en auraient pas. Ils s'aiment trop... Le feu, - qui dévore, - consume et ne produit pas. (BDC[14], p. 127)

Loin d'être un manque, l'absence de l'enfant confère au couple son autosuffisance et son unité. Hauteclaire rejette la maternité et se consacre à être l'amante.[15] Le couple n'aura pas de descendants, leur éternité est figée dans le moment de leur apparition et dans le 'feu' qui les lie.

On peut aisément constater comment l'amour 'qui dévore, - consume et ne produit pas' s'oppose à la représentation du mariage bourgeois à travers une autre nouvelle de Barbey d'Aurevilly, 'Le Rideau Cramoisi'.[16] Le vicomte Brassard, locataire chez une famille de bourgeois, est rejoint 'régulièrement toutes les deux nuits' (RC[17], p. 46) par Alberte, la fille unique de ses hôtes. Cette relation amoureuse apparaît immédiatement comme la manifestation d'un accomplissement des désirs contre la mutilation de l'être sentimental et sexuel imposée par la société. Il y a, dans ce texte du 'Rideau Cramoisi', une opposition frappante entre l'amour/l'érotisme, lié à une certaine conception d'une élite, et le mariage bourgeois, respectable, raisonnable mais sans passion. Cette passion produit l'image d'un couple qui s'oppose au reste du monde, qui se constitue comme un espace symbolique extérieur au monde réel, idées chères aux Romantiques. La conception de la sexualité, mise en place par un pouvoir bourgeois, dont Michel Foucault nous retrace l'histoire, est sans cesse défiée et transgressée dans ce texte, et cela à différents niveaux. L'érotisme incarne la transgression d'un triple interdit social, moral et religieux. Foucault nous dit que 'la famille conjugale confisque la sexualité': Alberte dans 'Le Rideau Cramoisi' s'approprie cette sexualité réservée au couple légitime pour la partager, hors de tout dessein matrimonial, hors du cadre institutionnel et légitime du mariage, avec le jeune pensionnaire de ses parents. Certes, la notion d'autorité parentale est bafouée, mais surtout, le couple légitime est dépouillé de son privilège d'accomplir seul l'acte sexuel. Cette transgression du domaine parental est encore illustrée et amplifiée par une violation de l'espace géographique du couple conjugal. Alberte, pour rejoindre Brassard, doit forcément passer par la chambre de ses parents: 'elle sortait de son lit, et, pour venir, elle avait... le croirez-vous? été obligée de traverser la chambre où son père et sa mère dormaient! (RC, p. 45), raconte Brassard. Notons que dans le texte, le couple n'est pas regroupé sous le terme générique de 'parents', mais sous les dénominations de 'père' et 'mère', ce qui les sexualise dans une perspective homme/femme tout en les identifiant à un rôle procréateur. La jeune fille traverse le lieu officiel de la sexualité, de son exercice et de sa productivité, ce sanctuaire impressionnant de la sexualité telle qu'elle est conçut au XIXème, dans un esprit puritain collectif. Le couple bourgeois voit non seulement son autorité transgressée, il est aussi fortement dépouillé de toute activité sexuelle par le narrateur. Ils sont, 'le mari et la femme, tous deux âgés' (RC, p. 29), ce sont encore 'de très braves gens, aux moeurs très douces, et de très calmes destinées' et 'la femme passait sa vie à tricoter des bas à côtes pour son mari, et le mari, timbré de musique, à racler sur son violon'. Les décrivant ainsi, le narrateur leur ôte toute passion bouillonnante, toute pulsion et les fossilise. Il en fait des êtres paisibles auxquels le lecteur ne peut prêter aucune activité érotique, autre que celle qui, dans un passé lointain, a mené à la naissance de leur fille. Et encore, peut-on parler d'érotisme? Ceci est souligné par la passivité de leurs corps qui dorment quand Alberte traverse leur chambre. Est-ce donc que les couples mariés et bourgeois conventionnels, 'c'était bien ce que vous pouvez imaginer de plus bourgeois' (RC, p. 29), sont représentés comme âgés, ternes, sans passion, sans sexualité autre que celle qui produit ou a produit? Barbey d'Aurevilly, dans sa description du couple, reproduit exactement l'image conjugale que la loi désire: un encadrement de la sexualité par le mariage, voire même une suppression de la sexualité dans le mariage. De cette manière, il recrée la représentation de ce qu'il combat; la vision bourgeoise du mariage. Toutefois, il semble qu'au-delà de la simple transgression sexuelle d'Alberte s'esquisse une réflexion sur l'amour et la sexualité qui l'accompagne, comme phénomène sinon anti-bourgeois, du moins hors des normes et moeurs bourgeoises. Alberte est sans cesse mise en évidence et différenciée de ses parents en termes de classe sociale.

> Leur fille! Il était impossible d'être moins la fille de gens comme eux que cette fille-là! Non pas que les plus belles filles du monde ne puissent naître de toute espèce de gens. J'en ai connu... et vous aussi n'est-ce pas? Physiologiquement, l'être le plus laid peut produire l'être le plus beau. Mais elle! Entre elle et eux, il y avait l'abîme d'une race... (RC, p. 31)

Alberte est certes belle, mais ce n'est pas ce critère de beauté sur lequel se base le narrateur pour créer le contraste, contraste exagéré au niveau du récit par le nom 'fille', qui porte en lui l'idée de lien familial et d'hérédité. 'Elle et eux', singulier et multitude, sont séparés 'par l'abîme d'une race'. Cet 'abîme' signale le gouffre que le narrateur établit entre les classes sociales. Cependant, Alberte, fille de bourgeois, devrait logiquement appartenir à la même classe que ses parents. La différence de classe aurevillienne n'opère pas sur le plan social mais sur des attitudes, sur une conception subjective et sentimentale de ce qu'est l'être noble et l'être bourgeois. C'est une différence de classe qui se fonde, non pas sur les critères politico-économiques auxquels nous sommes habitués, mais sur une hiérarchie intellectuelle, sentimentale, des codes de conduite, qui sont pour Barbey d'Aurevilly, après tout, aussi légitimes que les autres, sinon plus. Françoise Mugnier note que 'les personnages aurevilliens ne sont pas réductibles à leur statut économique ou social'[18] mais surtout que 'la perturbation des distinctions socio-économiques assure, en partie, la fascination de ces personnages qui ne correspondent à aucune définition sociale univoque'.[19]

> Mlle Albertine (c'était le nom de cette archiduchesse d'altitude, tombée du ciel chez des bourgeois comme si le ciel avait voulu se moquer d'eux), Mlle Albertine [...] ne semblait pas plus la fille de l'un que de l'autre. (RC, p. 32)

Alberte apparaît comme une infiltration de la noblesse dans la bourgeoisie. Les lois de cette dernière, elle refuse de s'y conformer. Notons cependant que cette transgression est interne et non pas une confrontation. Les valeurs de la bourgeoisie sont minées dans le secret de la nuit, pendant le sommeil des gardiens de la règle, et non pas ouvertement au grand jour. La passion, on pourrait aussi dire l'érotisme, qui prend des risques et s'alimente de danger, est opposée à la relation codifiée entre les sexes. L'intrigue a besoin de braver des interdits pour faire palpiter les coeurs, la raison est éliminée:

> Et jusque par-dessus son épaule, je regardais derrière elle si cette porte, dont elle n'avait pas ôté la clef, par peur du bruit qu'elle pouvait faire, n'allait pas s'ouvrir de nouveau et me montrer, pâles et indignés, ces deux têtes de Méduse, ces deux vieillards que nous trompions avec une lâcheté si hardie, surgir tout à coup dans la nuit, images de l'hospitalité violée et de la Justice! (RC, p. 46)

On peut bien sûr aussi penser au couple du 'Bonheur dans le Crime', à cette relation adultère, vivant dans l'incertitude du lendemain. Le narrateur du 'Rideau Cramoisi' parle de 'stupeur de la première fois'. Cette intrigue ne se transforme jamais en routine, elle ne vit que dans l'instant; contrairement à une conception traditionnelle du mariage, cette relation n'a d'autre but qu'elle-même, pas de dessein, pas de calcul hors du moment. Il n'est jamais question de mariage, d'enfants, de dot, ou de position sociale. C'est encore la beauté dandy de la gratuité, la recherche du plaisir pur. On pourrait même aller jusqu'à établir une opposition entre érotisme et activité sexuelle dans le cadre de la loi, en utilisant la définition de l'érotisme que donne Georges Bataille: 'ce qui différencie l'érotisme et l'activité sexuelle simple étant une recherche psychologique indépendante de la fin naturelle dans la reproduction et dans le souci des enfants'.[20] On est ici en plein coeur de la distinction, dans le domaine amoureux, que nous offre Barbey d'Aurevilly. Il semble que les moeurs codifiées du XIXème, le Code Civil, l'hypocrisie du puritanisme ambiant, transforment la relation sexuelle en acte utile dés-érotisé, de même que ces codes créent leur propres violations et transgressions en générant l'interdit au niveau érotique. L'excitation est toute entière contenue dans le danger de la transgression de l'interdit comme le souligne le Docteur Torty dans 'Le Bonheur dans le Crime' (p. 104), qu'il est des passions que l'imprudence allume, et qui, sans le danger qu'elles provoquent, n'existeraient pas'. Ceci produit un clivage entre la sexualité légale et légitime d'un côté, et l'érotisme qui est 'essentiellement [...] le domaine de la violence, le domaine de la violation'.[21] L'amour dandy s'identifie à l'érotisme, indissociable d'une idée de transgression. Or, pour qu'une transgression soit rendue possible, il faut qu'il y ait des codes, des structures d'interdits en place, à bouleverser et à violer. Le dandy ne cherchera donc pas à changer les codes en matière sexuelle. Il a besoin d'institutions à transgresser pour être (notamment dans sa conception de l'amour, de l'érotisme) et, ce XIXème siècle d'interdits lui offre un terrain d'exercice plus que favorable.

Ainsi donc le dandy s'attaque-t-il aux fondements de la bourgeoisie à travers son défi à l'utilitarisme et à la famille canonique. Il affiche son mépris contre ce système de valeurs mais, mépriser et haïr, c'est encore faire exister: le dandy a besoin de l'existence et du pouvoir de la bourgeoisie pour s'y opposer et donc pour exister lui-même en tant que différence. Plutôt que de créer un univers autre, il s'efforcera reconstruire un monde bourgeois type pour se permettre de l'affronter. De plus, le dandy s'appuie sur son mérite à être lui dans sa perfection et, par ce trait, il imite sans le vouloir cette classe bourgeoise qu'il rejette et qui est, tout comme lui, largement fondée sur une méritocratie: ce concept que l'on peut 'se faire', à partir de peu ou de rien, et réussir. Mais tenter de dominer la bourgeoisie et de lui échapper, ne suffit pas au dandy qui va créer une idée d'*aristocratie de l'esprit* comme philosophie de différenciation et de domination de l'aristocratie.

Dandysme et aristocratie semblent intimement liés par un sentiment anti-bourgeois apparent, même si le dandy n'est pas toujours noble et même si l'aristocratie ne profite pas de cette bourgeoisie. La connexion provient bien sûr du fait que le dandy, par son refus de l'utilitarisme, sa vie consacrée au culte du faste et de l'art de vivre, embrasse des valeurs traditionnellement attachées à l'aristocratie et, qui désormais constituent son seul prestige. Ceci est surtout remarquable chez Barbey d'Aurevilly, pour qui en fait le dandysme n'est qu'une déviance d'un idéal aristocratique dans lequel il a été bercé. Toutefois, pour lui, la chute de l'aristocratie lors de la Révolution, n'est que la punition divine et donc juste de cette classe qui s'est corrompue par le libertinage au XVIIIème siècle, les mésalliances, les mariages consanguins. Il retrace dans *L'Ensorcelée* (1854),[22] à travers son personnage de Jeanne Le Hardouey, née Feuardent, non seulement le récit de l'histoire de sa famille et sa lutte chouanne mais aussi la descente aux enfers d'une classe sociale qui a transgressé les barrières du sang et de la lignée:

> On savait la distinguer de son mari quand on en parlait. A elle, on ne lui reprochait rien, si ce n'est un peu de hauteur quand on pensait à son mariage, mais qu'on lui pardonnait quand on pensait à sa naissance. Les Feuardent avaient été une famille puissante.
>
> Des fautes, des malheurs, des passions, cette triple cause de tous les renversements de ce monde, avaient, depuis plusieurs siècles, poussé, de générations en générations, les Feuardent à une ruine complète. Avant que 1789 éclatât, cette ruine était consommée. (*L'Ensorcelée*, p. 708)

Vaincu politiquement, le noble s'accroche désespérément aux vestiges de son prestige pour tenter de légitimer sa position et sa raison d'être dans la nouvelle société. L'espoir d'un retour au pouvoir ne sera jamais vraiment concrétisé. La vieille aristocratie de souche se voit remplacée par la noblesse d'Empire sous Napoléon et Louis-Philippe, phénomène qui en fait imite, mais contourne, l'ancienne manière d'accéder à ce rang. La noblesse ruinée s'allie bon gré, mal gré, avec les finances de la bourgeoisie pour subsister dans son monde illusoire, son royaume des apparences comme le remarque cyniquement Lord Bulwer Lytton.

> La richesse servant à procurer l'alliance et le respect du noble, on affecte la richesse quand on ne la possède point; et la mode, qui est la créature de l'aristocratie, ne pouvant être atteinte que par la ressemblance avec les gens à la mode (fashionable), il s'ensuit que chaque individu imite son voisin, et se flatte d'acheter le respect dans l'opinion des autres, en renonçant à l'indépendance de sa propre opinion.[23]

Paraître noble devient donc possible à travers la mode et l'argent. Qui donc peut paraître plus noble que le noble si ce n'est le dandy qui lance la mode, qui dilapide l'argent dans cette *foire aux vanités*. De plus, l'aristocratie survivante offre au dandy un théâtre privilégié où il peut briller, rivaliser en magnificence et en mots d'esprit. Etre reçu dans les salons n'est-ce pas pour lui la concrétisation de la noblesse recréée de son personnage, de la hauteur de son esprit, dans ce milieu où l'on cultive encore l'art 'inutile' de la conversation, activité chère entre toutes à Barbey d'Aurevilly?

> Avec l'esprit et les manières de son nom, la baronne de Mascranny a fait de son salon une espèce de Coblentz délicieux où s'est réfugiée la conversation d'autrefois, la dernière gloire de l'esprit français, forcé d'émigrer devant les moeurs utilitaires et occupées de notre temps. [...] Rien n'y rappelle l'article du journal et le discours politique, ces deux moules si vulgaires de la pensée, au dix-neuvième siècle.[24]

L'attitude du dandy envers l'aristocratie va cependant et encore s'ériger comme un paradoxe de plus, car s'il s'y associe idéologiquement, par des valeurs partagées, il se dissocie de son héritage, de ses critères de légitimité liés au nom, au sang et à la gloire des ancêtres, signes, qui même s'ils sont devenus bien hypocrites et désuets, il ne possède pas nécessairement. Comment mieux se dissocier de l'aristocratie qu'en la dominant, sans posséder aucunement la légitimité d'un titre? Comment mieux le faire en s'arrogeant et en raffinant jusqu'à l'art absolu les qualités qu'elle prétend siennes? Là encore, plutôt que de défier de front les valeurs survivantes de la noblesse, le dandy va fonctionner par transgression interne, passer par-dessus ces lois implicites.

L'élégance du dandy va réussir dans cette société mobile à compenser l'absence d'un glorieux héritage par sa qualité même, à corriger les critères d'élection habituels et à les éclipser par les siens. L'élégance qui proclame la souveraineté du futile et de l'individualité créatrice, alliée à la vanité dandy, cette conscience en exercice de sa différence et de sa supériorité, s'érige au rang d'héroïsme: un héroïsme du *rien,* puisqu'il ne repose sur rien de solide, mais qui différencie et élève. Cette noblesse de l'esprit, impalpable et immatérielle, que le dandy crée pour remplacer la noblesse de titre, n'est-elle pas toute aussi légitime que la noblesse de tradition ancrée dans l'imaginaire social? En fait, elle lui est même supérieure car plus profonde selon Barbey d'Aurevilly, si l'on en juge par sa description de Mesnilgrand dans 'A un Dîner d'Athées':[25]

> Il était profondément aristocrate. Il ne l'était pas seulement de naissance, de caste, de rang social; il l'était *de nature,* comme il était *lui,* et pas un autre, et comme il l'eût été encore, aurait-il été le dernier cordonnier de sa ville. Il l'était enfin, comme dit Henri Heine, 'par sa grande manière de sentir', et non point bourgeoisement, à la façon des parvenus qui aiment les distinctions extérieures. (ADA, p. 182)

La 'vraie' noblesse serait celle du coeur et de l'esprit, ainsi doit-on lire les mots 'de nature'. Elle est inséparable d'une conscience aiguë d'être soi et 'pas un autre', donc d'une conscience d'être différent. C'est certainement à cette même conception de l'aristocratie que Baudelaire pense quand il parle d'aristocratie de l'esprit' dans *Le Peintre de la Vie moderne,* cette aristocratie qui ne s'appuie pas sur des signes extérieurs. Le terme 'de nature' est encore problématique à plus d'un titre. Cette aristocratie de 'nature' est une construction artificielle qui tente d'éclipser les critères usuels de l'aristocratie de souche. Or, tout le problème réside dans le fait que de tout temps l'aristocratie du monde occidental s'est toujours comme présentée comme 'naturelle' car de droit divin, élue de Dieu. Barbey renforce cette notion en voulant la supprimer. De plus, 'de nature' implique une prédestination, une vision essentialiste qui s'inscrit dans une fixité d'un état de choses: il n'y a donc plus de mobilité, mais surtout l'alternative du choix disparaît. Comment donc le dandy peut-il prétendre à une libération? Notons que Mesnilgrand est noble de naissance mais qu'il apparaît toutefois comme un îlot de supra-noblesse dans la noblesse, au-delà de son 'rang social'. Par cela, il illustre parfaitement le phénomène dandy qui selon Emilien Carassus 'procède à une démarche de ségrégation', qui 'veut être séparé mais être séparé à l'intérieur du groupe qu'il domine'.[26] Cette noblesse de la personne apparaît surtout chez Barbey d'Aurevilly dans ses héroïnes, qui représentent plus une caste qu'un sexe. La femme-dandy est une 'princesse de *substance*' comme il l'écrit dans 'Un Dandy d'avant les Dandys' à propos de la Grande Demoiselle;[27] elle est comme Hauteclaire encore, cette femme 'royale d'attitude' (BDC, p. 86). Il faut ajouter que, pour les femmes-dandys, la question de l'intégration sociale reste entière: Barbey d'Aurevilly ne montre pas de femme qui ait réussi au statut de dandy seule et célibataire, contrairement à ses person-nages masculins. L'indépendance de la femme aurevillienne n'existe que si elle est veuve et riche (*L'Amour impossible*). Les femmes ne sont socialement intégrées que par le mariage et on peut citer celui de Savigny et Hauteclaire ('Le Bonheur dans le Crime').

C'est sur ce principe d'une supériorité innée, due à la prise de conscience et à l'exercice d'une différence que s'appuie le mépris du dandy pour le *vulgaire*. Le *vulgaire* n'est pas forcément catégorisé par une appartenance sociale à une classe: Mesnilgrand eut-il été 'le dernier cordonnier de sa ville', il aurait quand même été un être extraordinaire. La différence entre le dandy et le vulgaire se joue sur 'sa grande manière de sentir' donc sur une super-sensibilité, un regard sur soi qui se veut nouveau et affranchi du poids d'une pensée collective soumise aux normes sociales et culturelles imposées par le pouvoir. Dans ce sens, le dandy se rapproche et s'identifie à l'artiste, mais à sa manière et selon sa volonté. Il est bien évidemment possible au lecteur de d'Aurevilly de faire le procès du sentiment de supériorité du dandy, de celui qui se croit mieux que tout le monde, qui illuminé par sa conscience d'avoir compris, refuse de se mêler au lot et au sort communs. On ajoutera que les dandys aureviliens, vu leur naissance et leur aisance matérielle peuvent d'autant plus facilement se détacher des préoccupations de ce monde qu'ils n'ont pas à les affronter et, s'adonner au loisir de cultiver leur égotisme. Grâce à la 'supériorité aristocratique de son esprit',[28] le dandy légitime sa philosophie de domination et de différenciation de l'aristocratie, qui va s'exprimer à travers l'art du vêtement, le privilège dérobé au Roi de lancer les modes, ou tout du moins d'apparaître comme l'ultime élégance.

Le dandy incarne le paradoxe de la modernité, flottant constamment sur l'espace tangent de la multitude et de l'individualité, de l'anonymat et de la différence, de la transgression et de l'obéissance.

University of Nottingham

1   Barbey d'Aurevilly, *Du Dandysme et de G. Brummell, Oeuvres Romanesques Complètes*, éd. J. Petit, 2 vols (Paris: Pléiade Gallimard, 1964-66), I (1964), 667-733 (p. 675).

2   Emilien Carassus, *Le Mythe du Dandy* (Paris: Armand Colin, 1971), p. 118.

3   Roland Barthes, 'Le Dandysme et la Mode' [United States Lines Paris Review 1962], in *Oeuvres Complètes*, éd. E. Marty, 3 vols (Paris: Editions du Seuil, 1993-95), I: *Ecrits 1942-1965* (1993), 963-967 (p. 963).

4   On peut citer, à titre d'exemple, le mariage d'Anastasie Goriot et de Monsieur de Restaud dans *Le Père Goriot* de Balzac.

5   Baudelaire, 'le Dandy', *Le Peintre de la Vie moderne*, in *Oeuvres Complètes*, éd. C. Pichois, 2 vols (Paris: Pléiade Gallimard, 1975-76), II (1976), 683-724 (p. 711).

6   Barbey d'Aurevilly, *Du Dandysme*, p. 689.

7   ibid., pp. 688-89.

8   Michel Foucault, *La Volonté de Savoir, Histoire de la Sexualité* (Paris: Gallimard, 1976), p. 161.

9   Pour se remémorer l'importance donnée au modèle de la famille patri-arcale, il suffit de s'en remettre à la lecture du Code Civil de 1804.

10   Lord Shaftesbury, cité dans *The Victorian Family, Structure and Stresses*, éd. Anthony.S.Wohl (London: Croom Helm, 1978), p. 9.

11   Pour une étude psychanalytique et biographique de la famille aurevilli-enne voir *Barbey d'Aurevilly, Le Roman familial*, éd. J. Petit, *La Revue des Lettres Modernes*, 11 (Paris, 1981).

12   Michel Foucault, *La Volonté de Savoir*, p. 9.

13   Barbey d'Aurevilly, 'Le Bonheur dans le Crime', *Les Diaboliques*, in *Oeuvres Romanesques Complètes*, II (Paris: Pléiade Gallimard, 1966), 81-128.

14   BDC: 'Le Bonheur dans le Crime', op. cit.

15   Ce thème de la femme qui refuse la maternité réapparaîtra dans le roman décadent de Rachilde (1860-1953), *La Marquise de Sade* (1887). L'héroïne déclare à son époux durant sa nuit de noces: 'La maternité

que le Créateur enseigne à chaque fille qui se livre à l'époux, moi, j'épuise son immensité de tendresse à cette minute sacrée qui nous laisse encore libre de ne pas donner la mort en donnant la vie, libre d'exclure de la fange et du désespoir celui qui n'a rien fait pour y tomber. Je vous dit cyniquement: je ne veux pas être mère' (Paris: Imaginaire Gallimard, 1996), p. 215.

16   Barbey d'Aurevilly, 'Le Rideau Cramoisi', in *Les Diaboliques*, op. cit.

17   RC: 'Le Rideau Cramoisi', op. cit.

18   Françoise Mugnier, 'Dissimulation des classes sociales, de l'économie et de l'histoire dans la fiction de Barbey d'Aurevilly', *Nineteenth-Century French Studies*, 19 (1991), 279- 89 (p. 279).

19   ibid, p. 281.

20   Georges Bataille, *L'Erotisme* (Paris: Editions de Minuit, 1957), p. 17.

21   ibid, p. 23. Notons que la transgression, aussi bien chez Bataille que chez Foucault, dépasse largement l'exercice qui consiste à enfreindre la loi et les structures en place. La transgression ne se limite pas aux infractions de la loi.

22   Barbey d'Aurevilly, *L'Ensorcelée,* in *Oeuvres Romanesques Complètes*, éd. J. Petit, I (Paris: Pléiade Gallimard, 1964), 553-741.

23   Bulwer Lytton, 'L'Angleterre et les Anglais' [trad. Jean Cohen, Bruxelles, 1837], in Henriette Levillain, *L'Esprit dandy* (Paris: José Corti, 1991), p. 27.

24   Barbey d'Aurevilly, 'Le Dessous de Cartes d'une Partie de Whist', in *Les Diaboliques*, op. cit, p. 130.

25   Barbey d'Aurevilly, 'A un Dîner d'Athées', in *Les Diaboliques*, op. cit.

26   Emilien Carassus, *Le Mythe du Dandy*, p. 113.

27   Barbey d'Aurevilly, 'Un Dandy d'avant les Dandys', in *Oeuvres Romanesques Complètes*, I, 719-33 (p. 721). Cet essai est un complément à *Du Dandysme et de G. Brummell* et traite de Lauzun comme prototype du dandy.

28   Baudelaire, 'Le Dandy', p. 710.

Preserves of Nature : Traffic Jams and Garden Furniture in Zola's La Curée

Larry Duffy

It has been observed that 'topography, history and biology all condemn Zola's characters to a life where free will is powerless to act, to bring about change'.[1] It is also often the case that topographical, historical (or at least socio-historical) and natural phenomena are represented in terms of each other. The case of *La Curée*, in particular, highlights the inseparability of representations of space from a distinctly nineteenth-century view of nature, whereby conclusions drawn from empirical observation are as moral and social as they are scientific. Two locations in particular illustrate very well how this view of nature creates implicit and often explicit links between physical, social and moral space, and importantly, facility of movement, or mobility, within space according to social and, particularly, gender, criteria. Both spaces, namely the Bois de Boulogne and the home of Aristide Saccard, are described in detail in the opening chapter, and are clearly dependent on one another. The former is the scene of a traffic jam, the latter of a display of conspicuous wealth and of what can only be described as 'garden furniture'.

Why such a designation is appropriate should become clear after consideration first of all of the Bois de Boulogne scene as a discourse of checked vehicular mobility. In a detailed enumeration of vehicles, human beings are mentioned in the same stroke as their means of conveyance, such that an instant of immobility yields a snapshot of middle-class society in terms of its chosen form of transport. Indeed, 'tout Paris était là'. No one, from 'Mme de Lauwerens, en victoria très correctement attelée', to an infant in 'un landau gros bleu',to 'Selim pacha, avec son fez et sans son gouverneur' to 'la duchesse de Rozan, en coupé-égoïste, avec sa livrée poudrée à blanc', is mentioned without reference to a specific type of vehicle, or in some cases, of animal.[2] Everyone is singled out, classified according to certain exterior qualities in the pseudo-Linnaean taxonomy (almost self-parodic to a late twentieth-century eye) characteristic of the *Rougon-Macquart* cycle. In the earliest stages of a novel whose chief subject is the transformation of *immobilier* into *mobilier* by the property speculation of the age of Haussmann, facility of movement is central to the depiction of human beings, such that, as Priscilla Parkhurst Ferguson observes, '[the] mobility encouraged by the transformation of the city [...] provides the model for relations in every domain'.[3] When movement actually does occur, the social relations of a society in movement remain static, and distinctions between individuals lose their importance; displacement may occur, but there is no change in distance between the separate sections of society being displaced: 'le défilé alla, dans les mêmes bruits, dans les mêmes lueurs, sans cesse et d'un seul jet, comme si les premières voitures eussent tiré toutes les autres après elles' (*RM,* I, 321). The only irregular motion here, which disturbs that of the *défilé,* is that of perceived social or sexual deviants, such as 'les deux inséparables' suspected of being lesbian lovers, whose motion diverges from that of the others in 'un huit-ressorts qui quittait à grand fracas le bord du lac pour s'éloigner par une allée latérale' (*RM,* I, 322). Otherwise, individuals in society seem capable of assuming distinct identities only when static. Movement has a definite moral and social significance.

While the descriptive motifs here might be part of a coherent and consciously-chosen frame of reference which pervades the novel, if not the *entire Rougon-Macquart* cycle, they have their antecedents, notably in the description of the second *embarras de voitures* of *L'Éducation sentimentale* (in Chapter IV of Part II). Superficial similarities between the two extracts are so striking as to suggest wholesale transposition by Zola of elements of one to the other. The naming of individuals in accordance with a hierarchisation of vehicles occurs first at the races; this goes as far as the identification of Mme Arnoux's (inevitably) disappearing *milord* with Mme Arnoux herself.[4] Once the traffic jam is in full swing there is an exhaustive listing of private modes

of conveyance; the *berline* of Frédéric and Rosanette, having left
the socially exclusive surroundings of the racetrack, progresses to
the Champs-Élysées 'au milieu des autres voitures, calèches,
briskas, wurts, tandems, tilburys, dog-carts, tapissières à rideaux
de cuir où chantaient des ouvriers en goguette, demi-fortunes
que dirigeaient avec prudence des pères de famille eux-mêmes'
(*ES*, p.209). This widening of the social hierarchy serves however
only to express the lack of cohesion of a society in which what
should be animate is inanimate. A marginal note to a manuscript
folio for this episode highlights '[des c]ontacts d'existences
diverses - expressions différentes de figure - les riches les pauvres
les insolents les envieux'.[5] There is mere contact, no interaction;
society may be in flux, as the *défilé*'s subsequent depiction as 'un
fleuve où ondulaient des crinières, des vêtements, des têtes
humaines' (*ES*, p.210) suggests, but, much in the same way as
Frédéric, who spends much of his time in motion, does not actually
reach any destination he might have, social relations do not
undergo any real displacement. Real movement is restricted by
boundaries, much in the same way as the 'river' of vehicles is
hemmed in by rain-soaked trees which become 'murailles'.
What appears 'natural' becomes artificial, contrived, socially
determined. Representations of nature in the nineteenth century
are indeed essentially a function of Metropolitan discourses of
spatial organisation and modernity, whereby, as Nicholas Green
outlines, there is not simply an opposition, but an inter-
dependence between the non-natural and the natural, between
the country and the city, exterior and interior, such that boundaries
between the two are blurred.[6]

Central to this 'blur' are representations of light and
visibility. In both *L'Éducation sentimentale* and *La Curée*, the fluid-
like movement of society along predetermined paths in its
'menagerie' of carriages, captured in instantaneous exposure, is
'illuminated', in the former by 'une lumière roussâtre, qui faisait
étinceler les moyeux des roues, les poignées des portières, le bout
des timons, les anneaux des sellettes' (*ES*, pp. 209-210), in the
latter by a last ray of sunlight 'baignant d'une lumière rousse et

pâlie la longue suite des voitures devenues immobiles' (*RM*, I, 319). The imagery of water and reflection is crucial to the immersion of man-made objects into the discourse of nature.[7] Nature and the artificial coexist here; the *calèche* of Renée and Maxime reflects 'des coins du paysage environnant', so that it almost becomes part of the 'natural' world. It is the occupants of the vehicle who, at least at this stage, are disconnected from nature, concerned with social rather than natural phenomena. They may as well be in a drawing room or an opera house. In Flaubert's traffic jam, there is no 'natural' interaction of individuals: they merely stare at each other: 'On s'examinait. Du bord des panneaux armoriés, des regards indifférents tombaient sur la foule; des yeux pleins d'envie brillaient au fond des fiacres; des sourires de dénigrement répondaient aux ports de tête orgueilleux [...]' (*ES*, p.209). The only factor linking people is visibility; the side-panels of vehicles become windowsills from which the outside world can be viewed. Similarly, in *La Curée*, Renée, as if leaning from an opera box, has to resort to 'son binocle, un binocle d'homme' to examine Laure d'Aurigny and to establish that 'tout Paris était là'. As in Flaubert, 'il y avait des échanges de regards muets, de portières à portières; et personne ne causait plus, dans cette attente que coupaient seuls les craquements des harnais et le coup de sabot impatient d'un cheval' (*RM*, I, 320). The occupants of vehicles, as if waiting for a show to start or as if posing for a photograph against a background which is nothing if not 'picturesque', do not interact in any way other than by seeing and being seen; the horses can move, since they are 'natural', instinctual, and not 'social'. The humans here are removed from their indoor, artificial *milieux*, and yet paradoxically remain in them, since they are equally removed from the nature which surrounds them. As Florence de Chalonge observes: 'Habitée et mobile, relativement transparente, la calèche crée une opposition entre un intérieur et un extérieur: deux mondes – sans autre intersection que le regard – cohabitent'.[8] Rather than simply being opposed, however, interior and exterior to an extent become one another. We can see already that although outdoors, Zola's characters behave as if indoors, and are simultaneously in

public and in private. As elements of the urban spectacle, they
also become part of the contrived 'natural' spectacle of the urban
park, conceived itself so that nature is at no distance from the
city, and is in fact urbanised, socialised. Individuals, especially
women, are decorated in such a way that they appear almost as
botanical specimens. Renée herself wears a hat 'orné d'une touffe
de roses du Bengale'; the visible aspect of the motion of the
cavalcade is enhanced by 'les livrées éclatantes perchées en plein
ciel et les toilettes riches débordant des portières', so that clothes
play the role of foliage (*RM*, I, 320-321).

What is most striking here is the manner in which the park
itself is interiorised. It is most definitely an artificial and contrived
'coin de nature' in an unnatural environment, subject to 'interior
decoration', according to which its manufactured, lifeless
contents might as well be furniture, becoming *mobilier* as a
function of their immobility. The 'lac immobile' is a mirror, in
which the 'verdures noires' of the 'lignes théâtrales' of trees are
'pareilles à des franges de rideaux savamment drapées au bord de
l'horizon'.[9] The layout of the park is in no way natural; its
spatial organisation has been planned to the last detail. Light
conspires with 'ce décor qui semblait fraîchement peint' to create
'un air d'adorable fausseté' (*RM*, I, 322). Tree-trunks become
colonettes, lawns become carpets, 'plantés çà et là d'un bouquet de
grands arbres' (so that trees in turn become 'carpet flowers'); the
park gate is a lace curtain shielding this outsize drawing-room
from the 'exterior', creating a semi-transparent boundary which
becomes further blurred as the sun goes down (*RM*, I, 324). And
it is in fact at this point that the boundary between nature and
'the world' becomes least clear. When the light, such a significant
factor in the ordering of perceptions in the modern city, disappears,
everything becomes hazy, including, notably, moral as well as
physical boundaries. Light and colour, in their scarcity, take on
moral qualities and moods, simultaneously with Renée's drift
into melancholy as her carriage, paradoxically, moves back to the
world. The Bois becomes part of a natural rather than social
universe:

> Ce grand morceau de ciel sur ce petit coin de nature, avait un frisson, une tristesse vague; et il tombait de ces hauteurs pâlissantes une telle mélancolie d'automne, une nuit si douce et si navrée, que le Bois, peu à peu enveloppé dans un linceul d'ombre, perdait ses grâces mondaines, agrandi, tout plein du charme puissant des forêts.
>
> (*RM*, I, 326)

And the full implication of what 'nature' is becomes clear, at least in the moral universe of this particular novel: it is a locus of divergence from social norms, and of transgression, particularly sexual transgression, untrammelled by social convention. It is the prospect of the transformation of 'cette nature si artistement mondaine' into 'bois sacré' where 'les anciens dieux cachaient leurs amours géantes, leurs adultères et leurs incestes divins' which brings about in Renée 'une singulière sensation de désirs inavouables', and sets the scene for further transgression in the novel, which, true to Zola's subtitle for the entire cycle, relates what happens when 'natural' actions determined by extra-societal factors are placed in a social framework. Elsewhere in the novel, as here, the organisation of space has profound social and moral significance, and physical boundaries are blurred with social and moral ones. That this is part of a coherent 'Naturalist' system employed throughout the novel and not isolated use of particular forms of representation of space and its boundaries becomes clear in the latter half of this opening chapter, where the detailed description of the Hôtel Saccard reflects the same confusion of interior and exterior, of inanimate and animate, of social and natural as appears in the Bois de Boulogne. And central to this Naturalist topography are visibility, furniture and foliage.

The Hôtel Saccard is in many respects a labyrinth of spaces and invisible boundaries which define and restrict movement. Spaces are distinguished by their contents and by their accessibility. 'Tout Paris' might once again be assembled for an evening at Saccard's house, but there is only one space where access is guaranteed to all, namely the *grand salon*. The *salon*'s defining feature is gold, which is unsurprising given the money-obsessed character of the society inhabiting it, and much of their conversation. Genuine, uninhibited intercourse cannot of course occur here; other rooms are reserved for that, and distinguished most obviously here by gender, which in turn dictates the layout and decor of gender-specific spaces.

The most obviously gendered spaces in the Saccard residence are the *fumoir*, to which the men retire after dinner, and the small *salon bouton d'or*, situated at the other extremity of the larger, 'unisex' *salon*. These two rooms are of the same size and shape, and remote from each other. Their depiction, as we shall see, is in complete accordance with nineteenth-century notions of separate spheres, of male activity and female passivity, approval of male sexuality, censure and concealment of female sexuality. On this point, it is interesting to note even the positioning of these rooms in the house. 'Le fumoir *occupait*...une des pièces rondes formées par les tourelles', and is actually named, whereas the other room is 'une pièce ronde *dont on avait fait* un adorable petit salon' (*RM,* I, 349-350, italics added). The male space is thus active, the female space passive. The *fumoir*, 'de style...très sobre', is devoid of any frivolity perceived as feminine, and its furnishings are cylindrical, bare, exposed, and 'recouvert de peau de chagrin couleur de bois' (*RM*, I, 349). In this locus of male intimacy, where confidences are divulged around the incense-bearing totem of the cigar, and where anecdotes can be related between men in their uncensored form, 'foliage' is markedly absent. There are no trees in bloom, only wood; the only leaves present are those rolled into cigars, which constitute a recurring motif of male potency and sanction of overt discussion of 'private' matters in the novel (as in the *fiacre* episode in Chapter IV, where the light of the cigar is a catalyst for Renée's and Maxime's transgression and where Renée, ordering Maxime to hold on to his cigar, declares herself to be a man (*RM*, I, 442)).[10] Maxime must relinquish his cigar before crossing the asexual *grand salon*, populated by ladies and 'quelques jeunes gens et des viellards

[...], ayant le tabac en horreur' (*RM*, I, 349), who are, by such implication, impotent. When he has reached his destination, he only gets as far as the threshold of this 'cénacle de...dames', not quite as exclusive as the *fumoir* (there is a man present, though he is asleep), but described in much greater detail, since, of course, there is much more detail to describe, particularly with regard to furniture. In contrast with the austere surroundings of the *fumoir*, luxury and decoration are what define the *salon bouton d'or*. Like the Bois de Boulogne before nightfall, the room is possessed of 'un charme voluptueux, d'une saveur originale et exquise'. Light creates 'une symphonie en jaune mineur'; the interior is exteriorised into 'un coucher d'astre s'endormant sur une nappe de blés mûrs'. Most importantly, the furniture is foliated in the extreme: 'On ne voyait pas le bois de ces meubles; le satin, le capiton couvrait tout'. What is exposed in the male space is concealed here, covered in flowers. The carpet, 'semé de feuilles sèches', becomes a lawn. The room contains every variety of decorated furniture; it is a botanical garden containing a multitude of species: 'Les causeuses, les fauteuils, les poufs, étaient recouverts de satin bouton d'or capitonné, coupé par de larges bandes de satin noir brodé de tulipes voyantes. Et il y avait encore des sièges bas, des sièges volants, toutes les variétés élégantes et bizarres du tabouret' (*RM*, I, 350).

'Nature' has thus been recreated indoors in an artificial garden. The *fumoir* is no less artificially 'natural'; it merely contains different 'plant life'. Both spaces are in fact restricted in terms of the botanical variety they contain, and, simultaneously, of the society they can entertain. False, socialised exteriors have been placed into these interiors; restrictions have been placed on natural, rather than social, behaviour. Public and private, male and female worlds, cohabit separately, remote from each other. The only ambiguity here is between exterior and interior; other, even more ambiguous, spaces are required for unhindered circulation and transgression.

The most obvious such space in *La Curée* is the *serre chaude*
adjoining the house. As before, species are enumerated: the
naturalism here is explicit, with plants referred to with initial
capital letters. However, there are no restrictions on the room's
contents: all types of plant are here with covered and bare
species coexisting. Vegetation here is not furniture; the descriptions
of individual species do not render them lifeless; nature, even if
artificially installed, remains natural, and an incitement to 'natural'
activity. The *serre* is outside and inside at the same time; it is
transparent, yet remote from the surroundings which its trans-
parency reveals. It is 'a patch of nature artificially sustained,
whose exotic exuberance acts on the lovers' senses like a heady
philter...'.[11] Indeed, it is what most of all facilitates the sexual
transgression of Renée and Maxime. Its walls are glass, and it
is accessible via a window, which, for Naomi Schor, represents
'a neuralgic point where Zola's aesthetic, sexual and political
concerns intersect'.[12] A glass structure attached to a stone
building, it brings to mind the railway station and the exhibition
palace, structures simultaneously opaque and transparent in
which 'circulation' (of people and goods) can occur. Like the
railway station, the *serre* is part of the urban environment and at
the same time part of 'somewhere else'; the nineteenth-century
elimination of distance between city and 'not-city', society and
nature, extends to all structures, and moral mobility (in this case
the capacity for moral transgression), as much as physical mobility,
is a function of this. In Chapter IV, some time after their incestuous
relationship has been consummated in the *cabinet particulier*, that
most ambiguous combination of private and public space, we
find Renée and Maxime in the *serre*, amid 'une débauche de
feuilles' and overcome by 'des désirs fous de croissance immédiate',
'à mille lieues de Paris, en dehors de la vie facile du Bois et des
salons officiels, dans le coin d'une forêt de l'Inde...' (*RM*, I, 487-
488). Blurring of natural categories combines with an overpowering
and immediate (that is, direct, transparent and unobstructed)
sense of fertility and potency to remove the couple from the city
completely, paradoxically as a function of their being in it.
Distance is conceived in terms of its absence, and exteriority in

terms of of interiority. The lovers are 'en dehors' precisely on account of their being in the enclosed space of the *serre*. The Bois, conversely, is perceived as an interior, of the same stamp as the *salon*; it performs an unambiguously social role, reproducing a version of nature acceptable to the Metropolitan gaze. In the *serre*, however, plants remain natural, and become people, not furniture, as people become as 'natural' as the vegetation surrounding them. Plants take on human attributes, affected by the lovers as much as the lovers are affected by them:

> La serre aimait, brûlait avec eux. [...] Les Palmiers, les grands Bambous de l'Inde...mêlaient leurs feuilles avec des attitudes chancelantes d'amants lassés. Plus bas, les Fougères, les Ptérides, les Alsophila, étaient comme des dames vertes, avec leurs larges jupes garnies de volants réguliers[...].
>
> (*RM*, I, 486)

Transgression, then, is a function of an ambiguous environment, where socially-defined boundaries and distinctions become transparent and ultimately non-existent. Identities, whether of plants or of people, are uncertain and interchangeable, and to a large extent dependent on the environments in which they exist. Renée's demise comes about as a result of the incompatibility of her natural environment with her social one. She may at one point appear in command, or believe herself to be so ('C'était surtout dans la serre que Renée était l'homme'), but once Maxime decides to opt for society rather than nature, she loses control, her doomed motion unchecked due to her immersion in nature. Physical space and motion determine the possibilities of social mobility and moral transgression, in a highly systematised imaginative complex.

Zola's Naturalist project, then, works alongside other nineteenth-century strategies of representation of space, society and gender in order to link physical, social and moral movement. No doubt the passages cited could stand alone and similar conclusions could be drawn about Zola's representation of society. The traffic jam is a good example of this; it closely resembles the traffic jam in *L'Éducation sentimentale*, where the listing of vehicles has no particular biological significance. It is only when Zola's *encombrement* is contextualised in nature by way of the subsequent descriptions of the park itself and of the Hôtel Saccard that its fuller Naturalist significance develops. Similarly, nineteenth-century descriptions of interiors often employ great detail with regard to furniture, windows and so on. Again in *La Curée* it is the organic relationships between such descriptive passages which add further meaning to individual extracts. We only become aware of the full significance of the depiction of plants as furniture, for example, when we see furniture depicted as vegetation. Similarly, gendered spaces and the public/private dichotomy exist independently of any nature motifs, and indeed of Zola, but are given particular resonance by their induction into the Naturalising scheme of things. Most importantly, however, it is the organic combination of different representations of space which ultimately informs behaviour, movement and interaction of individuals. In *La Curée*, it is precisely because topography is so impregnated with social, historical and biological significance that it does indeed despatch Zola's characters to sealed fates.

University of Hull

1   Naomi Schor, 'Zola: From Window to Window', *Yale French Studies,* 42 (1969), 38-51 (p.51).

2   Émile Zola, *La Curée* (1871), in *Les Rougon-Macquart. Histoire naturelle et sociale d'une famille sous le Second Empire,* ed. by Henri Mitterand, 5 Vols (Paris: Gallimard, 1960-1967), I (1960), 320. This edition hereinafter referred to as *RM* with volume and page numbers in the text.

3   Priscilla Parkhurst Ferguson, *Paris as Revolution* (Berkeley: University of California Press, 1994), p.134.

4   Gustave Flaubert, *L'Éducation sentimentale* (1869), ed. by P.M. Wetherill (Paris: Garnier, 1984), pp.207-208.

    This edition hereinafter referred to as *ES* with page numbers in the text.

5   Bibliothèque Nationale, NAF 17605, f° 44.

6   Nicholas Green, *The Spectacle of Nature* (Manchester: Manchester University Press, 1990), pp. 11ff.

7   For an extensive discussion of the fictional exploitation of water imagery in *L'Éducation sentimentale*, see Bernard Masson, 'L'Eau et les Rêves dans *L'Éducation sentimentale*', *Europe,* 47 (1969), 82-100.

8   Florence de Chalonge, 'Espace, regard et perspectives: La promenade au bois de Boulogne dans *La Curée* d'Émile Zola', *Littérature,* 65 (1987), 58-69 (p.59).

9   Compare the 'rideau de peupliers' at the beginning of *L'Éducation sentimentale*.

10 This is a recurrent motif in the nineteenth-century novel, a most notable exponent being Flaubert. See in particular P.A. Tipper, 'Frédéric's "pro-Coital" cigarette: Causal Indeterminacy in *L'Éducation sentimentale*', *Neophilologus,* 80 (1996), 225-241.

11 Mario Maurin, 'Zola's Labyrinths', *Yale French Studies,* 42 (1969), 89-104 (p98.).

12 Naomi Schor, op. cit. , p47.

PART THREE

Twentieth-Century Perspectives

Homosexuality and Transgression in Three Political Novels of the 1930s

Angela Kershaw

What follows is not a study of 'homosexual literature', however that might be defined. My analysis does not consider texts by self-proclaimed homosexual writers and it does not address questions about literary projections of a homosexual self-image.[1] The texts it examines do not present homosexuality as a dominant theme. My focus is the different ways in which three authors, writing in the 1930s from diverse political standpoints, present homosexuality as a transgression, and how that motif relates to the political messages of the texts. The novels of the two female authors in question remain undeservedly neglected. Louise Weiss is known to students of women's history for her high-profile political career between the wars in France in the suffrage movement and in the peace movement. Her 1936 novel *Délivrance*[2] tells the story of the relationship between two women, one politicised and emancipated, one not, who meet in Geneva at the time of the demise of the League of Nations. Weiss's own political convictions could be broadly characterized as right of centre. Edith Thomas, whose novel *Le Refus*,[3] also from 1936, will be the focus of the second part of my analysis, writes from an overtly communist standpoint. *Le Refus* describes the political apprenticeship of a central female protagonist attempting to free herself from her bourgeois origins to achieve solidarity with the proletariat. The third text is Pierre Drieu la Rochelle's *Gilles*,[4] a rather better-known text, famous, or perhaps infamous, for its fascist ideology and for its misogyny.

Homosexuality has variously been constructed as embodying a positive transgressive force. According to Monique Wittig, '[h]omosexuality is the desire for one's own sex. But it is also the desire for something else that is not connoted. This desire is resistance to the norm'.[5] This sort of resistance to established norms of female sexuality in inter-war Paris was largely focused on the communities of women which sprang up in the 1920s around Anglo-American expatriates such as Natalie Barney, Djuna Barnes, Gertrude Stein and Alice B. Toklas.[6] These *salons*, frequented by French women such as Colette, Rachilde and Adrienne Monnier, were concerned with lesbian self-expression and with the redefinition of a female sexual identity through art and literature. Women writing about politics in the period were in a similar way deliberately engaged in transgressing and redefining conventional gender boundaries in their attempt to access what was legally and culturally a male domain, in order to redefine a female political identity. Drieu la Rochelle's writing appears vehemently to assert the sort of assumptions about gender and politics against which such women were fighting. Nonetheless, the novels of Weiss, Thomas and Drieu la Rochelle provide comparable instances of the coming together of sexual and political transgressions when they make use of the motif of homosexuality as a means of clarifying a particular facet of their political ideology.

Their literature is, in political terms, necessarily engaged in transgression in that it sets itself against prevailing political norms in order to recommend a different political ideology to the reader. Stallybrass and White, in their introduction to *The Politics and Poetics of Transgression*, make a useful distinction between discursive transgression as an inversion or a contradiction of existing cultural norms as opposed to a conception of transgression as 'movement into an absolutely negative space *beyond the structure of significance*'.[7] The novels with which I am concerned here do not transgress in any formal sense the structure of significance. Rather, they adopt conventional novelistic techniques to propose a political transgression that is beyond the literary. In so doing, they may remain aesthetically conservative, but they escape the problem of the potential dependance of the transgressive discourse on the norm which it sets out to transgress. The extra-textual transgressions proposed by Weiss, Thomas and Drieu la Rochelle demand the abolition of the oppositional term and the establishment of a new structure of political significance.

Louise Weiss's *Délivrance* offers a rethinking of politics itself. For Weiss, it is the inclusion of women in the polity and a concomitant rejection of war that constitute political progress. The power to achieve this political transgression is to be found in a uniquely and exclusively female mode of relating to the world and to other people. Initially, the reader wonders whether the model for such relationships is to be provided by lesbianism. The response of the narrator, Marie, to Noémi has erotic overtones from her first sight of this well-known politician in a newspaper photograph: 'Je portai l'image sous la lampe, la lissant, la caressant...'[8] Noémi's body becomes the focus of Marie's erotic fantasies:

> L'etoffe moulait ses formes. Moi, je devinais en elle l'amante
> aux seins fermes, aux hanches drues, sans autre ornement en
> sa nudité que ses nattes. Mon désir fit un bond et je compris
> la jouissance d'aimer un être au pouvoir.[9]

However, the text is categorical in its rejection of any possible political potential of female homosexuality. Noémi, the text's female political mouthpiece, gently but firmly rejects Marie's sexual advances because '[l]es lesbiennes sont des impuissantes: nous n'en sommes pas'.[10] Not lesbians or not powerless? The phrase remains ambiguous but either way homosexuality and power are deemed to be mutually exclusive. Furthermore, it becomes clear that the structures of domination and submission which Marie actively desires in her heterosexual relationships also characterize her response to Noémi:

> Mon sentiment pour Noémi m'étonnait par sa ressemblance
> avec mes amours masculines. Androgyne, il oscillait entre les
> deux stratégies de la domination: la soumission ou l'emprise.
> C'est que de son inspiratrice émanait une extraordinaire
> virilité d'esprit; je me délectais en mon goût pour elle.[11]

Délivrance represents homosexual desire in terms of a conventional oppressor/oppressed dichotomy. It cannot then symbolize personal female liberation or political liberation, since the pacifism the text recommends depends precisely on the erasure of the oppressor/oppressed structure on the macro level.

The specifically female mode of relationship that is to guarantee political progress is instead connoted by the maternal role. The assertion of a 'natural' link between motherhood and pacifism, and a logical one between feminism and pacifism, gained considerable symbolic resonance in relation to pacifist politics between the wars.[12] Thus Weiss proposes a feminized politics which will orient humanity towards peace rather than war and which is based on women's life-creating capacities. Accordingly, the text presents Noémi as an arch-mother and a positive example of female political commitment. Her campaign for peace through the League of Nations is described as 'l'enfant de son esprit'[13], a symbolic maternity which is provoked by the death of her own baby son. Her political commitment to pacifism is infused with a maternal commitment to the protection of innocent children: 'En souvenir du bébé que j'avais totalement chéri, j'entrepris de plaider à travers le monde sa cause, celle des innocents, la paix'.[14] *Délivrance* offers its unemancipated first person narrator the possibility to seize power through 'la maternité libre', to define her existence by bringing up her child on her own, excluding any subsequent male participation. This individual maternal power parallels the text's representation of a more general feminized political power. Male influence must be excluded from both because it represents death. The narrator's (male) ex-lover symbolically 'kills' her child by persuading her to opt for abortion, parallelling the text's political association of the male with the death of innocent children in war.

I find the text's celebration of female specificity through maternity less than convincing, since maternity presupposes an initial heterosexual relationship, and also since it is only the bearing of *sons* which the text presents as politically enabling. These are paradoxes which the text fails to address. Lesbianism might seem to be a more logical motif of Weiss' political ideal, especially given the resolutely negative representation of male characters in the novel,[15] and its celebration only through *female* eyes of the female body as a desirable object. Lesbianism is not an option for Weiss however, because it cannot incorporate the presumed equivalence between a woman's capacity to create life and pacifism's desire to prevent its destruction. The text's political ideal is therefore mono- but not homosexual. Weiss's text rejects sexualized, embodied lesbianism but at the same time attempts to harness the political potential of female specificity and separatism which more recent theorists such as Wittig have exploited through a lesbianism which is both sexual and political. Weiss transgresses conventional constructions of politics by positing a single-sex politics that is female. However she rejects the transgressive potential of lesbianism, unable, or unwilling, to translate her celebration of femaleness into a positive politicization of lesbianism.

Edith Thomas sets out from a very different starting point as regards the relationship between femininity and politics. Whilst Weiss seeks an exclusive integration of femininity and politics, Thomas rejects femininity as antithetical to politics. Part of the political revolt of the main female protagonist of *Le Refus* is her rejection of bourgeois constructions of the female as wife and mother. As a result, homosexuality appears in the text in the first instance as a positive political transgression because it constitutes an attack on the bourgeois construction of women as a commodity for exchange in the marriage market.[16] This would seem to correspond to Wittig's conception of lesbianism as a solution to oppression:

> Lesbianism is the culture through which we can politically question heterosexual society on its sexual categories, on the meaning of its institutions of domination in general, and in particular on the meaning of that institution of personal dependence, marriage, imposed on women.[17]

The homosexuality of Brigitte, the text's central female protagonist, is initially connoted intertextually by her reading of authors such as Proust, Rimbaud and Baudelaire.[18] The question of Brigitte's sexuality is developed through a highly ambiguous relationship with her close friend Anna. Their relationship is presented in covertly sexual terms and as exclusive and extremely close both physically and mentally, although it is never openly labelled as lesbian:

> Anna, mon amie. A qui donc rendre grâce de ce don qu'est l'amitié d'Anna, sinon à Anna elle-même. Elle va dire "mon amour", car elle n'en a pas d'autre. Elle dit "mon amie"et c'est beaucoup plus que tout ce que l'on peut dire. Ah! le coin de la rue! Nous nous étions avancées si lentement l'une vers l'autre, les mains hésitantes et tendues, car nous avions peur de ne rien saisir et d'avoir ensuite à nous retirer, le coeur ardent de désir, mais toujours vide. Ce jour-là...Mais quel jour? Il n'y a pas eu de jours saillants dans la suite des jours, car si on déclare son amour, il n'est pas de déclaration d'amitié.[19]

This presentation is foregrounded by a brief incident at the start of the novel concerning Brigitte's sister, Annie:

> -Comme tes bras sont froids, Brigitte, laisse-moi me coucher dans ton lit et te réchauffer.
> Une légère hésitation, un court moment où le coeur de Brigitte semble s'arrêter de battre: le danger rôde encore.
> -Non, dit-elle, tu vois, je vais me lever. Et elle rejeta ses couvertures et s'assit au bord du lit.[20]

The text seems to suggest the danger that something inadmissible might be inadvertently revealed, but the actual nature of that danger is not explained. However, the similarity of the names suggests a symbolic pairing and legitimizes a reading in terms of the Brigitte-Anna relationship.

Brigitte wants further to develop this unspoken union, however Anna refuses to pursue this path. She opts instead for a 'respectable' academic career, a choice which the text uses to defines Anna as a true daughter of the bourgeoisie: 'Si votre oncle n'était pas professeur d'histoire à la Sorbonne, auriez-vous choisi l'histoire plutôt qu'autre chose, Anna? Est-ce que vous ne regrettez pas tout ce que vous devez laisser de côté?'.[21] According to the value system of the text, this decision conforms to bourgeois standards because it is dependant on contacts rather than ability and represents opportunism rather than a pursuing of one's real passions. A relationship with Brigitte will not fit with the ordinances of the bourgeois sociocultural milieu with which Anna allies herself, and which she is not prepared to disrupt: '...je tiens surtout à pouvoir vivre tranquille'.[22] Anna, by her rejection of Brigitte, appears as one of the text's political traitors, refusing the opportunity to contravene the bourgeois code through a transgressive sexual relationship. Brigitte however offers a positive example of a communist political apprenticeship[23], and her homosexuality is presented as one manifestation of her revolt against bourgeois ideology.

Despite all this, the text ultimately rejects the political potential of lesbianism. The text suggests that the development of the Brigitte-Anna relationship would simply amount to inauthentic self-definition via the lover, which the text also somewhat Existentially condemns as the inevitable position of the female subject in heterosexual relationships in a bourgeois cultural environment. Brigitte's sister, despite her professional success as a scientist, is just such a female subject, defined by her husband: 'une Catherine, par Serge, accomplie'.[24] The passage continues, 'Elle [Brigitte], elle était encore latente et endormie. C'est ainsi du moins que parlent les hommes et qu'ils ont appris aux femmes, à parler. "Mais moi, je m'accomplirai bien moi-même. Et seule, s'il le faut. Anna d'ailleurs m'a déjà aidée et m'aidera"'. There is a degree of *mauvaise foi* in the contradiction - resisting conventional self-definition through the male lover, Brigitte proposes to substitute a female to fulfil the same function and call this autonomous self-definition. As in Weiss's novel, homosexual desire is not free from the dangers presented by heterosexual desire. It is precisely the refusal of the inauthenticity which seems to characterize all sexuality in Le Refus which allows

Brigitte to come to politics. By the end of the novel, the theme of homosexuality has been lost. Thomas does not embrace Wittig's vision of politically productive lesbianism. Lesbianism in *Le Refus* is socially and politically transgressive, but not ultimately politically enabling.

Drieu la Rochelle's representation of homosexual characters in *Gilles* is as homophobic as his representation of women is mysogynistic. The brief description of Antoinette's opium-induced cavorting with 'une vieille lesbienne célèbre' in her apartment which is dubbed 'ce petit cimetière bourgeois'[25] is represented in terms of the degeneracy, self-destruction and death which Drieu equates with the French nation and with the bourgeoisie. Lesbianism functions as a motif of the decadence and sterility of France and of the Modernist age. Christopher Robinson, in his *Scandal in the Ink*, finds such presentations of homosexuality typical also of turn-of-the-century literature.[26] Antoinette's male lover, Galant, is also linked with social and political disorder because of his sexuality. Antoinette is the wealthy bourgeois wife of his half brother: by contact with her, Galant is tainted by incest and by lesbianism as well as by his own homosexuality. The decadence of the French nation is a sexually transmitted disease. It is the February riots of 1934 which represent for Gilles the apex of this decadence. Gilles himself contracts decadence by participating in the riots, mistakenly believing that they contain the seed of a French fascist state, and this is expressed in terms of homosexuality: 'Je viens de te faire une scène de femme. Prends-moi, fais-moi mal. Une scène d'inverti. Nous sommes pire que des tantes'.[27] Not only a homosexual position, this is also a 'feminine' one: Gilles is the one taken, the masochistic subject. Drieu creates a network of equivalences between social and political degeneracy, femininity and sexual 'deviance', thereby associating a female or a feminized homosexuality with all that the text presents as politically repulsive.[28] Homosexuality in *Gilles* appears as an abhorrent transgression which is antagonistic to the political ideology recommended by the text.

For Drieu, that political ideology - fascism - is exclusively male. Femininity is as destructive to his politics as masculinity is in the case of Weiss. The coincidence of fascism and virility is made explicit when Gilles, stranded in Ibiza in the Epilogue and certain to be executed if he falls into the hands of the Spanish communists, takes a life and death decision, which turns out to be justified, on the basis that the face he sees must be fascist because it is masculine: 'Il avait confiance dans cette figure jaune et mâle, si sévère qu'elle fût'.[29] Drieu's ideal of virile political commitment is expressed in terms of the coincidence of thought and action and is symbolized by ancient forms of combat:

> Tu comprends, autrefois, les hommes pensaient parce que penser, pour eux, c'était un geste réel. Penser, c'était finalement donner ou recevoir un coup d'épée...Mais, aujourd'hui, les hommes n'ont plus d'épée...Un obus, ça les applatit comme un train qui passe [...] ce sont des hommes sans épée.[30]

Here Gilles looks back to an ideal past when thought and action formed a single unity and the phallic sword was an integral part of warfare. The sexual nature of the image is obvious. For Gilles, male sexuality and politics are one and the same thing. The Epilogue provides a political resolution of problems posed in terms of sexuality in the main part of the text concerning Gilles's male identity. The complete absence of sex in the Epilogue contrasts sharply with its abundant presence in the rest of the novel. Desire however is not absent from the Epilogue: it has simply found a different outlet. The quest for the virile male sexual identity which women in their decadence fail to provide for the male subject ends in fascism: only in fascism can male desire find authentic and fertile self-expression.

However it is problematic for Drieu to propose an exclusively male, virile, sexualised fascism. *Donner un coup d'épée* is clearly an active, masculine position. But *recevoir* here implies that the male subject might also be the object of the action, a conventionally female position. If fascism is to exclude femininity completely, then male subjects must necessarily occupy both active and passive positions. If male desire cannot be authentically channelled through women then perhaps it is to be expressed through male-male relations. As David Carroll notes, 'this is where the question of homosexuality comes in. In fact, it comes in everywhere, in all those places left empty by the suppression of the woman, everywhere men desire their own phallic rigidity and themselves to the exclusion of women'.[31] Drieu's fascism would indeed seem to imply a male desire that is homosexual.[32] His rejection of femininity leads him to posit a positive, if disembodied, homosexuality *malgré lui* which is quite the opposite of the feminized homosexuality of Galant and Antoinette. Their sexuality is decadent in its sterility; this other homosexuality on the contrary leads to a tangible political product: fascism. Robinson suggests that in the work of Cocteau and Genet, sexual sterility is justified by aesthetic fecundity; in Drieu's sexualized fascism there is a comparable justification by political fecundity.[33] Despite itself, the text permits a reading of homosexuality as a transgressive force that is positive within the political value system of the text.

I would like to argue that this symbolic homosexuality finds expression in the relationship between Gilles and his mentor, Carentan. Here, Drieu chooses a motif highly charged with positive homosexual connotations, the 'Greek love' motif, as a means to present a political ideal of fascism and virility.[34] The positive homosexual connotation is cemented by two references to Greece in the Normandy episode: Gilles's active service in Greece is mentioned, and, perhaps more significantly, we learn that Carentan is writing a book about Greek influences on Christian culture.[35] The tutor's alignment with the text's political ideal is also made clear. Carentan, associated, by extension, with the virile force of nature manifested in the Normandy coast where he lives, displays ideological virility in his distance from the decadent and feminine modern period and the capital.[36] Declaring 'je ne connais pas ton époque', preferring 'un univers complexe et ancien', he cites a hatred of modernity as the source of his anti-Semitism: 'Eh bien! moi je ne peux pas supporter les

juifs, parce qu'ils sont par excellence le monde moderne que
j'abhorre'.[37] That the relationship between Gilles and Carentan
is set away from Paris is not an attempt to neutralise homosexuality by situating it in an Other, distant geographical location,
but rather a means of endowing the relationship with a positive
political connotation.[38] Here then, a male-male relationship
positively charged with homosexuality is fused with positive fascist
commitment. Through the Gilles-Carentan relationship the text
provides clear justification for a reading of its fascist ideal in
terms of homosexuality. That which is to be inferred from the
exclusion of femininity from male desire is overtly present in this
relationship: sexualized fascism, which is in direct opposition to
femininity, Paris, modernity, sterility and the physical desiring
body, is in a continuum with a symbolic (because disembodied)
and virile homosexuality which the text therefore recommends.

I should like now to begin to draw the strands of the analysis
together. Drieu and Weiss both associate one sex exclusively
with positive politicisation. In so doing, Drieu suggests a positive
politically transgressive homosexual position which contradicts
the text's otherwise conservative and negative portrayal of
homosexuality. His sexualization of politics and his politicization
of virility imply that authentic masculinity can only be achieved
through the expression of male desire between men via fascism.
In Drieu's text then, it is difficult to argue that the political position
reached at the novel's conclusion is not a homosexual position.
The case of Weiss is rather different. Weiss contentiously uses
the motif of maternity, which colludes with, rather than transgresses, conventional and oppressive constructions of femininity,
in order to express a political ideal which is transgressive in relation
to the contemporary political environment. Homosexuality in
Délivrance transgresses the political value system the text is
recommending rather than the one it is demolishing. Weiss and
Drieu transgress further in their reformulation of the nature of
politics itself to include, in Weiss' case, the maternal body, and
in Drieu's case, a disembodied homosexuality. Thomas is more
concerned with the substitution of one political ideology for

another than with transgressing the established parameters of politics. In *Le Refus*, homosexuality is presented as a transgression against the value system to which the text is hostile. And yet it does not function as a manifestation of female political power. Thomas's political ideal is asexual, whilst Weiss proposes a monosexual political model and Drieu's text offers a homosexual politics despite itself.

The apparent refusal of 1930's female political authors to adopt homosexuality as a positive motif of political transgression must be considered in relation to their general refusal to conceive of female politics in terms of sexuality. It is a frequent feature of such literature that the female protagonist must forgo an active sexual identity in order to achieve full politicization. Female politicization in the 1930s implied transgression of norms of femininity and of politics which associated women with the private sphere and men with the public, the polity. Male-authored political texts of the period almost invariably suggest close links between male sexuality and politics whilst rejecting female sexuality as apolitical or as an impediment to politics. Their female counterparts do little to redress the balance. So it is that a male writer such as Drieu, who is so obviously homophobic, can paradoxically produce positively political discourses about homosexuality, whereas a writer such as Thomas, who acknowledges the political potential of homosexuality, will not make it part of her politics. An active and positive politicization of female sexuality did not come until much later with the feminists of Wittig's generation.

All of the texts in question ascribe a positive value to trans-gression in their quest for the establishment of a new political order. The relationship of homosexuality to that transgression however appears to be problematic. Weiss perceives the maternal role to be more liberating than a lesbian identity. Thomas rejects lesbianism as more of a hindrance than a help in political terms. Drieu's acceptance of a positive political role for homosexuality is perceptible only by reading against the grain of a text that

otherwise uses homosexuality as a motif of all that is wrong
with the French nation. Stambolian and Marks assert, in their
introduction to *Homosexualities and French Literature*, that 'the
finest achievement of the French writers derives from their
profound understanding of the value of homosexuality as a
transgression'.[39] The examples I have considered from the
political genre suggest that this is not universally the case.

University of Nottingham

1   What critical literature there is concerning homosexuality and French
    literature generally has such a focus. Two full-length studies exist:
    Christopher Robinson, *Scandal in the Ink: Male and Female Homosexuality
    in Twentieth-Century French Literature* (London: Cassell, 1995) and
    Homosexualities and French Literature: Cultural Contexts/Critical Texts, ed.
    by George Stambolian and Elaine Marks (Ithaca and London: Cornell
    University Press, 1979). For a historical angle, see Antony Copley,
    *Sexual Moralities in France: New Ideas on the Family, Divorce and
    Homosexuality* (London: Routledge, 1989).

2   Louise Weiss, *Délivrance* (Paris: Albin Michel, 1936).

3   Edith Thomas, *Le Refus* (Paris: Éditions Sociales Internationales, 1936).

4   Pierre Drieu la Rochelle, *Gilles* (Paris: Gallimard, 1939).

5   Monique Wittig, 'Paradigm', in *Homosexualities and French Literature*,
    ed. by Stambolian and Marks, pp.114-121 (p.114).

6   Shari Benstock offers a very detailed account of these literary and artis-
    tic activities in inter-war Paris in her *Women of the Left Bank: Paris
    1900-1940* (London: Virago, 1987).

7   Peter Stallybrass and Allon White, *The Politics and Poetics of
    Transgression*, (London: Methuen, 1986), pp.17-18.

8   Weiss, *Délivrance*, p.28.

9   ibid., p.92.

10 ibid, p.94.

11 ibid., p.68.

12 For an analysis of women's participation in the peace movement
    between the wars, see Christine Bard, *Les filles de Marianne* (Paris:
    Fayard, 1995), particularly 'Sauvegarder la paix', pp.129-44 and 'La
    paix menacée', pp.289-313, and Siân Reynolds, *France Between the
    Wars: Gender and Politics* (London: Routledge, 1996), particularly chap-
    ter 8, 'War and Peace: Assent and Dissent', pp.181-203.

13 Weiss, *Délivrance*, p.109.

14 ibid., p.215.

15 The one exception is L'Enchanteur, a fictional representation of
    Aristide Briand.

16 See Robinson, *Scandal in the Ink*, p.15 where the author considers the repression of lesbianism under the Second Empire precisely on these grounds.

17 Wittig, 'Paradigm', in *Homosexualities and French Literature*, p.118.

18 See Robinson, *Scandal in the Ink*, p.167-72 for a discussion of intertextuality in homosexual literature.

19 Thomas, *Le Refus*, pp.40-41.

20 ibid., pp.26-7.

21 ibid., pp.44-5.

22 ibid., p.91.

23 See Susan Suleiman, 'Pour une poétique du roman à thèse', *Critique*, 30 (1974), 995-1021 and also her *Authoritarian Fictions* (New York: Columbia University Press, 1983) for a discussion of the apprenticeship structure in political literature.

24 Thomas, *Le Refus*, pp.32-33.

25 Drieu la Rochelle, *Gilles*, p.433, p.458.

26 See Robinson, *Scandal in the Ink*, pp.11-12 and p.70 for a discussion of the motif of homosexuality in Proust and Zola.

27 Drieu la Rochelle, *Gilles*, p.603.

28 See Robinson, *Scandal in the Ink*, for a discussion of the homophobic association of the male homosexual with femininity.

29 Drieu la Rochelle, *Gilles,* p.655.

30 ibid., pp.487-88.

31 David Carroll, *French Literary Fascism: Nationalism, Anti-Semitism and the Ideology of Culture* (Princeton, New Jersey: Princeton University Press, 1995), p.156.

32 As a point of comparison, see Klaus Theweleit, *Male Fantasies*, trans. by Stephen Conway, Erica Carter and Chris Turner, 2 vols (Cambridge: Polity Press, 1987-88), I, p.277 and II, p.30 and p.339 where the author discusses the issue of the focus of male desire where women are expressly rejected as love objects but insists that this desire is not homosexual.

33   Robinson, *Scandal in the Ink*, p.71.

34   See ibid., p.46, where Robinson suggests, in relation to Proust, that the Greek model was the only positive model for homosexuality for early twentieth century writers.

35   Drieu la Rochelle, *Gilles*, p.147, p.155.

36   ibid., pp.143-44.

37   ibid., p.156, p.159.

38   See Robinson, *Scandal in the Ink*, p.14, where the author identifies geographical distancing as a means of neutralizing homosexuality as 'other'.

39   *Homosexualities and French Literature*, ed. by Stambolian and Marks, pp.25-26.

(Re-)Mapping the (Post)Colonial City : Gender and Economics in the African Novel in French.

Shona Potts

[..] the reinscription, enclosure and hierarchization of space
[..] provide an analogue for the acquisition, management and
reinforcement of colonial power. [1]

Issues of space, power and difference have long been central to the ideology of colonialism. Edward W. Said defines imperialism as 'an act of geographical violence' perpetrated against the native by the imperial power which explores, charts and finally brings under control the local place of the native.[2] Imperialism, Said continues:

> achieves the domination, classification, and universal commod-
> ification of all space under the aegis of the metropolitan
> center [...] To the imagination of anti-imperialism, *our* space
> has been usurped and put to use by outsiders for *their* purpose.
> It is therefore necessary to seek out, to map, to invent, or to
> discover [another space] that derives derives historically and
> abductively from the deprivations of the present.[3]

It is this assumption of a decolonized space by the formerly colonized peoples which is of interest in the exploration of the theme of transgression. Examining three texts, I aim to demonstrate the way in which the African novel in French has explored the topology of the the colonial and postcolonial city, focusing on the city's function within the text as a site of disruption and challenge of the established boundaries. In the colonial urban environment, the paradigm was established of the city divided in two: the native slum and the privileged colonial quarter. Native Africans were socio-politically marginalised, living on the periphery of the city and excluded from the political and administrative centres of colonial authority which were located in the colonial quarter. Racial separation was maintained by means of colonial laws, some of which were of specifically racial orientation, and/or purely economic barriers which made it impossible for native Africans to afford to live in the colonial quarter. Entry to this quarter was restricted; the area was accessible only to those Africans who were employed by Europeans to perform menial tasks such as cooking, cleaning and gardening and, at particular times of day, to Africans, usually women, who sold their wares in traditional markets. The importance of African women in the reappropriation of urban space is particularly significant in the novels of Ousmane Sembène. The position of women in the urban environment has traditionally been a site of some ambiguity. Writing with reference to the Muslim countries of North Africa, Fatima Mernissi highlights the Islamic religion's inherent fear of *fitna*: 'chaos provoked by sexual disorder and initiated by women'.[4] The potential for sexual licence represented by women and the fear such licence inspires as a threat to established masculine order manifests itself in the preoccupation of urban Francophone literature with female prostitution, the portrayal of sexual licence reflecting concern with a wider moral disorder.[5] For Ousmane Sembène, the role of women is integral to the development of post-independence African society :

> L'Afrique ne se développera sans la participation concrète de
> la femme. La conception que nos pères avaient de la femme
> doit être enterrée une fois pour toutes. La femme est l'élément
> le plus solide d'une communauté, d'une société.[6]

Les bouts de bois de Dieu by Sembène Ousmane, written in the post-independence period but set prior to independence, examines the way in which the native population challenges the existing geographical and conceptual boundaries in the colonial city, transgressing the limits which are designed to safeguard the colonial population both physically and in terms of its position of authority. This essay will examine Sembène's 1973 novel, *Xala* and Aminata Sow Fall's *La Grève des battù*, both of which explore the dynamics of the postcolonial city. Socio-economic divisions have replaced racial segregation as the colonial quarter is now inhabited by the educated African elite. According to Alessandro Triulzi, the post-colonial city is a unique site of colonial memory and political challenge by the margins in the negotiation of an independent future.

> [..] the African city becomes the visual symbol of post-colonialism, both the meeting place and battle-ground for two opposed worlds, with their contrasting features: power and impotence, poverty and ease, new immigrants and old inhabitants, centre and fringe. [..] It must be remembered that the contemporary African city is , by definition, the visual space of the political. It is also the 'site of memory of colonisation, with its divisions, [...] its visible remains [of colonialism] [..] and its obligatory 'synthesis' of tradition and modernity [..]. The post-colonial city is, then, *the* site for the challenge to the political and at the same time the locality for negotiation and agreement where new freedoms, new services, autonomous spaces and the delegation of previously centralised powers can be gained.[7]

Ousmane Sembène and Aminata Sow Fall portray the subversion of the neo-colonial authority represented by the urban elite by those Africans who continue to experience marginalisation and hardship in the postcolonial urban environment. The effectiveness of the challenge to and transgression of the established power structure, I will argue, lies in the unique position of women and the poor outwith the dialectic they seek to disrupt. Homi K. Bhabha points out that in an introduction to an anthology of black feminist criticism, Henry Louis Gates, Jr. :

> describes the contestation and negotiations of black feminists as empowering cultural and textual strategies precisely because the critical position they occupy is free of the 'inverted' polarities of a 'counter-politics of exclusion'.[8]

Bhabha goes on to cite Gates' explanation of the way in which :

> They [black feminists] have never been obsessed with arriving
> at any singular self-image ; or legislating who may or may
> not speak on the subject ; or policing boundaries between 'us'
> and 'them'.[9]

While the indiscriminate application of black American
feminism to the situation of African women would demonstrate
insensitivity to the profound socio-cultural differences between
the two groups, it is interesting to note the rejection of the binary
opposition between centre and margin which Henry Louis
Gates, Jr. highlights as a productive element of black feminist
criticism. I would argue that a similar position outwith the
dialectic of (neo)coloniser/(neo)colonised is occupied by the
marginal characters in the urban environment explored by
Ousmane Sembène and Aminata Sow Fall. Those living on the
margins assert their right to be heard, legitimising their new
position in the centre by drawing attention to the artificiality of
the boundaries which divide the city and breaking down the
structures of containment which characterise the colonial
ideology. Robert Holton comments that:

> the transgression of the boundary between the two groups
> exposes the artificiality and brutalising effect of the boundary
> itself. What has appeared natural - the segregation and
> stratification of the races is thus shown to be an arbitrary
> social and historical creation, subject to further historical
> alteration.[10]

The colonial city

The colonial city, then, differed from other urban lanscapes
in that it was a city divided iredeemably in two.[11] According to
Peter Gutkind : 'Nowhere is the colonial imprint on these
towns seen more clearly than in the racial distribution of the
population'.[12] In his 1961 treatise, *Les Damnés de la Terre*, Frantz
Fanon spells out the dichotomy between the two areas. The
colonial quarter is described by Fanon in terms which emphasise

its permanence and socio-economic well-being based on racial segregation.

> La ville du colon est une ville en dur, toute de pierre est de fer. C'est une ville illuminée, asphaltée[..] La ville du colon est une ville repue, paresseuse, son ventre est plein de bonnes choses à l'état permanent. La ville du colon est une ville de blancs, d'étrangers.[13]

The native quarter is denied even a stable identity, being referred to by several different terms. Fanon's description mediates ironically between a negative perspective which might reflect the views of the colonial population, emphasising the threat posed by the inhabitants of the native quarter and more sympathetic references to the difficulties facing the native population : poverty, overcrowding, inadequate sanitation.

> La ville du colonisé, ou du moins la ville indigène, le village nègre, la medina, la réserve, est un mal famé, peuplé d'hommes mal famés. [..] C'est un monde sans intervalles, les hommes y sont les uns sur les autres. [..] La ville du colonisé est une ville accroupie, une ville à genoux. C'estune ville de nègres, une ville de bicots.[14]

It is important to consider the fear with which European expatriates regarded the native quarter of colonial cties, emphasising the exclusionist nature of European attitudes and the resulting marginalisation of the native population. The European fear of disease and contagion associated with the native quarter acts as a metaphor for the fear of disorder represented by the indigenous population's 'marginal' way of life which threatens the order of the European centre. By maintaining segregation from the native population, the colonial authorities expressed their desire to protect Eurocentric socio-political space. By inscribing their surroundings with European points of reference, cultivating European-style gardens, surrounding themselves with European goods and maintaining a

European lifestyle, the colonial population retains 'a comforting set of references which help secure the community's links with their cultural origins'.[15] Ironically, however, the Eurocentric extremes of the ex-patriate population promotes an idealised image of a Europe which does not exist. The ideal according to which the colonial population is defined exists only in opposition to what it is not : the native other.[16]

> The native city, with its different set of cultural, ideological and architectural values was marked as a potential source of danger to the Anglo-Indian inhabitants. The native city was associated with infection and disease; segregation operated as a means of safeguarding the welfare anddentity of the colonial settlement. Where contact was necessary, a set of rules regulated the terms of the encounter. The semantic violence meted out in the word 'native' parallels the socialand political. Far from being defined as 'autochthonous' or indigenous to the region, the word 'native' was taken to refer to something unnatural or foreign.[17]

In his discussion of colonial cartography, Graham Huggan highlights the way in which Derridean deconstruction :

> undermines the claim to coherence of cartographic discourse by revealing that the exemplary structuralist activity involved in the production of a map (the demarcation of boundaries, allocation of points and connection of lines within an enclosed, self-sufficient unit) traces back to a point of presence whose stability cannot be guaranteed.[18]

A similar instability is manifest in the attempts of the colonial population to exert control over urban space and thereby promote the discourse of colonialism, a rhetoric of containment by marginalisation of native inhabitants. The 'centre' to which the European centre refers itself is in fact an idealised product of colonial discourse.[19]

Les bouts de bois de Dieu : Ousmane Sembène

In Ousmane Sembène's *Les bouts de bois de Dieu*, the contrast
between areas inhabited by the native population and the colonial
is emphasised, highlighting the increased socio-economic hardship experienced by the African miners and their families during
the 1947-48 strike which forms the historical backdrop of the
narrative. The native quarter of the town of Thiès is described as
a barren landscape where poverty and hunger reign and death is
omnipresent.

> Thiès : un immense terrain vague où s'amoncellent tous les
> résidus de la ville, des pieux, des traverses, des rues de loco-
> motives [..] des carcasses de chats, de rats, de poulets dont les
> charognards se disputent les rares lambeaux. [..] Des gosses
> nus, perpétuellement afamés, promenaient leurs omoplates
> saillantes et leurs ventres gonflés: ils disputaient aux vautours
> ce qui restait des charognes. Thiès : la zone où tous, hommes,
> femmes, enfants avaient des visages couleur de terre.[20]

The colonial quarter of Thiès, however, is built on the ordered
pattern of the European urban model. The area is described as
being fertile, with flourishing European-style gardens. The care-
free lives of the European children who have no conception of
the daily suffering of their native counterparts acts as a telling
point of contrast.

> Toutes semblables avec leurs toits de série, leurs pelouses
> vertes bien entretenues, leurs allées ratisées, leurs perrons que
> ceinture une balustrade de ciment, les villas des employés
> blancs de la Régie s'alignaient pour former un quartier bien
> à part de la ville [..] Dans les jardins qu'ombrageaient les
> bougainvilliers, des massifs de roses, de marguerites, de gueules
> de loup faisaient des vaches vives. Le long des trottoirs et des
> allées des bandes d'enfants rieurs se poursuivaient, poussaient
> leurs trottinettes ou jouaient avec les tuyaux d'arrosage.[21]

Even prior to independence, however, the European community in Africa portrayed by Ousmane Sembène is aware of the potential threat to its security posed by the political agitation of the African population. Since the railway strike's beginning, the atmosphere in the colonial quarter has altered somewhat, initially in reaction to a transgression of the previously inviolable boundaries designed to protect the European population by young African apprentices which highlights the French population's awareness of its growing vulnerability and causes the men to form 'en secret des groupes de vigilence'.[22] While the colonial population is conscious of the potential physical threat posed by native discontent, the underlying threat to the socio-political order of colonialism is of far greater consequence.

> Ce n'était pas tant les pierres et les boulettes de plomb que l'appréhension de voir des corps noirs se glisser dans l'ombre qui transformait, la nuit venue, chaque foyer en un petit fortin.[23]

Roger Chemain identifies the insecurity which underlies the deceptive comfort of the colonial quarter as the European inhabitants become conscious of their own status as 'other' within the African environment.

> C'est que, malgré le confort et la salubrité de leur quartier complaisamment opposés par les romanciers à la promiscuité et à l'insalubrité du quartier indigène, les Européens se sentent isolés, etrangers.[24]

The dramatic alterations which threaten the structures of colonial authority equally call into question the relationship between African men and women as traditional gender roles are reversed and women take on an active role, manifested particularly in their changing relationship to the colonial topography. In his study of Sembène's work, Martin Bestman highlights the importance of geographical displacement in the affirmation of individual autonomy: 'ceux qui aiment les habitudes séculaires ne se déplacent guère, tandis que les personnages qui veulent reconquérir leur liberté sont en constant mouvement'.[25] While initially, the transgression of established boundaries will take the form of the rejection of those borders which restrict population movement, the subsequent action is offensive in nature.

The ultimate example of female activity is the march which takes place from Thiès, the strike headquarters, to Dakar, Senegal's capital, where negotiations are to take place between trade union officials and their French employers. Within the narrative context, the women's march is a dynamic movement which marks a shift away from the fragmentary nature of the narrative structure, providing a link between the two most significant geographical locations in the novel. The women's initiative is a radical break in the underlying stasis of the narrative which has characterised the deadlock of the strike situation: 'Tandis que les hommes discutaient à la maison du syndicat, les femmes se préparaient au départ'.[26] The march proves to be fundamentally important for the women as a movement towards altering their traditionally contained role within African society. Following the success of their march, the women of Thiès will work 'à quelques kilomètres de la ville' as '[l]a marche ne leur faisait plus peur', demonstrating their new confidence and autonomy in the world outside the boundaries of the compound, although the domestic space of the compound remains the point of reference around which the women circulate.[27]

In *Les bouts de bois de Dieu*, in the aftermath of the women's march, tension between the native and colonial quarters in Dakar has risen to such a degree that the security forces are called upon to prevent further instances of confrontation. However, increased segregation of the French and African inhabitants of the town serves only to reinforce mutual suspicion and hostility and the boundaries which are being upheld are revealed as artificial constructions designed to reinforce the authority of the ruling regime.

D'ailleurs, depuis plusieurs jours, l'atmosphère s'était alourdie dans toute la ville [..] [L]es autorités avaient considérablement augmenté les services d'ordre: policiers, marins, gendarmes, tirailleurs, patrouillaient inlassablement les rues. Entre les bas-quartiers indigènes et les avenues résidentie-lles ou commerçantes, on avait établi de véritables cordons de protection et, de part à d'autre, cette ségrégation créait un malaise.[28]

Towards the conclusion of the novel, any illusion of European security in Thiès is finally destroyed beyond repair when the African women of the town march upon the European residences in order to demand the departure of Isnard, the French foreman, a condition of the men's return to work which has not been met. The women's action is fundamentally offensive as they assert their right to a place and a voice in the centre. The initiative taken by the African population to transgress the accepted spatial boundaries of the relationship between colonised and coloniser is symbolic of the transformation of the colonial power structure, heralding its imminent demise and highlighting its arbitrary nature. The African women alone, can initiate such a challenge due to their marginalised position within the seemingly exclusively masculine colonial regime, a marginalisation which ensures that they are free from the direct implication within the dialectic of *colonisateur/colonisé* which prevents the African men confronting their colonial oppressors. According to Frederick Case, 'it is as though Sembène is telling us that it is only women who can organize themselves and undertake their own struggle against oppression'.[29] Case points out that in his portrayal of the railway workers, Sembène gives little impression that the experience of the strike has altered the relationships between the men or with their employers, whereas for the female characters in the novel, their active contribution to the struggle has dramatically altered their position in society.

Herd-like creatures in their socialization, men appear to be incapable of meaningful social and economic revolt. [..] This surely is the final test of meaningful change in society that women arecapable of the positive transformation of gender relationships through the consciousness-raising process of revolt.[30]

Even prior to independence, the colonial city is portrayed as having become a site of racial confrontation as the native population challenges the implicit authority of colonial rule by transgressing the geographical boundaries which segregated them from the European quarter, claiming their place in the centre.

Post-Independence

While the granting of independence to the majority of former European colonies in Africa might have been expected to combat the situation of inequality, the socio-economic barriers between Africans themselves were in fact strengthened as racial division ostensibly diminished. Following the European departure, the positions they left empty in the political, commercial and administrative structures they had created in the colonies were filled by Western-educated Africans. This new bourgeois element had assimilated European values and would continue to promote the structures of colonialism while the majority of the urban African population continued to exist in poverty. According to Peter Gutkind, writing in 1974 :

> ...[T]his urban racial ecology has changed little. The exclusive residential areas occupied by expatriate Europeans are now occupied by senior, and elite-minded, African civil servants and African housing estates are becoming more congested, therefore producing increased personal deprivation, frustration, and serious slum conditions.[31]

Gutkind goes on to emphasise the potential for political conflict which characterised the continents of the so-called 'Third World' at this time as socio-economic disparity between the poor members of the African population and the educated elite increased. While granting a voice to the privileged few, independence reinforced the boundaries which it was expected to have destroyed.

> It is, therefore, not unreasonable to suggest that the towns of Africa, Asia and Latin America might become the arena of major class confrontations. [..][A]s migration to the towns increases, as unemployment rises to an even more accelerated rate, inequity, poverty and misery steadily increases. Squatter settlements rise faster than they can be removed by governments offended by urban blight, and under these conditions the towns become tinder boxes of discontent.[32]

In the post-independence African novel in French, the city provides a locus for the interaction of questions relating power, gender and economics, becoming a site of class transgression as the strict boundaries which divided the colonial city are further challenged and subverted by the marginalised members of the urban population. According to Islamic belief, the less fortunate members of society ; those who due to physical disability, age or unemployment are forced to beg for their daily subsistence, are an essential element of human society. By giving money to these beggars, the better-off members of society receive their blessing and are believed to find favour with Allah, experiencing good fortune in return for their good deed. By the nature of their situation in Muslim society, therefore, beggars are not strictly confined to one area of the city. Martin Lemotieu comments that:

> L'aumône est alors ce lien indissoluble qui lie les deux groupes sociaux et devrait normalement les unir dans un état de solidarité et de complémentarité.[33]

In both *Xala* by Sembène Ousmane and *La Grève des Battù* by Aminata Sow Fall, the authors have chosen to portray beggar characters as a means of foregrounding the disruption of the socio-political boundaries of the neo-colonial power structure by the margins. The urban environment is no longer segregated according to racial criteria; instead, economic disparity maintains the rigid segregation of the city. Ousmane Sembène and Aminata Sow Fall explore the moral issues surrounding the marginalisation of which the beggars become nonetheless the victims in the modern secular city. In both novels, the beggars challenge their marginalisation by subverting the existing power structures and transgressing the boundaries which perpetuate their disadvantaged socio-economic situation.

Xala : Sembène Ousmane

Writing with reference to the literature of the Anglo-Indian city, Gail Chiang-Ling Low comments that the European quarter 'is figured within a topos of linearity and geometry'. As well as describing the physical geography of the settler community, Low argues, such descriptions reflect the community's 'persistent interest in demarcation, naming and segregation'.[34]

> The obsession with walls, detachment and spaces-in-between signals a fear, an imagined pressure from the native quarters, whose bodily secretions threaten to run riot and spill over established boundaries. Lines of demarcation are also lines of defense. [..] The language of the disciplinary and regulatory discourses produces an Other city which is always sinister, mysterious, and dark, and whose shadow falls on the city of light. The Other, expressed through the [..] privilege of the body as transcoder of difference, always threatens to spill over the geometric divisions of the civilised body, oozing its contaminated bodily wastes, disgusting odours and noxious smells.[35]

In *Xala*, the ultimate fear of the ruling elite is realised when the beggar population moves into the former colonial quarter and takes over one of the homes of El Hadji Abdou Kader Bèye, representative of the African bourgeoisie. The description of the beggars' invasion of El Hadji's home will be seen to clearly reflect the preoccupation of the new African elite with segregation and the fear of disorder, concerns analagous to those of the former colonial occupiers described by Gail Chiang-Ling Low. In Sembène's novel, the body of the native beggar becomes a sight of potential threat to neo-colonial order, their description focusing on their diseased and less than human condition.

In *Xala*, Ousmane Sembène describes the way in which, as a young man in pre-independence Africa, El Hadji Abdou Kader Bèye was seen as a hero of the younger generation. Politically active and a militant trade union member, he would speak out against the colonial occupation and those Africans who had assimilated Western values.

> Papa Jean savait beaucoup sur ce musulman, sur ses activités syndicales, on lui avait rapporté ses discours dans les meetings politiques sur la présence française, ses alliés, les assimilés.[36]

Following independence, El Hadji's business activities become such that he depends upon the former colonial authorities and finds himself compromising his revolutionary ideals for financial gain. Throughout the novel, an indication of El Hadji's distance from the beliefs of his youth and the religious premises of the Muslim faith is his attitude towards the beggar who begs outside El Hadji's shop. The businessman finds the beggar's singing and chanting irritating and rather than giving him charity, frequently has the beggar arrested.

> Le mendiant était très connu à ce carrefour. Le seul qui le trouvait agaçant était El Hadji. El Hadji, maintes fois, l'avait fait rafler par la police. Des semaines après, il revenait reprendre sa place. Un coin qu'il semblait affectionner.[37]

Only Modu, El Hadji's chauffeur, himself a marginalised figure, converses with the beggar who, referred to simply as *'le mendiant'*, has no individual identity. Most of the initial references to him describe him only in terms of a disembodied voice rather than an individual, further denying the beggar humanity. It is somewhat ironic, therefore, that the beggar should reveal himself as the only person who can cure El Hadji's *xala*, or sexual impotence, which is the focus of the narrative. The significance of the unexpected association between the beggar and the business-man is revealed only when, in a dramatic act of subversion of the established power structure, the beggar leads his fellows in a march upon the villa of one of El Hadji's wives. The destruction of pre-existing socio-economic boundaries is expressed when the beggars enter the bourgeois residential stronghold, transgressing the borders which have previously offered protection to the entrepreneurial elite.

'Le quartier', prior to the beggars' arrival, 'respirait la bienfaisance d'une vie de pleine de quiétude'.[38] The peace and tranquillity of the early morning scene is soon broken as the marginalised members of the urban landscape enter the bourgeois residential stronghold, asserting their right to claim a position in the centre. The description of their arrival ironically reappropriates the metaphors of dirt and disease which were typical of colonial portrayals of the native quarter in the colonial city.

> Du front, occupant la largeur du talus, avançaient en procession éclopés, aveugles, lépreux, culs-de-jatte, unijambistes, hommes, femmes et enfants sous la conduite du mendiant. Un bruissement d'insectes planait. La progression avait quelque chose d'horrible, laissant traîner la senteur fétide de leurs hardes variées.[39]

Frantz Fanon's description of the fears of displacement by the native population which haunt the colonial mentality are a valuable reference point in reading Sembène's description of events in El Hadji's home.

> Le regard que le colonisé jette sur la ville du colon est un regard de luxure, un regard d'envie. Rêves de possession. Tous les modes de possession : s'asseoir à la table du colon,

coucher dans le lit du colon, avec sa femme si possible. Le
colonisé est un envieux. [..] C'est vrai, il n'y a pas un colonisé
qui ne rêve au moins une fois par jour de s'installer à la place
du colon.[40]

El Hadji, as a representative of his socio-economic class,
experiences the realisation of their underlying anxieties as the
beggars displace him within his own home. Ousmane Sembène
presents a lengthy description of the way in which the beggars
avail themselves of El Hadji's possessions, invading all areas of
his private domain and molesting his wife. El Hadji and his
family are subjected to the experience of marginalisation in their
own home, unable to react to a situation which overturns all
expectations which habitually govern human relations in the
city. El Hadji and his daughter are forced to assure the police
that there is no problem, and are thus denied any means of
protection from the representatives of former colonial authority
as the beggars invade the villa. El Hadj's wife, we learn:

> était statufiée, rivée au sol, incapable d'articuler un mot. A la
> hauteur de ses mollets, un homme-tronc la frôlait, Angoisée,
> le frisson de l'écouerment lui montait jusqu'aux cheveux. La
> nausée gagnait tout son être. Une des boîteuses, d'un geste
> rapide, lui ôta son écharpe et s'en couvrit la tête, provoquant
> l'hilarité générale. [..] [El Hadji], abasourdi par tant
> d'audace, de sans-gêne, regardait sans réagir. Il fixait des
> yeux le mendiant avec étonnement, comme paralysé.[41]

Reduced to silence, El Hadji himself becomes the centre of the
spectacle. In a profound act of physical violation, El Hadji is
denied all dignity and forced to stand naked on a chair while the
beggars spit on him and his trousers are passed from hand to
hand. He is stripped of his manhood and subjected to the ultimate
humiliation of being ridiculed by those he has always considered
to be his inferiors. The truth concerning El Hadji's ill-gained
fortune is unveiled as the beggar's voice is heard for the first
time. El Hadji becomes a representative of his whole class, being

punished for their behaviour and attitudes as much as his own individual actions. Even if El Hadji claims to have seen the error of his ways and returned to the revolutionary discourse of his youth, he cannot deny his previous oppression of the poor and it is retribution for these actions which the beggar seeks to obtain. For the first time, the beggar has a voice and berates El Hadji for the hypocrisy of his class :

> Toi et tes collègues ne construisent que sur l'infortune des humbles et honnêtes gens. Pour vous donner une bonne conscience, vous créez des oeuvres de bienfaisance, ou vous faites l'aumône aux coins de la rue...[42]

The chilling final line of the novel, however, indicates a return to the status quo. The apparent assumption of power by the beggars, subverting the traditional balance of power, is shortlived as the forces of order reinstate control by the authorities and the discourse of law and order reinforces the neo-colonial power structure and its polarisation of centre and margin : 'Dehors, les forces de l'ordre manipulaient leurs armes en position de tir'.[43]

It is important to consider the extent to which transgression is necessary within society in order to legitimise the position of the dominant order. According to Jonathan Dollimore, a limited degree of controlled insubordination is an important element of an authoritarian regime's reinforcement of its own position of power. By being seen to repress a challenge (albeit relatively insignificant) to its authority, the ruling regime can promote itself as maintaining order, ensuring a shift in public attention away from concern with the activities of the authorities to the potential threat posed by the insubordinate minority. In this way, the ruling regime ensures the continuation of public support for its oppressive government.

> Tyranny endlessly provokes social disruption within those it subordinates, intentionally or not. [...] Equally certain however is that tyranny relegitimates itself in they eyes of some or

many precisely by suppressing the discontent it provokes. It deploys its 'superior' forces in the name of law and order; in other words it is a suppression working simultaneously in terms of brute force and intense ideological work at the level of representation. At the same time or separately, tyranny typically displaces crises generated within the dominant (for example between competing factions) onto the subordinate, whose control and extra-repression again serves to relegitimate and sometimes reintegrate the dominant.[44]

While Dollimore acknowledges that the inversion of the binary opposition between centre and margin is 'a necessary stage in its displacement' he also points out that this is only a beginning in the strategy of resistance which is potentially reductive if not taken a stage further in the creation of a new space from which to speak located outwith the boundaries have previously governed the relationship of the margins with the centre.[45] Nevertheless, the beggars' taste of power in Sembène's novel has fundamentally undermined the previously unquestioned superiority of the bourgeoisie and the lower caste is unlikely to accept a return to the former situation. While shortlived, the transgression of the boundaries which protect the bourgeois elite is an important symbolic challenge to its authority, highlighting its vulnerable position and the refusal by the margins of their condemnation to silence.

La Grève des Battù : Aminata Sow Fall

Aminata Sow Fall's *La Grève des Battù* is another critique of the social situation in contemporary urban Africa. Sow Fall high-lights the disparity between the minority bourgeois ruling elite and the majority of the urban African population which suffers from extreme financial deprivation due to a high proportion of urban unemployment and difficult social conditions. In Senegal in the late 1960s and early 1970s, extended periods of drought and the fall in the price of peanuts, the principal crop, led to a mass rural exodus and a dramatic increase in the urban population.

Greater government intervention in city life resulted from the problems of rapid urban growth and, simultaneously, a new generation of 'technocrats', more concerned with bureaucracy than politics, began to fill positions of authority.[46] This historical situation forms the backdrop of Aminata Sow Fall's novel. Blurring the boundaries between historical fact and fiction, Aminata Sow Fall's novel satirises the persecution of the marginalised members of urban society which took place in Dakar in the late 1960s and early 1970s.

> In the urban milieu, the policy of '*déguerpissement* ' (chasing away) and the battle against those who in administrative vocabulary are referred to as 'human congestion', beggars, street-hawkers, the handicapped, the mentally ill, has been the subject of an impressive judicial announcement that can be seen as indicative of an official intent to the control, segregation, and locking up of hitherto uncontrollable 'marginal' or 'abnormal' people.[47]

The technocrats of the ruling regime are a particular object of Sow Fall's satire, fictionalised in the character of Mour N'Diaye, the Director of the Department of Public Health and Hygiene who arranges for the streets to be cleared of the beggars as a means of obtaining the approval of the country's president and subsequently, he hopes, promotion to the much coveted position of Vice-President. In *La Grève des battù,* Aminata Sow Fall's beggar characters give a voice to this previously marginalised and silent majority of the urban African population. The existing power structure is subverted as the beggars reject their former position of acquiescence to the authority of the ruling elite and assume an essential degree of autonomy and self-respect by calling into question the neo-colonial power base.

In *La Grève,* Nguirane, one of the beggars, remembers the begging which formed part of the Coranic school training in the countryside where he grew up and the importance of the reciprocal relationship between giver and receiver.

> La mendicité n'était pas considérée comme un fléau. Elle
> était toute naturelle pour ceux qui se trouvaient dans
> l'obligation de mendier et pour ceux qui donnaient, elle était
> considérée comme un devoir...[48]

Towards the end of the colonial period, the growth of urban
agglomerations resulted in a population exodus from the rural
regions to the new cities. For Nguirane and many other peasants,
the dream of life in the capital contained the hope of a better
existence in a situation where jobs and resources would be readily
available to all : 'Nous pensions pouvoir nous en sortir en venant
à la ville qu nous voyions dans nos rêves comme un paradis ou
rien ne manquait' .[49] The reality of urban life proved to be very
different and begging became the only means of survival, devoid
of its religious significance. In Aminata Sow Fall's modern urban
African society, the presence of the beggars throughout the city
is considered by the authorities to be an unfortunate and
unnecessary eyesore. The beggars are portrayed as aggressive
and an offensive encroachment upon the lives of ordinary, hard-
working people. Most importantly, in the post-Independence
period, Africa's new situation as a tourist destination ensures
that the claimed detrimental effect of the beggars' presence
upon the tourist image of the capital is one of the most important
considerations in the decision 'd'assainir les voies publiques' by
moving the beggars to remote villages.[50] The problem of the
beggars' presence is dealt with by removing them from the
capital rather than investigating the root causes of the social
conditions which force the beggars to live on the streets. The
image presented to Europe by Africa is considered to a great deal
more important than the beggars' religious significance : 'Leur
présence nuit au prestige de notre pays; c'est une *plaie* que
l'on doit cacher, en tout cas dans la ville'.[51] The reference to
concealment and an open sore is an important reflection of the
ruling elite's attitude towards the beggars, once again appro-
priating the metaphors of disease and contagion which characterised the European view of the native population during the
colonial era.

In *La Grève,* the pursuit of the beggars during the street clearance operation is portrayed as an inhumane action whose perpetrators conceal themselves behind a screen of bureaucratic procedures. The beggars live in increasing fear for their lives under a regime of constant police harassment and gradually will not go out in daylight, a situation which underlines their alienation from human society.

> Sur les visages d'épaves, la peur et la mélancolie ont appliqué un masque de terreur. Las d'être traqués, las de courir. Depuis quelques temps, ils ne sortent plus en plein jour...Ils sont désespérés, terrorisés;...[52]

The beggars do not understand the alteration in their relationship with the authorities which had previously tolerated their presence and are forced for the first time to call their role into question and define their position in society.

> Ils se sont toujours considérés comme des citoyens à part entière, qui excercent un métier comme tout un autre, et à ce titre ils n'ont jamais cherché à définir d'une manière particulière les liens qui les unissent à la société. Pour eux le contrat qui lie chaue individu à la société se résume en ceci: donner et recevoir. Eh bien, eux, ne donnent-ils pas leurs bénédictions de pauvres, leurs prières et leurs voeux?[53]

However, the beggars have great deal of self respect and a strong community spirit which is encouraged by their oppression as they draw together against their common enemy, the anonymous 'authorities'.

The mysterious death of beggar Gorgui Diop following further police aggression proves to be a turning point in the beggars' attitude towards the way in which the authorities are treating them. Having lived in constant fear for their lives, the beggars finally decide to take a stance. They realise that 'l'heure du choix a sonné: mener une vie de chien, être poursuivi, traqué et matraqué ou vivre en homme'.[54] The only means of exerting power open to the beggars is to refuse to accept charitable offerings and they gradually become fully aware of the power they wield as the remainder of the population relies upon the beggars to bring them good fortune.

> Notre faim ne les dérange pas. Ils ont besoin de donner pour survivre, et si nous n'existions pas, à qui donneraient-ils ? Comment assureraient-ils leur tranquillité d'esprit ? Ce n'est pas pour nous qu'ils donnent c'est pour eux ! Ils ont besoin de nous pour vivre en paix ![55]

As in *Les bouts de bois de Dieu*, physical displacement proves to be an important element in the power structure. Following their persecution and eventual assumption of pride, the beggars retreat to the suburbs, forcing the bourgeois population to enter the poor areas and raising their consciousness of the situation of the urban poor. The beggars previously travelled to the inner urban landscape governed by the ruling elite. Now, the elite are forced to travel to the beggars in order to obtain favour.

Having successfully overseen the beggars' removal from the capital's streets, Mour N'Diaye is told by his religious guide, the *marabout*, that in order to guarantee his promotion to the vice-presidency, he should sacrifice a bull and distribute the meat amongst the beggars in the capital. Mour is forced to humiliate himself by pleading with the beggars to return to their former positions. At the novel's beginning, Mour's position of authority was reflected in the fact that he controlled the beggars' fate from the safety of an eighth floor office, a potent phallic symbol of masculine neo-colonial authority. Mour's increasing desperation as the novel progresses and the evident determination of the beggars to refuse to cooperate with his scheme renders the Director ridiculous. Chasing through the town in search of beggars to whom he can distribute the meat, Mour loses any semblance of authority. In a powerful illustration of the inversion of the former power structure, Mour is now forced to travel to the beggars to plead for their aid. The bourgeois population, represented by Mour N'Diaye, find the experience fundamentally disconcerting as they have both literally and figuratively no reference points in this altered situation and are rendered powerless by the beggars' initiative, forced to leave the security of the mapped centre behind and enter the unmapped marginal districts.

> Dès qu'ils ont perdu de vue la route goudronnée. Mour a eu la sensation que la voiture s'égarait dans un désert qui semblait s'étendre a l'infini: paysage tristement nu, sans vie, fouetté par un vent d'une rare violence... Mour n'a jamais mis les pieds dans ces coins, il en connaissait seulement l'existence par des cartes géographiques où ils sont colorés en rouge.. Il est en train de découvrir d'autres réalités sans même s'en rendre compte...[56]

The unmapped border district outwith the city boundaries becomes the locus of an alternative discourse of power and authority. Mour is forced to accept that the power dynamic which has until this point guaranteed his superior position exists no longer. and the beggars are free to come to his aid or not as they choose as *'la force est de leur côté'*.

> Il y a des aberrations dures a avaler..ces gens que je n'aurais jamais côtoyés s'il n'y avait eu ce sacrifice..et qui sont peut-être les seuls, a travers la ville, a oser me recevoir avec si peu de considération..Mais aujourd'hui, c'est moi qui ai besoin d'eux...il va falloir tout supporter...[57]

When asked by one of the many *marabouts* he has consulted in his desperate bid for promotion : 'Vous vous êtes battus contre les mendiants...Qui a gagné ?' Mour is forced to concede that his is a hollow victory.[58] While he has succeeded in his mission of clearing the streets of the beggars, Mour has lost his dominant position in the power structure and his action has been in vain as the beggars deny him the promotion he desires.

Force lui est de constater que l'angoissante incertitude dans laquelle il vit depuis le verdict de Kif Bokoul montre bien que le rapport des forces s'est inversé...[I]l s'est convaincu qu'a partir de ce moment, tout son destin est entre les mains des mendiants.[59]

The verb 'to transgress' is fundamentally ambiguous in its definition: literally 'to step across' but also with powerful negative moral connotations of 'trespass'. Mae G. Henderson points out that:

> breaking down structures of resistance not only speaks to breaking the ramparts that bolster the systems of contain-ment, as Derrida insists : it also concerns the modifying of limits in order to transform the unknown or forbidden (metaphorical borderlands) into inhabitable, productive spaces for living and writing.[60]

More than any other characters we have examined, Aminata Sow Fall's beggars affirm the viability of the margins as a productive site of transgression. The novels of Sembène Ousmane and Aminata Sow Fall illustrate the changing face of the African urban environment as the racial segregation which governed the topology of the colonial city is replaced with a class division based on economic status following the departure of the colonial population. However, both authors seek to illustrate the inherent instability of the barriers which divide the urban environment as the native population is portrayed as trans-gressing the boundaries which have traditionally reinforced its subordination and marginalisation. Those living on the margins are increasingly seen to be asserting their right to be heard, claiming their place in the centre which they have previously been denied. As Robert Holton affirms :

> the legitimacy of social groups depends on their ability to articulate publicly a perspective, to assert with legitimacy their view of the world and their position in it.[61]

In *La Grève des battù*, Aminata Sow Fall presents an act of transgression which fundamentally challenges the authority of the dominant discourse, rejecting the binary opposition between centre and margin and constructing an alternative spatiality from which the marginalised of post-independence African society may speak.

University of Aberdeen

1   Graham Huggan, 'Decolonizing the Map : Post-Colonialism, Post-Structuralism and the Cartographic Connection' in *Past the Last Post : Theorizing Post-Colonialism and Post-Modernism*, ed. by Ian Adam and Helen Tiffin (London: Harvester Wheatsheaf, 1991), p.125.

2   Edward W. Said, 'Yeats and Decolonization', in Terry Eagleton, Frederic Jameson and Edward Said, *Nationalism, Colonialism and Literature* (Minneapolis: University of Minneapolis, 1990), pp. 69-95 (p.77).

3   ibid., pp. 78-79.

4   Fatima Mernissi, *Beyond the Veil : Male-Female Dynamics in Muslim Society* (London: Alsaqi Books, 1985) [First published 1975] , p.31.

5   For further treatment of the theme of prostitution in the Francophone African novel see, for example, V.Y. Mudimbe, *Le bel immonde* (Paris: Présence Africaine,1976), Calixthe Beyala, *C'est le soleil qui m'a brûlée* (Paris: Presses Pocket, 1987).

6   Sada Niang, 'An interview with Ousmane Sembène by Sada Niang: Toronto 1992', in *Ousmane Sembène: Dialogues with Critics and Writers*, ed. Samba Gadjigo, Ralph Faulkingham, Thomas Cassiere and Richard Sander (Amherst: University of Massachusetts Press, 1993), pp.87-112 (pp.99-100).

7   Alessandro Triulzi, 'African Cities, Historical Memory and Street Buzz' in *The Post-Colonial Question: Common Skies, Divided Horizons*, ed. Iain Chambers and Lidia Curti (London: Routledge, 1996), pp.78-91 (p.81).

8   Homi K. Bhahbha, 'The Postcolonial and the Postmodern' in *The Location of Culture* (London: Routledge, 1994), pp.171-197 (p.178).

9   ibid., p.178.

10   Robert Holton, *Jarring Witnesses: Modern Fiction and the Representation of History* (London: Harvester Wheatsheaf, 1994), p.174.

11   In his valuable study, *La Ville dans le Roman Africain* (Paris: L'Harmattan, 1981), Roger Chemain identifies three distinct areas within the quarter of the African city which can be defined as the 'colonial quarter' : a residential, administrative and commercial quarter. For the purposes of this study, I have chosen to focus on the residential quarter alone.

12   Peter C.W. Gutkind, *Urban Anthropology ; Perspectives on 'Third World'*

Urbanisation and Urbanism (Assen, The Netherlands: Van Gorcum & Comp B.V., 1974), p.19.

13   Frantz Fanon, *Les damnés de la terre* (Paris: Gallimard, 1991) [First published 1961], p.69.

14   ibid., pp.69-70.

15   Gail Ching-Liang Low, *White Skins/Black Masks : Representation and Colonialism* (London: Routledge, 1996), p.163.

16   ibid., pp.69-70.

17   ibid., p.158.

18   Graham Huggan, op.cit., p.128.

19   Jacques Derrida, 'Structure, sign and play in the discourse of human sciences' in *Modern Criticism and Theory : A Reader*, ed. by David Lodge (Essex: Longman, 1993)[First published 1988], pp.107-123.

20   Ousmane Sembène, *Les bouts de bois de Dieu* (Paris: Presses Pocket, 1991) [First published 1960], pp.35-36.

21   ibid., p.252.

22   ibid., p.252.

23   ibid., p.250.

24   Roger Chemain, *La Ville dans le Roman Africain* (Paris: L'Harmattan, 1982), p.88.

25   Martin Bestman, *Sembène Ousmane et l'Esthétique du Roman Négro-Africaine* (Quebec: Editions Naaman Sherbrooke, 1981), p.294.

26   *Les bouts de bois de Dieu*, p.291.

27   ibid., p.371.

28   ibid., p.317.

29   Frederick Ivor Case, 'Aesthetics, Ideology and social Commitment in the Prose Fiction of Ousmane Sembène', in *Ousmane Sembène: Dialogues with Critics and Writers*, ed. by Samba Gadjigo, Ralph Faulkingham, Thomas Cassiere and Richard Sander (Amherst: University of Massachusetts Press, 1993), pp.3-13 (p.7).

30   ibid., p.8.

31   Peter C.W. Gutkind, op.cit., p.19.

32   ibid., pp.37-8.

33   Martin Lemotieu, 'Interférence de la religion musulmane sur les struc-
      tures actuelles de la société négro-africaine : l'exemple de la *Grève des
      Battù* d'Aminata Sow-Fall', in *Nouvelles du Sud* 1986-1987, VI, 49-60
      (p.57).

34   Gail Ching-Liang Low, op.cit., p.163.

35   ibid., p.165.

36   Sembène Ousmane, *Xala* (Paris: Presence Africaine, 1973), p.44.

37   ibid., pp.54-55.

38   ibid., p.179.

39   ibid., p.179.

40   Frantz Fanon, op.cit., p.70.

41   *Xala*, p.181.

42 . ibid., p.185.

43   ibid., p.190.

44   Jonathon Dollimore, *Sexual Dissidence : Augustine to Wilde, Freud to
      Foucault* (Oxford: Clarendon Press, 1991), pp.90-91.

45   ibid., p.65.

46   Christian Coulon and Donal B. Cruise O'Brien, 'Senegal', in
      Contemporary West African States, ed. by Donal B. Cruise O'Brien,
      Jonathon Dunn and Richard Rathbone (Cambridge: Cambridge
      University Press, 1989), pp.145-164 (p.152).

47   ibid., p.152.

48   Aminata Sow Fall, *La Grève des battù* (Dakar: Les Nouvelles Editions
      Africaines, 1979), p.83.

49   ibid., p.84.

50   ibid., p.6.

51   ibid., p.7.

52   ibid., pp.50-51.

53   ibid., p.30.

54   ibid., p.53.

55   ibid., p.53.

56   ibid., p.105.

57   ibid., p.121.

58   ibid., p.88

59   ibid., pp.88-89.

60   *Boundaries, Borders and Frames : Cultural Criticism and Cultural Studies*,
      ed. by Mae G. Henderson (London: Routledge, 1995), p.2.

61   Robert Holton, op.cit., p.167.

Transgression and the Exploration of the Writing Self in the Novels of Eugène Savitzkaya

Patrick Crowley

This essay sets out to look at the texts of the contemporary Belgian writer, Eugène Savitzkaya, and will argue that they can be read as explorations of self-identity.[1] The exploration in question is manifested, in particular, by the transgression of generic and narrative conventions. The underlying assumptions of my argument are informed by two antagonistic approaches. The hermeneutics of Paul Ricœur offer the notion that narrative is a mediator of self-identity. For Ricœur the self cannot come to know itself directly but only through the mediation of language. Ricœur, however, does not see the self as being constituted by and in language but, more fundamentally, by its prelinguistic experience as a being-in-the-world. This appropriation of the Heideggerian concept of *Dasein* is used by Ricœur to support his presupposition that experience precedes language. Language, for Ricœur, is simply a means of expression: a mediator. In the light of this philosophical position each text is a referential testament. Each text refers not only to itself but to a world beyond it and beyond texts. Each text has an ontological import. There is something attractive in this idea given the autobiographical content of Savitzkaya's writing. In this respect, it could be said that Savitzkaya's texts are fractured, poetic, configurations of what Ricœur would call the *pre*narrative symbolic order of experience. Savitzkaya's texts suggest that the subterranean theme is that of seeking to understand that site of language and body, the self.

Many would disagree with Ricœur's premises. The word 'self' comes laden with the philosophical baggage of presence, autonomy and essence. To talk of the self is to reassuringly suggest stability and ultimate truth. This idea has been rigorously contested over the past thirty years. Linguistics, structuralist anthropology and psychoanalysis argue that the self is constituted within and by a system of signs. The term 'self' has lost favour and has been usurped by the word 'subject'. Derrida writes that:

> Le sujet de l'écriture n'existe pas si l'on entend par là quelque solitude souveraine de l'écrivain. Le sujet de l'écriture est un système de rapports entre les couches : du bloc magique, du psychique, de la société, du monde. A l'intérieure de cette scène, la simplicité ponctuelle du sujet classique est introuvable.[2]

The subject is viewed as an 'effet de discours', an intertext characterised by heterogeneity and rupture. The most problematic signifier of the subject is the first person pronoun. The *je* of literary texts has become foregrounded yet its referential function is considered an illusion or even a delusion. Louis A. Renza writes:

> For some years now, the first person pronoun has been in disarray as a transparent signifier of an authorial signified. Instead of referring to the writing self, the "I" (a word authorising and authenticating the discourse of fictional as well as autobiographical narrative self-references) places this self 'under erasure' as a rhetorico-linguistic shifter, figure or trope. Struck down by this smallest of pronouns, self-reference thus becomes another illusion of self-presence: of the writer's or even narrative persona's autonomous self-identity.[3]

The self is both process and product and its textual representation an illusion. The textual *je* is other.

Yet to overemphasise this would be to the neglect of the self's capacity to produce. There is a link between the *je* and the writer. There is a 'who'. This 'who' may be a particular effect of institutions and language but it can be keenly aware of its status as effect, its own heterogeneity and the absence of self-transparency. At times, it is the who of the act of writing which is seeking to understand, however obliquely, its particular constitution through the mediation of language. In order to pursue this idea I would like to examine the nature and function of transgression in Savitzkaya's texts at the level of genre, theme and language.

Each of Savitzkaya's texts under consideration in this paper is marketed and published as '*un roman* '. However, such a generic category cannot be reduced to a simple descriptive judgement. As Schaeffer has argued, there is an expectation that the specificity of the genre partakes in the generation of the text and facilitates the act of interpretation.[4] Savitzkaya disrupts this presumed generative relationship between genre and text. In an interview in which he talks about his first novel, *Mentir*, Savitzkaya remarks ' J'ai appelé ce livre *Mentir* parce que cette forme [*that of the novel*] était immédiatement un mensonge. Vouloir dire le vrai est illusoire'.[5] Though aware of the illusion of enunciating truth, Savitzkaya's texts also suggest a desire to engage the illusion. This illusion is flagged by Savitzkaya when, on occasion, he uses the paratext of his novels to play with the reader's expectations. The *prière d'insérer* of his second novel, *Un jeune homme trop gros*, declares that:

> Ce roman est la biographie exemplaire d'une célèbre vedette de la chanson, qui n'y sera jamais nommée. Certes, l'ouvrage est dédié à la mémoire d'Elvis Presley, mais l'auteur ne repecte guère les lois du genre. Il transforme certains épisodes réels, il ajoute des détails inexistants et saugrenues, il affabule, il ment.

Biography's reference is to what has happened, to what is true. It is bound by the restraint of archive and event. It is, however, lying, the hallmark of the novel, that is acknowledged by Savitzkaya in the *prière d'insérer* above. By admitting the lie of fiction into the biographical enterprise he transgresses the boundary between both suggesting perhaps that a truth is best serviced by both the trace of the past and the possible worlds of fiction. However, if the pact between reader and writer is based on a lie, (the premise of fiction), the introduction of the non-lie (the aspiration, if not the premise of biography and autobiography) draws the founding premises of fiction, biography and auto- biography into a zone of proximity and mutual contamination.

Un jeune homme trop gros includes verifiable facts about Elvis's life which are shifted into a new setting. We are given the year of his birth, details of his life such as the death of his twin brother, his job as a truck driver, his stage performances, his mansion in Memphis. But other details are distorted, fabricated. Colonel Parker is referred to as 'le Colonel, son père', Elvis's mansion 'Graceland' becomes 'La Maison de la Grâce'. Surreal episodes, such as a train journey through China in search of a Diva, pepper the text. And though the text is declared to be both a novel and a biography, it also contains hints that it is a covert operation to explore Savitzkaya's own childhood. When the dark-haired youth is abruptly described as having 'les cheveux blonds'(p.16) and exhibits the same preoccupation with the mother as the previous text, *Mentir*, the suspicion that the text is a palimpsest begins to find support. It is also worth noting, just to thicken the plot, that the text is written in a parody of a medieval hagiography – a genre never too fussy about factual accuracy and nearly always a reading of the past as a fore- shadowing of the present.

Savitzkaya's sixth novel, *Sang de Chien*, appears to be the most openly autobiographical of the texts he had written until then. Yet the *prière d'insérer* tells the reader that what is about to be read is neither a diary nor a biography. It ends with the following: 'Mais *Sang de Chien* n'est ni un manuel didactique, ni un recueil de psaumes, encore moins une biographie de l'auteur. *Sang de Chien* n'est qu'un roman, dont l'usage, c'est bien connu, reste à découvrir'. It is interesting to note that within a *prière d'insérer* of five sentences there are two disclaimers to biographical intention. This renouncement of an autobiographical subtext serves to strengthen the desire to find one. Savitzkaya seems to transgress the parameters of genre in order to create a tension in the reading process. His texts might also be interpreted as a sign of the writer's delight in the perverse pleasure of playing with a reader's expectations. In this respect, his use of transgression may also be a device to better exercise the licence of writing.

I would suggest that Savitzkaya both acknowledges the referential hankering of the act of writing but refuses the static entrapment of representation. His novels are autobiographical, biographical and quite obviously fictional. They slip from one genre into another and in doing so transgress an implied reader's expectations of generic norms. Such a reader is forced to become involved in the act of producing meaning and to experiment in what Guy Davenport has called narrative's interest in the 'functional liberty of the lie'.[6] By transgressing the boundaries of genre the generative process has been transferred from genre to reader.

Writing autobiographically in the third person about the genesis of his first novel *Mentir* (1977) he notes '. Se rappelle qu'il a une mère. Écrit *Mentir* comme s'il venait de découvrir l'alphabet'.[7] The theme of the absent yet present mother and the theme of childhood, his own and more recently his son's, are constant in Savitzkaya's texts. Of his childhood, Savitzkaya has said: 'si je pense à ce qu'était mon enfance, j'ai des souvenirs de pourriture, d'immobilité. La plupart des souvenirs qui me restent ne sont pas agréables, pourtant je sentais que j'avais une grande force, que j'existais très fort'.[8] Of writing and childhood Savitzkaya has written: 'mon enfance perdue est mon seul avenir, mon seul but véritable et cohérent'.[9] Of childhood in general Savitzkaya has said that it is 'un monde extrordinaire' and that the child is 'habité par une ferveur, une énergie à l'état pur'.[10] Savitzkaya's texts seem to articulate this thirst for energy and force, to recreate a state of childhood possibility in order to re-experience its flux between being and becoming, its tension between *immobilité* and *ferveur*, and its promise of transformation. The motif of this desire to recreate and to transform is metamorphosis. It is a motif which gives expression to the possibility of change and it also acts as an agent and product of transgression.

In *Mentir* the metamorphosis of the mother is a recurring motif yet the transformation never achieves a completed or definable state: 'Comment après de longues métamorphoses, le visage se changea en faciès de mammifère, de loup ou de chien. La façon dont la jeune femme est léchée, mais pas mordue' (p.63). Here, whilst the use of the past historic is towards a specific moment in time the drift of the 'longues métamorphoses' is towards the imperfect tense. There is a sense that each time a transformation takes place it is as if for the first time, even if subsequently repeated. The confusion of the moment is reflected in the uncertain nature of the metamorphosis. The text returns constantly to this motif, the young woman, the mother, appears to change into a panther, a wolf, a large dog and yet even this is unclear for she is herself licked by the beast. The mother, then, is evoked yet never anchored to the specifics of appearance or personality, traditionally associated with the construction of a literary character.

The young singer in *Un jeune homme trop gros* undergoes a metamorphosis on stage which returns him to a primordial state, making him '*infatigable*'. The transformation involves such force and energy that impulses are expressed which are normally repressed or inhibited as a result of socialisation :

> Il rampera vers le public, le visage tordu, murmurant des paroles de haine. Il demandera qu'on l'aime. Il criera comme un chien de chasse. Il crachera des mots obscènes et la foule tremblera de plaisir. Il invitera à danser et à faire l'amour. Chaussé de blanc et vêtus de noir, confondu dans la pénombre. (...) Il cassera la baraque. Le théâtre tremblera et sera incendié le même jour (p.59).

Metamorphosis gives thematic expression to transgression. It is an unleashing of energies and violence and a confusion of form as the narrated subject becomes 'confondu dans la pénombre'. The identity of the narrated subject is even more ellusive in *La*

Disparition de Maman. This text teems with proper names never to be developed as characters and the *je*, though ubiquitous, is foregrounded as a linguistic shifter rather than as a referential index. It is in this text, too, that transgression becomes more directly thematised. The word *'interdiction'* makes sudden and repeated intrusions into the text: ' Malgré l'interdiction, il entra dans l'armoire' [...] 'Il avait rangé ses poupées'(p.57), [...] 'il fut découvert et sévèrement chatié'(p.58). The phrase 'malgré l'interdiction' occurs again on page 99 and later we read: 'Malgré l'interdiction, elle ouvrit la targette et entra dans l'armoire infestée. Mais elle fut découverte et sévèrement châtiée. Maintenant, elle est morte et pétrifieé'(p.102). The trope is iterated on page 114:

> Malgré l'interdiction et la puissance du feu, elle se rasait la tête et se peignait les lèvres. Sous la glace de ses ongles défilaient les petits nuages blancs. Ses défauts remontaient à la surface, ses minuscules fautes. Découverte, elle fut sévèrement châtiée.

On page 126 of *La Disparition de Maman* the phrase 'Malgré l'interdiction' is repeated three times. The point being delineated here is that transgressive behaviour is portrayed, on the surface of the text, as dangerous, something to be punished, yet transgression, as a trope, appears to be validated as part of a process of exploring different aspects of a self or even selves; the boy plays with the dolls in the wardrobe, the girl experiments with a different appearance. The text, however does little to provide a reassuring conclusion to the question of identity:

> Qui ouvrit la porte ? Qui précipita la fin ? Qui délivra les porcs malgré l'interdiction ? Qui fut méchant et désobéissant, fourbe et un peu veule, sale, morveux et puant ? Qui boucha les tuyaux? Qui détraqua la machine ? Qui brisa les carreaux, tous les carreaux de la villa sur le mont, sur la montagne qui bouge ? Qui trahit, déchira, déterra ? [...] Et qui, puni, prêt

à être dévoré, s'échappa à la faveur de la nuit ? Moi, toujours
moi (pp.140-141).

The text of *La Disparition de Maman* ends on the following page
with ' Qui blanchit le toit et le muret ? Qui, sale et fourbe, plus
sale et plus fourbe chaque jour? Moi Moi Moi ' (p.142). There is
an interweaving between the transgression of the interdiction
and the questioning of the subject's identity. There is, in much
of Savitzkaya's writing, an interplay between the operant of
transgression and an active engagement with the search for an
identity and the play of identities.

This interplay becomes frenetic in *Les morts sentent bon*. This
text is, in broad terms, organised around the figure of Gestroi,
the King's young envoy who is sent in search of a *'lieu paisible'*,
a place of rest for the king. The journey undertaken by Gestroi
takes him across a wordscape which refers to the Vogols of
Siberia, the calligraphy of the Chinese, the cities of Hamburg
and Liège. It is a voyage of initiation but without outcome; the rite
of passage from the imagined biological state to the constructed
social being is never completed. The transgressions which take
place do not serve the function of leading to social integration
but multiply and abound to a point where disintegration seems
to be the end. Gestroi is reported to eat children; we are told
that some say he eats little girls with wild thyme and marjoram.
He sells his sperm to pigs. He has sexual intercourse with a ewe
who gives birth to a lamb. The ram awakens, rapes Gestroi who
immediately gives birth to a kid goat. There is an account of an
orgy and the incestuous advances of a boy in the text result in
violent punishment: ' le violent poison lui tordit brutalement
les vertèbres et le sang bouleversé fit éclater les veinules de ses
trempes [...] On le dépouilla pour le brûler'(p.29).

Gender definition is transgressed. Gestroi gives birth and
there are several references to androgyny in the text. We read
that 'La morte fut repêchée à l'aide de gaffes [...] elle fut deposée

271

et, sous ses vêtements, les fossoyeurs qui la caressaient reconnurent son corps de garçon' (p.89). Later we read 'De la fille qu'il était, l'enfant deviendra garçon (p.119)'.

The theme of androgyny has an ancient pedigree and gives voice to a longing for the erasure of differences, a reconciliation of opposites and a nostalgia for a return to an utopian state of being which preceded the split consciousness of dualism. It expresses a yearning for the wholeness of self. Jean Labis links the myth to others and concludes that 'l'androgynat, l'inceste et la gémelité pourraient bien constituer des éléments réversibles d'une même mythogène' and adds that 'Chacun de ces termes, d'une certaine manière, transgresse un ordre, s'oppose à ce qui est donné, s'érige en fantasmagorie. Chacun d'eux abolit une distance et gomme, dans une certaine mesure, une dualité. Chacun d'eux restitue une intimité perdue'.[11] This notion of a search for wholeness, fusion, or a *regressus ad uterum* is common to Savitzkaya's texts. However, equal stress is given to fusion's apparent polar opposite namely that of things coming apart, of things incomplete. In this way a dynamic is created between two mythical states; the primordial, formless state of chaos and the illusion of the finality of form. The *prière d'insérer* of *Les morts sentent bon*, like a medieval gloss, tells the reader that in Lublin Gestroi almost becomes a girl. The word 'almost' is significant for it signals that the process of transformation never reaches a state of completion. At every turn in Savitzkaya's texts the nostalgia for wholeness is rigorously countered.

The countering of fixity and wholeness is evident in Savitzkaya's use of language. Savitzkaya's first text, *Mentir*, was, he has said, triggered by the memory of his mother and a professed rediscovery of the alphabet. Such a declaration draws our attention to a perceived inaugural moment where memory and the desire to write converged. The texts which followed are difficult to describe. They place before the reader language brought to the fore and freed from the binds of the habitual and the constraints of function which have jaded its force. The word *scriptible* comes to mind. Savitzkaya's texts radically foreground language. The delineation and construction of character is schematic. Narrative is undermined. In *La Disparition de Maman* plot is replaced by a spaghetti junction of intrigues. Syntax is denied its prescriptive authority. The texts are fragmented and disjointed.

The transgression of genre also operates at the level of language. The effect is similar; the structure of the texts is such that convention is flouted and it is the process of producing a text and a meaning which is inscribed.

In *Mentir* memories and photographs of the mother are translated from images to words. They are modified, iterated and compose a text of fragments linked by the sound track of white silence, the generous empty spaces between the paragraphs. The text does not represent the mother within the frame of standard characterisation but mobilises a circular movement between the outline of presence and absence. The repetition of sentences recalling the mother creates a process of textual stratification; her absence is given a textual density. This simulacrum of presence is in turn undermined by confronting the reader with gaps in information, linear disruption and empty space. As a consequence, it is the interstice between text and emptiness which becomes the site of meaning. It is here that presence and absence overlap and confront a reader grappling to produce a sense of the mother despite the uncertainty of a narrative which foregrounds the problematics of recall, writing and interpretation.

> Elle souriait. Elle marchait vite vers sa maison. Mais j'exagère. Elle ne souriait peut-être pas, ou alors à peine et son pas paraissait plutôt lent. Et ce n'était pas ma mère débarquée dans cette gare, sortie de ce train en pleine journée (p.41).

By introducing irreconcilably differing accounts into a single recollection of the mother, Savitzkaya keeps the image free from a limiting definition but unsettles the reader's trust in the narrative.

At times it is narrative itself which is disrupted as the stress patterns and associative logic of poetry converge to shape the text. Here is an example from *La Disparition de Maman* :

> Le petit garçon voit le ciel: un monstre rose y menace les arbres. Arrive du bout du jardin, secouant sa lourde tête, éternuant, étincelant, maigre, un cheval d'une très grande blancheur qui détruit les barrières et va se percher sur le petit toit de la cabane à lapins; les rongeurs s'en échappent et tondent la prairie.
> Beaucoup de menthe dans la salade, et du blé.
> Un beau vélocipède rouge contre le sorbier.
> Nous sommes en Juillet 1933. Il faut songer à entrer sous terre. Où est ma petite sœur? (p.34).

In this example narrative sequentiality is replaced by a disjointed poetic passage.

Further rupturing takes the form of doing violence to syntax. The disruption of the ordering function of syntax in the earlier texts articulates, I would argue, a desire to escape the repression of syntax's prescriptive imperative in order to celebrate language in a less restricted state. One upshot of this is that the poetic structure of the text recreates those two experiences characteristic of his childhood *immobilité* and *ferveur*. There is an example of this conflict of states, articulated by transgressing syntax, in *Les morts sentent bon*:

> Dans les hauts arbres, les hommes de la forêt, les barques, les drapeaux aux pointes déchiquetées, les archers tendus, les balcons aux draps agités, les terribles chuchotements, l'air (p.49).

Here the combination of nouns and adjectives such as 'archers tendus' suggest incipient movement restrained by the absence of a verb and hushed by the final word which seems to envelope the sentence. The words, unharnessed from the verb, create a static, pictorial sensation. The immobility, the impediment to follow the forward momentum of narrative, leads to its opposite, creates out of ocular suspension the impulse to move. Here, as in all of Savitzkaya's writings, text and theme resonate. In so doing they become part of the underlying ontological enterprise to explore a sense of a self immersed in language and subverted by language.

In *La Disparition de Maman* this enterprise is thrown into apparent disarray by the use of contradiction and oxymoron in respect of an named yet unknowable subject:

> Pierre est semblable à la fourmi, au ver, au canrelat, à la mangouste, car il est semblable au bois, à l'eau, à la pierre; il est dur et vide; il est plat et dur; il est liquide et froid; il est froid et sec; il est transparent; il est invisble; il est déjà pourri; il est déjà mort, ayant déjà craché le salive sur le feu et rendue le sel à la mer (p.35).

This is metamorphosis pushed to a paroxysm of transformation. It puts pressure on the buttresses of form by connoting the proper noun with the use of contradictory adjectives and the appearance of animals with the result that 'Pierre' is stripped of human specificity and becomes a rhetorical figuration for the theme of transformation. The subject is dispersed by the text and becomes a function of language; at once liberated and imprisoned.

> J'étais la porteuse d'eau, marchant sur les feuilles, sur la tourbe poreuse, m'approchant des viviers, tremblant au soleil, pieds nus et ongles en deuil, la fille de Czarek, la femme d'Evorian, de l'ogre de la forêt, l'enfant du planteur du café, du cultivateur, la cousine d'Evoé, l'amie de Pierre noire, de Pierre perdue, de Pierre percée, l'ennemie de François l'enterré, l'ourse du Poisson somnolent, la belette et la souris d'Eloé, la louve de Simon le tari, la chatte éspiègle de Dominique, le cheval cabré contre l'arbre ou le mur, la laitière, la feuille du robinier, de Robur centenaire, la flamme

du feu, la courroie du Fusil, la carabine du Tueur de buffles, l'amande de l'Amandier, l'eau du Ruisseau, la maman du Bébé (p.82).

The list goes on and the tension builds up putting pressure on meaning and syntax. Here, once more, *la ferveur* is stoked up within the core of *immobilité*. The list of nouns linked to that single verb translates a sense of things concrete and static and the forward flow of the narrative is momentarily immobilised as the text before us resists an easy reading. However, the accumulated pressure of so many referents attributed to a paradoxically unidentifiable and unidentified *je* is, however, so great that it has the effect of dispersing and multiplyng the subject to the point where it is either everything or a chaotic constellation of referents from which each reader must discern a design. A difficult task for Savitzkaya's texts resist form whether it be generic or syntactic. The obfuscation of genre and the transgression of conventional syntax are, I would argue, the supra- and infra-manifestations of an ontological enterprise which is aided, abetted and mischievously undermined by the text. And yet, innocent as it may seem to suggest, there is a writer behind these texts. Savitzkaya is the linker and unlinker of words.

Starting with *Sang de Chien* Savitzkaya's later texts appear to be overtly autobiographical. They feature a narrator who narrates his relationship with his parents in *Sang de chien*, his new born son in *Marin mon cœur*, and the ordinariness of living in a house with his family in *En Vie*. These autobiographical novels feature the names of Savitzkaya's children and partner, *En Vie* gives the address where the writer lives. The mood is one of reconciliation. Creation and chaos seem to be harmonised or reconciled:

> Le monde de Marin est constitué de particules infines. A chaque second il peut le réorganiser à sa guise. La place de chaque particule n'a aucune importance, car rien n'a de place ni de forme définitive sur la terre. Il ne bâtit que jusqu'au moment ou il détruit (...) Une belle construction est une

construction dont on aura autant de plaisir à défaire les
éléments qu'on en a eu à les assembler. Un beau désordre
vaut mieux qu'une inerte ordonnance (p.71).

Marin mon cœur can be read as a reflection on the theme of
childhood from the perspective of the father but also as a reflection
on the act of writing from the perspective of writer and first
reader. Savitzkaya's text, *En Vie,* exhibits an increasingly stoical
attitude towards the otherness of the body and its transitory
form: 'Peu à peu, au fil de la journée, s'accentue le caractère
disparate de mon corps. Des morceaux menacent de
tomber'(p.16). Later, in the same text, we read that ' le bain du
soir est à la fois une réconciliation avec les éléments disparates
qui nous forment et une consolation puérile, mais combien
douce, des pertes et des désastres du jour. Demain sera lundi'
(p.19). Though there is a mood of reconciliation it is not a forced
fusion of opposites but an attitude, a way of coming to terms
with the facticity of existence and the ineluctability of change:
'Chacun ne devrait jamais ignorer qu'il se trouve au milieu du
mouvement général'(p.104).

But these pointers to reconciliation and identification are
falsely lulling. The *je*, though orbited by apparently identifiably
autobiographical referents, remains as opaque as ever. The *je*
remains an emblem. Robert Smith writes that autobiographical
literary theory has traditionally focused on the subject of writing
becoming the object of writing. However, he writes that 'when
the relation of object to subject is deranged and reordered, when
there ceases to be an object (me) to be interiorised (by me), a
different kind of connection is opened up'.[12] The undermining
of self-presence requires a reworking of its traces within
language. Savitzkaya alerts the reader to the confusion The
subject consumes the object and is consumed by it. Savitzkaya
alerts the reader to this confusion of subject and object. In *En Vie*
he writes that, when eating, there is ' un moment d'intense
fusion dans le mélange des levures et des sédiments que l'on
mange. On ne sait plus si on mange ou on est mangé' (p.66).

The radical dispersal of the subject in *La Disparition de Maman* finds a soft echo in the *je* of *En Vie* which is portrayed as having moments of transitory fusion or dissolution: 'Il y a quelque utilité à plonger le bras, puis le corps entier, dans l'eau trouble d'une rivière [...] On ne peut vivre que dans la clarté. Il n'est pas mauvais de parfois disparaître, de tenter de se dissoudre dans l'opacité, d'être dissous'(p.117). To link such sensory epiphanies with the writer would be to commit the sin of intentional fallacy. But, like some sins, it is attractive. What is clear, however, is that the subject is not self-contained but remains open within the text.

But if all is movement and dissolution transgression is deprived of the rules that define it. In a world where fluidity has a greater purchase on our sense of reality than form, need one worry about an answer to the question of self? Read chronologically, these texts allow at least this reader to trace an evolution in the outcome of transgression. The transgression of generic and narrative expectations in the early texts serves to problematise the narrative enterprise and articulate a pained return to the affective state of childhood. The frenzy of taboo transgression in *Les morts sentent bon* foregrounds the thematic qualities of transgression and brings violence and manic disruption to a text which drives towards creating a sense of the writing subject and strives to evade the strait-jacket of formal identity. *Marin mon cœur* and *En Vie* offer a gentler, more playful, mood, yet continue to transgress by resisting the orthodoxies of form. These texts draw together fiction, philosophical reflection and the observance of the everydayness of living to a point where one is informed by the other. Transgression, then, is a tool of refiguration. It counteracts the deadening process of solidification.

Transgression is also an agent of understanding. Savitzkaya's texts read like explorations of the teasing illusion of identity whilst affirming the specificity of the act of writing. Who is it that writes the text? Who is it that strives to recreate the unending movement between form and formlessness? There is the pitfall of intentional fallacy, the danger of domesticating the text, and every chance of being duped by the writer. The signifiers of Savitzkaya's texts relate more, perhaps, to themselves than to the presumed signified of the self. Nevertheless, I would hold to the argument that each of Savitzkaya's texts experiments in transgression in order to refigure an experience of living and writing. I would happily express the opinion that each act of trangression, whether it be generic, textual or thematic, articulates a perspective on a process of becoming and that it is through the mediation of the text that the writer gathers some understanding of a self immersed in language.

Royal Holloway, University of London

1   Eugène Savitzkaya was born in Liège, Belgium in 1955. His father was Polish and his mother Russian. 1972 saw the publication of his first collection of poems *Les lieux de la douleur.* His first novel entitled *Mentir* was published in 1977 by Minuit. Since then Minuit has published all seven of his novels: *Un jeune homme trop gros* (1978), *La Traversée de l'Afrique* (1979), *La Disparition de Maman* (1982), *Les morts sentent bon* (1983), *Sang de chien* (1989), *Marin mon cœur* (1992) and *En vie* (1994). All references to Savitzkaya's novels are to the editions specified above and are referred to hereinafter with page numbers in the text.

2   Jacques Derrida, 'Freud et la scène de l'écriture', in *L'écriture et la différence*, (Paris: Éditions du Seuil, collection Points, 1967), p.335.

3   Louis A. Renza, Book Review, *Comparative Literature*, 39 (1987), 172-176, pp.172-173.

4   Jean-Marie Schaeffer, 'Literary Genres', in *The Future of Literary Theory*, ed. by R. Cohen (London: Routledge, 1989), p.168.

5   Antoine de Gaudemar, 'Le jardin d'Eugène', *Libération*, 2 April 1992, p.20.

6   Guy Davenport, *The Geography of the Imagination* (London: Picador, 1984), p.308.

7   Eugène Savitzkaya, 'Éléments Biographiques' in *Mongolie, plaine Sale, L'Empire, Rue Obscure*, (Bruxelles: Éditions Labor, 1993), pp.196-198 (p.197).

8   Hervé Guibert, 'Entretien avec Eugène Savitzkaya', *Minuit*, 49 (1982), 5-11 (p.10).

9   Eugène Savitzkaya, 'L'Écriture en spirale', in *Revue Estuaire*, 20 (1981), 103-104 (p.103).

10   Antoine de Gaudemar, op.cit., p.21.

11   Marie Miguet, 'Androgynes', in *Dictionnaire des Mythes Littéraires*, ed. by P. Brunel (Paris: Éditions du Rocher, 1988), pp.71-72.

12   Robert Smith, *Derrida and Autobiography* (Cambridge: Cambridge University Press, 1995), p.131.

Jacques Réda et le discrédit du cérémonial de la transgression

Fabienne Reymondet

'Transgresser, c'est passer une limite interdite' écrivait Roland Barthes, auteur d'une oeuvre toute entière traversée et travaillée par le thème de la transgression.[1] Il y aurait quelque mauvaise grâce à ne pas donner raison à Barthes tant il est clair que la notion de transgression est étroitement liée à celle d'interdit, à tout ce qui est réprouvé, discrédité, socialement et moralement mais aussi et surtout littérairement. Or, pour en venir au sujet plus particulier de cette étude, y a-t-il des interdits en poésie ? La question n'est au fond que rhétorique et la réponse est bien sûr affirmative. L'on pourrait même être tenté d'ajouter: en poésie plus qu'ailleurs sans doute, dans la mesure où la poésie est une forme extrêmement ritualisée et codifiée de la parole. Pourtant, il est vrai, la poésie française du XXème siècle, qui vit l'apparition du vers *libre*, qui fut le théâtre d'une 'révolution du langage poétique' sans précédent et sans pareil, pour reprendre les mots de Julia Kristeva, peut à bien des égards sembler s'être libérée d'un long assujettissement à des formes fixes, considérées comme archaïques et désuètes. En un mot, en violant un certain nombre de règles, et refusant implicitement un nombre au moins égal d'interdits, par de multiples transgressions libératrices, elle paraît s'être abrogée de toute contraintes. Devrait-on alors revenir sur l'assertion précédente et affirmer que la poésie française ne connaît plus d'interdits ? Rien n'est moins sûr. En fait, plus qu'une disparition des interdits, sans doute faut-il conclure à un déplacement. Et peut-être les interdits ne sont-ils que plus forts de s'être transportés et de s'être greffés sur certaines pratiques et procédés.

Autant que de tenter de les déterminer, l'objet de cette étude est de souligner, à travers l'exemple de la poésie de Jacques Réda, laquelle va à l'encontre de ces interdits, une pratique de transgression des dogmes implicites de la modernité poétique.

Mais parce que celle-ci n'est ni éclatante ni revendiquée, parce qu'elle ne se donne nullement sous un mode solennel ou inaugural, il s'agira aussi de mettre en évidence une mise à distance de la transgression dans ce qu'elle a de cérémonial.

Traversée et exploration des chemins de traverse

Tout d'abord, pour ne pas perdre de vue l'oeuvre et rentrer à brûle-pourpoint dans l'examen de pratiques purement textuelles, sans doute convient-il de s'attacher à la dimension transgressive que présente les parcours inlassables de Jacques Réda dans Paris et ses environs, parcours qui sont l'origine et le sujet de tant de ses proses et poèmes.

C'est en toute liberté buissonnière que se déploient les pérégrinations rédiennes dans l'espace urbain et en particulier suburbain. Empruntant ce mode archaïque de locomotion qu'est le vélo-solex, Réda déambule dans la ville, n'hésitant pas à emprunter les rues en sens interdit - petite transgression du code de la route - comme les chemins non carrossables qui s'offrent à la périphérie de la ville. En poète nuageux et vagabond, il se refuse aux itinéraires trop bien définis. Quand bien même il semble en adopter un, celui-ci soudainement s'infléchit, vers un talus, une berge désaffectée, un espace abandonné, un sentier en marge des chemins battus. Ses traversées sont ainsi le plus souvent exploration des chemins de traverses. En mode mineur, la traversée rédienne est ainsi une pratique transgressive, en ce qu'elle hante avec prédilection des lieux de la déshérence comme des espaces mis au ban de la ville. Parfois, certes, elle se donne explicitement comme une transgression, comme dans ce texte des *Ruines de Paris*:

Ainsi je prends tout à coup les sentiers que signale une pancarte jaune marquée de lettres au pochoir en noir un peu de traviole: DANGER TERRAIN MILITAIRE ACCÈS INTERDIT, car je me fous pareillement et plus de ces pancartes. [2]

S'il n'y a toutefois pas systématiquement de franchissement d'une limite ou de transgression d'un interdit, insidieusement elle y prépare. Le goût prononcé de Réda pour les déviations, les dérives de l'errance, qui, notons le au passage, se traduisent dans l'écriture par un recours immodéré aux procédés de la digression et de l'adjonction parenthétique, trahit en effet un attrait pour la douce *déviance*. Au niveau de la locomotion, nombre d'éléments illustrent cette inclination à s'écarter subrepticement de la norme, que ce soit le recours à un engin aussi archaïque que le solex ou le choix arbitraire de destinations qui lui donnent l'allure d'un original un brin farfelu.[3] Mais j'en voudrais aussi pour preuve l'emploi révélateur que Réda fait de cet accessoire qu'est le rétroviseur. Jouant des possibilités que lui offre ce miroir fiché sur son guidon, Réda détourne l'objet de sa fonction première pour permettre au paysage de se déployer, de l'encercler, de le ravir, lui donnant finalement 'le sentiment d'être un peu hors du monde'.[4] Une forme de franchissement se dessine ici, qui accrédite une lecture transgressive des pratiques erratiques du promeneur rédien.

Quand il arpente à pied la ville et ses faubourgs, une même logique régit les déambulations du poète. Dans l'optique qui est la nôtre, il semble à cet égard révélateur que Réda délaisse le centre de l'agglomération pour parcourir inlassablement ses limites extrêmes. Attiré par les espaces périphériques, il est également fasciné par ces symboles des limites que sont les grilles qui se dressent le long de ses promenades, les murs masquant des jardins ou les palissades recelant des terrains vagues. Toutes ces limites, Réda rêve de les franchir. S'il se contente la plupart du temps de contempler les espaces interdits à travers les barreaux des grilles ou à travers les trous des palissades, il lui arrive d'effectivement franchir ces obstacles dressés devant lui. Mais plus saisissant encore, et plus révélateur aussi, s'avère ce passage vers ce que Réda nomme 'l'autre côté des choses' ou 'l'envers du décor'. A de multiples reprises, face à des tableaux, des fresques aperçus au cours de ses promenades, Réda, absorbé dans la contemplation, s'imagine arpenter les contrées représentées.

'J'entre aisément dans les images, en flâneur'[5] souligne au demeurant Réda dans un des poèmes de la section intitulée 'Un monde peint' de *Beauté suburbaine*. Un bon exemple de cette traversée de l'espace qui se prolonge en une traversée de l'espace de la représentation est fourni dans *Châteaux des courants d'air*. Après avoir brièvement décrit la scène figurant sur un panneau de bois peint découvert dans le XIV° arrondissement, le texte transcrit la progression au sein du tableau sur le même mode que celui de la promenade elle-même:

> On avance avec légèreté sur l'herbe élastique de la prairie, attiré plus qu'on ne le voudrait par le son monotone et doux de la flûte. Bientôt voici la lisière de la forêt. C'est alors qu'il faut décider, et vite (car la lumière s'est épaissie comme la chair d'une reine-claude), si l'on continue tout droit devant soi, malgré le chien, dans cet univers immobile qui communique peut-être avec le coeur enchanté de l'arrondissement; ou si l'on préfère, une fois de plus, reprendre pied dans celui des métamorphoses ordinaires, un soir de septembre, à Paris. [6]

Polarisé par les limites, le parcours rédien n'est ainsi pas pure exploration de lisières, plus ou moins concrètes et saisissantes, mais une traversée au sens le plus riche du terme, un passage *dans et au travers*, en l'occurrence, de l'espace de la représentation. Reste toutefois que le passage demeure, dans cet exemple, nettement marqué et que la transgression est stigmatisée. Ce n'est pas toujours le cas. Il arrive qu'au cours d'une promenade, Réda se sente comme projeté de l'autre côté des choses, sans pour autant que des limites semblent atteintes ou du moins qu'elles soient indiquées. Ainsi en est-il dans le poème de *L'Herbe des talus* intitulé 'Dialogue de la petite gare'. Après avoir évoqué la traversée d'une paisible ville de province à la tombée de la nuit et l'arrivée à la gare, le poète, 's'éloign[e] distraitement' vers 'le revers de ce paysage inconnu'. Placé désormais comme de l'autre côté d'un miroir sans tain, il contemple la ville qu'il vient de parcourir, laquelle réapparaît sous des traits légèrement altérés mais indéniablement reconnaissables. Ainsi, l'évocation de la gare qui ouvrait le texte:

Souvenez-vous:

n'était-ce pas un petit bâtiment orné d'une frise de
céramique

dans des tons indécis comme le vert-bleu, le rose-jaune, le
mauve-gris,

avec des murs en brique et en fortes poutres métalliques

à boulons à tête ronde très doux,

le tout peint d'une nuance un peu terne d'ocre

devient:

> et tôt ou tard en suivant cette voie en courbe on arriverait
> devant une construction modeste égayée d'un motif de
> céramique
> aux nuances hésitant entre le vert-jaune, le rose-mauve ou le
> bleu-gris,
> avec un corps en brique sous un badigeon d'ocre pâle
> entre d'épais montants de fonte aux boulons ronds très doux [7]

L'ensemble du texte perpétue ce jeu entre ressemblances et
dissemblances. Le poème se présente alors comme une sorte de
diptyque juxtaposant deux visions similaires. A la vision première
succède une vision diffractée, sorte de 'double infidèle' pour
reprendre des mots de 'Tombeau de mon livre', dernier poème
du recueil. La traversée se fait traversée du sensible.

Sous le mode de la traversée, se fait jour dans l'imaginaire
rédien un rêve persistant de franchissement de limites, franchissement très clairement associé, comme la phrase de Roland
Barthes placée en ouverture de ce développement le rappelle, à
la transgression. L'ensemble de la démarche rédienne est au
demeurant polarisée par un mouvement d'échappée auquel le
rêve de franchissement est très étroitement associé. Les différents
recueils de Réda sont sous-tendus par ce mouvement de fuite
vers les banlieues. Ainsi la composition des *Ruines de Paris* met
très clairement en évidence ce mouvement centrifuge, puisque la
deuxième partie du recueil s'ouvre sur ces mots: 'Quand on sort

de Paris'. Mais cette échappée était déjà sensible à l'issue de la première partie de l'ouvrage qui se refermait sur la section intitulée, de manière fort significative, 'Aux environs' et qui conduisait le promeneur dans les périphéries de la ville. Empruntant le titre emblématique d'un des premiers recueils de poème de Jacques Réda, on pourrait donner à l'ensemble de l'oeuvre ce mot d'ordre: 'Hors les murs' ou encore, pour reprendre un autre titre, celui-là d'un ensemble de textes critiques, celui de: 'Affranchissons-nous'. Mais peut-être serait-ce là un peu forcer le trait et généraliser abusivement. Quoiqu'il en soit, transgressif, ce mouvement associant échappée et franchissement l'est indéniablement, Réda se présentant d'ailleurs bien souvent comme un 'bandit', un 'rôdeur'.[8]

Sous le mode de la subreptice déviance ou plus nettement de la marginalité et de la délinquance, les traversées rédiennes se rattachent ainsi, quoique obliquement, à la problématique de la transgression, qu'elles mettent en scène concrètement avant de l'inscrire au niveau textuel. La dimension transgressive des parcours rédiens peut en effet être mise en parallèle avec des pratiques d'écriture elles-mêmes transgressives.

Transgressions génériques et prosodiques

Tout d'abord, il faut souligner la très profonde hybridité des textes rédiens. Des ouvrages tels que *L'Herbe des talus*, *Recommandations aux promeneurs* ou *Le Sens de la marche* sont tout à la fois une suite de récits, des écrits d'essence autobiographique, des relations de voyage se commuant parfois en traité didactique sur l'art de la flânerie, et des proses émaillées de poèmes. Virtuose bric-à-brac poétique pourraient conclure certains. Mais c'est sans doute oublier un peu vite la composition très soignée qui régit ses ouvrages. Surtout, cette assertion est porteuse d'un jugement de valeur implicite, fondé sur des canons littéraires à la vérité très polémiques. Car si elle reconnaît le caractère inclassable des oeuvres rédiennes, elle discrédite son manque d'orthodoxie générique – perçu comme manque de rigueur, capharnaüm – sans mettre en évidence le jeu d'entrelacement des genres, travail d'alliance et de déviance génériques qui est l'un des grands intérêts de l'oeuvre. Pour l'illustrer, attardons-nous sur ces deux textes que sont *Aller aux mirabelles* et *Aller à Elisabethville,* véritable diptyque comme le souligne le parallélisme des titres. Tous deux furent publiés dans la collection 'L'un et l'autre' de Gallimard, collection qui tend à restaurer le biographique, tant discrédité dans le monde des lettres, sans prétendre à l'objectivité mais bien au contraire en valorisant le caractère subjectif de l'entreprise biographique.[9] Autant que biographique, l'entreprise est ainsi – obliquement – autobiographique.[10] Certes Réda ne choisit pas d'évoquer la vie d'un être admiré, auteur, musicien ou figure, mais des espaces. Les évoquant, il ne semble pas *a priori* faire autre chose que ce qu'il a coutume de relater dans ses proses ou poèmes. C'est omettre que le statut d'énonciation n'est plus le même et que ce n'est plus le poète mais un écrivain engagé dans une entreprise autobiographique oblique qui prend la plume. Proto-auto-biographies toutefois que ces deux ouvrages puisque, si l'espace est indéniablement autographe, *Aller aux mirabelles* se donne comme le récit d'un bref retour à la ville mythique de l'enfance et *Aller à Elisabethville* comme une parodie du récit d'enfance. Peu clairement biographiques, les deux oeuvres ne sont pas non plus nettement autobiographiques.[11] Une incertitude quant à la nature générique comme au statut des textes reste ménagée. L'oeuvre en prose de Jacques Réda se place ainsi, délibérément, au carrefour des genres. Le caractère transgressif de cette hybridité générique s'avère toutefois doux, ne compromettant en effet pas la lisibilité de l'oeuvre. Le brouillage générique n'affecte jamais chez Réda l'intelligibilité des écrits. Il ne sert pas un hermétisme du texte.

Le passage de la prose au poèmes, si important dans certaines oeuvres et notamment dans *L'Herbe des talus*, participent lui aussi de ce brouillage générique, encore qu'il faille ici être prudent dans la mesure où la prose peut se rattacher au genre poétique, la technique du vers n'étant nullement, en effet, un attribut de

la poésie. Si donc prose et poèmes alternent parfois sans pour
autant que l'on passe d'un genre à l'autre, on relève tout aussi
bien des juxtaposition de textes se rattachant aux genres
romanesque ou autobiographique et des strophes appartenant
indéniablement au genre poétique. J'en prendrai pour exemple
un extrait du 'District des Lacs' dans *Le Sens de la marche*. Après
avoir évoqué dans un poème son attente à la gare de
Windermere, Réda s'étend longuement dans un passage en
prose nullement poétique sur l'opposition véhémente de
Wordsworth contre l'installation du chemin de fer dans la région
des Lacs et à la fin de cet exposé biographique, Réda reprend:

En attendant la correspondance à Oxenholme, j'écrivis cet

Adieu

Et pour vous, ombres, qu'aurai-je été ? Moins qu'une
ombre
Parmi d'autres le long de la route, passant
Désinvolte parfois mais toujours ressassant
A part soi quelques vers dont l'accent et le nombre
Sont dans l'air maintenant d'impalpables décombres... [12]

Le changement de ton entre la phrase introductive banale et le
poème aux accents graves mais aussi l'emploi de rimes dans le
poème, tout stigmatise le passage d'un genre à l'autre. Parler de
transgression ici serait toutefois abusif. Un élément justifie cette
réticence. Il s'agit de l'inclusion du titre 'Adieu' dans la phrase
finale ('En attendant la correspondance à Oxenholme, j'écrivis
cet / Adieu'). Ce faisant, Réda assure une transition entre les
deux éléments profondément hétérogènes que sont ici proses et
poèmes, plus que ne ménage un contraste déroutant. Une fois
encore, l'effet transgressif est minoré.

La seule pratique *nettement* transgressive que présente alors
ce passage est de nature prosodique puisqu'au milieu des alexandrins
se glissent des vers auxquels sont rajoutés deux syllabes, comme

c'est par exemple le cas du vers liminaire. On peut regretter toutefois que l'exemple cité ici ne présente pas de ces vers spécifiquement rédiens que leur auteur nomme 'vers mâchés' qui doivent être lu sans tenir compte des *e* muets que le langage parlé élimine naturellement. En utilisant un mètre beaucoup plus long que la moyenne, puisque le vers mâché est un vers de quatorze syllabes, Réda rapproche le langage poétique de la parole ordinaire et le poème de la prose.[13] Ce faisant, il déstabilise, encore plus qu'il ne le fait dans l'exemple cité, les catégories prosodiques mais surtout génériques. Mais force est de reconnaître, que aussi transgressif que soit ce procédé particulier, il reste assez timide par rapport aux déconstructions du langage poétique dont l'oeuvre de Rimbaud, Mallarmé ou plus près de nous celle de Denis Roche fournissent de multiples et, convenons-en, nettement plus saisissants exemples.[14]

Avouons le, la transgression reste une caractéristique de l'oeuvre rédienne assez peu éclatante au premier abord. Pourtant l'oeuvre est très profondément transgressive. Mais jamais elle ne se donne comme telle, jamais elle ne se drape dans les poses de la transgression. S'arrêter ainsi sur des aspects qui peuvent ne paraître que *légèrement* transgressifs, en regard de pratiques nettement plus subversives respectivement d'errance ou de brouillage générique, répondait au double souci de ne pas donner image à l'emporte-pièce de l'oeuvre rédienne mais aussi de rendre mieux compte d'un mode très subtil de transgressions ayant cours dans les oeuvres poétiques contemporaines.

Pratiques transversales ... et transgressives d'écriture poétique

Pour en prendre la juste mesure, sans doute faut-il remonter à cette "révolution du langage poétique" signée par Rimbaud, Lautréamont et surtout Mallarmé. En dissociant la poésie de 'l'instrument héréditaire' qu'est le vers, pour reprendre un mot de Mallarmé, en reconnaissant à la prose la même capacité et qualité poétiques, les poètes furent du même coup renvoyés à la définition de ce qu'est la poésie. La déclaration qui fit date est celle de Mallarmé, distinguant 'langage essentiel' et 'langage brut'. La poésie, 'langage essentiel', est définie par opposition à 'l'universel reportage' qui est le propre du langage brut. 'Narrer, enseigner, même décrire', voilà ce que n'est pas la poésie.[15] Amplifiée par Valéry, relayée par Breton et même Sartre, disant dans *Qu'est-ce que la littérature ?*: 'Si le poète raconte, explique ou enseigne, la poésie devient prosaïque, il a perdu la partie',[16] cette conception de la poésie devenue prépondérante exclut catégoriquement le narratif, le descriptif, le didactique ou l'anecdotique. Beaucoup plus que l'alexandrin ou la métrique traditionnelle en général; le récit, la description, l'anecdote, tels sont les interdits majeurs quoique implicites de la modernité poétique post-mallarméenne.[17]

Et c'est au fond à l'encontre cette tradition poétique que s'inscrit l'oeuvre poétique de Jacques Réda. Les différents recueils rédiens - nettement narratifs, descriptifs - transgressent, discrètement certes, sans déclarations d'intention retentissantes ni revendications de rupture, les interdits les plus forts car les moins contestés de la modernité poétique. Le récit, la description, l'anecdote ne sont nullement interdits de citer chez Réda. Nullement enclin aux recherches formelles entravant l'intelligibilité du poème, refusant une conception idéaliste de la poésie 'pure', Jacques Réda s'attache au simple, à l'ordinaire, au banal même diront ses détracteurs, sans s'interdire le moins du monde de décrire ou de raconter. Telles sont bien au contraire les fins que le poète s'assigne. Contemplant un balayeur, véritable démiurge qui 'ayant la haute main sur les bouches à eaux de son territoire, [...] déchaîne du ciel en torrents au creux des caniveaux', ne conclut-il pas dans une des proses des *Ruines de Paris*:

> Mon travail est de voir, de décrire et de balayer en somme
> sans excès de zèle mais avec conscience [...] [18]

L'oeuvre de Jacques Réda se développe ainsi aux antipodes de la poétique mallarméenne ou plus exactement à rebours des poétiques post-mallarméennes. Réconcilier la poésie et le récit, réintroduire le descriptif et le narratif au sein du poétique, tel est l'un des paris de l'entreprise rédienne. Récits, descriptions, commentaires, dialogues sous-tendent et structurent ainsi les écrits. Ainsi dans 'Episode', l'une des proses (poétiques[19]) de *L'Herbe des talus*, passager d'un train s'arrêtant inopinément sur la voie ferrée, le poète surprend, à l'intérieur d'une maison, une scène anodine en apparence, mais visiblement douloureuse pour ces protagonistes. De cet échange entre un homme et une femme, qui, après le départ de son interlocuteur, s'assoit 'comme s'il n'y avait plus rien à faire, à espérer et, les yeux dans le vague, [...] grignote des noix, qu'elle prend une à une sur la table dans une corbeille qu'on ne peut voir.', naît une ébauche de récit.[20] Le poème naît de la fictionalisation de cette scène. A la manière de Baudelaire, Réda à travers les fenêtres contemple 'dans ce trou noir ou lumineux, vi[vre] la vie, rêv[er] la vie, souffr[ir] la vie'.[21] Il est d'ailleurs révélateur que, plus que dans la lignée de Mallarmé, l'oeuvre se place dans la filiation de Baudelaire dont personne ne conteste la narrativité, nombre de critiques ayant en particulier souligné la structure narrative des *Fleurs du Mal*. A de nombreuses reprises, Jacques Réda a en effet exprimé son admiration pour l'oeuvre baudelairienne et l'influence que celle-ci exerce sur ses écrits. Ainsi, selon les propres dires du poètes, le titre de son plus important recueil de poème en prose, *Les Ruines de Paris*, a été choisi par référence au *Spleen de Paris*. Sans doute peut-on alors lire dans la tonalité profondément baudelairienne des *Ruines de Paris* la nostalgie d'un temps où la poésie assumait encore tout naturellement le récit et l'obscure volonté de renouer avec cette conception du poétique. Certes, Réda nourrit également une vive admiration pour Mallarmé dont il partage le goût pour une syntaxe disjonctive. Mais il renie une certaine lecture faite de son oeuvre, largement tributaire de celle qu'en fit Valéry et Brémond notamment. En un mot, s'il ne renie pas l'héritage mallarméen, il n'appartient pas à ce que l'on a coutume de nommer les poétiques post-mallarméennes.

En réintroduisant le descriptif, le didactique, l'anecdotique et surtout le narratif au sein du poétique, Réda invalide également toute une classification générique gauchie par une définition somme toute contestable de la poésie. Car l'exclusion du récit, de la description, de l'anecdote est à la vérité issue d'une perception essentialiste de la poésie - 'langage essentiel' - comme du rêve mallarméen et surtout valéryen de la 'poésie pure'. Or, dans un système cohérent des genres, la poésie ne s'oppose qu'à la prose, et encore convenablement définie. Le récit pour sa part, comme la description, le commentaire didactique ou le dialogue, est, pour reprendre la terminologie élaborée par Bakhtine, une catégorie 'transversale' puisqu'on est susceptible aussi bien de le retrouver dans la prose que dans la poésie. Le récit, la description, l'anecdote interviennent en effet aussi bien dans une épopée, un roman que dans un reportage télévisé ou le compte-rendu d'un événement. Si la réintroduction du narratif, du didactique et du descriptif subvertit et transgresse des dogmes et interdits poétiques, elle remet aussi en question la manière dont est pensée la poésie comme les présupposés implicites sur lesquels repose désormais le système des genres. Mais la réintroduction du descriptif, du didactique et du narratif ne doit pas seulement être lue comme une pratique transgressive. Le souci de la transgression et surtout celui de l'afficher, de la revendiquer est, rappelons le, étranger à la démarche rédienne, toute en modestie et humilité. L'oeuvre rédienne est nettement en marge des poétiques de la rupture et de la discontinuité, au demeurant devenue des lieux communs. Non pas qu'elle ne connaisse pas cette problématique. Bien au contraire, elle est toute entière innervée par un décentrement fondamental. Mais elle est surtout en quête de jointures. Et, dans une oeuvre qui progresse aventureusement comme la marche et où la périphérie l'emporte sur le centre, où aucune pensée centralisatrice ne prévaut et, symptomatiquement, où aucune poétique n'est formulée, où enfin aucune finalité n'est assignée à l'oeuvre, tout entière dévolue à l'aléatoire et au contingent; la réintroduction du descriptif, du didactique et du narratif trahit le souci d'ancrer l'oeuvre: de l'ancrer dans la *représentation* au sens que Paul Ricoeur donnait à ce mot.

La transgression n'est pas ainsi pas nécessairement synonyme chez Réda de rupture ou de nouveauté, mais bien autant de retour à des pratiques délaissées, voire franchement réprouvées, que ce soit le recours à l'alexandrin ou la réintroduction du récit. Mais par souci de justice, sans doute faut-il noter que cette réintroduction du récit comme d'autres catégories transversales en poésie à laquelle l'on vient de plus longuement s'attacher, n'est pas le seul fait de Réda. S'esquisse en effet dans la poésie contemporaine un mouvement plus général de retour, comme de retrait par rapport à la rhétorique d'exclusion du narratif, du descriptif, de l'anecdotique née avec la postérité mallarméenne. Dominique Combe, au terme de sa magistrale étude, *Poésie et récit: une rhétorique des genres*, met ainsi en évidence ce 'mouvement apparu récemment, qui tend à réhabiliter le récit en poésie - comme la description et le didactisme, ainsi qu'on peut s'y attendre - à la faveur d'une autre manière de concevoir le poétique'[22] qu'il discerne chez des poètes comme Jean Daive, Denis Roche, James Sacré mais aussi - de manière certes plus confuse chez cet auteur dont l'oeuvre s'est amorcée sur la base d'esthétiques héritées du siècle précédent - dans l'un des derniers recueils de Bonnefoy, *Ce qui fut sans lumière*, 'qui explorant la voie ouverte par *Dans le leurre du seuil* semble revenir sur le refus du récit exprimé dans la postface à *L'Ordalie* qui avait déterminé, en son temps, la transformation d'une fiction en poème'.[23] Les poétiques contemporaines, et celle de Réda en particulier, si elles transgressent les interdits majeurs de la modernité poétique, sont toutes en *retraits*.

Retrait: le terme ne désigne pas seulement ce mouvement de repli par rapport à une perception du poétique devenue prépondérante et sclérosante. Il se décline dans l'oeuvre rédienne sur différents modes et s'applique à des aspects aussi divers que l'habitation poétique du monde ou la perception des fins et des limites de la poésie. Mais avant de s'y intéresser plus précisément, sans doute convient-il de préciser les rapports qui s'établissent entre cette notion de retrait et celle de transgression. Etre en retrait, c'est à la fois, certes, se replier, mais aussi se placer en marge. Dans l'optique qui est la nôtre ici, se dessine ainsi conjointement - et paradoxalement - une mise à distance de la transgression dans ce qu'elle a de retentissant, voire de cérémonial, et une position implicitement subversive, transgressive. En un mot, à la transgression un rien solennelle se substitue une transgression comme clandestine.

En marge des poétiques de dévoilement ontologique

Pour revenir à la traversée dont on a vu qu'elle était soustendue par le rêve d'affranchissement et possédait une indéniable dimension transgressive, celle-ci connaît aussi des limites et surtout des retraits. Si Réda parvient parfois à passer, imaginairement, de 'l'autre côté des choses', dans une sorte d'envers du décor, bien vite, il est amené à retourner dans le monde des 'métamorphoses ordinaires', comme le suggérait la clausure du texte de *Châteaux des courants d'air* cité précédemment. Le passage reste toujours, ultimement, intermittent, de même que la survenue de la poésie, moment privilégié de présence au monde et comme de regénérescence du monde, est toujours plus ou moins un rapt vite suivi d'une dépossession. Réda, dans cet ouvrage qui lui tient d'art poétique intitulé *Celle qui vient à pas légers*, souligne au demeurant, utilisant toujours cette thématique du franchissement des limites, des murs:

> ... de quelque certitude qu'elle m'ait effectivement comblé, il m'arrive de considérer la poésie avec [...] désenchantement [...]: elle m'a rejeté de ce côté des murs. [24]

L'impossibilité d'un séjour durable en poésie, dans sa fulgurance, est chose certes inévitable. Ce qui est en revanche moins banal est le refus croissant de Réda de trop s'approcher de ce qui se discerne de l'autre côté des murs, à travers les brèches que sont métaphoriquement ces trous dans les palissades, ces fenêtres ouvrant sur le ciel, ou les arrière-pays des tableaux. Car la traversée du sensible est bornée par un seuil que Réda ne se résout pas à franchir. Si le monde s'entrouvre et laisse discerner une profondeur insondable, une vérité éblouissante, un ordre tout autre, si une brèche apparaît; le poète ne franchit jamais - comme le dit métaphoriquement l'un des tout premiers poèmes de Réda - la porte donnant sur cette dimension essentielle du monde:

> **La Porte**
>
> Et pourtant c'est ainsi: l'on voit, par la porte battante,
> Une lumière qui s'approche, hésite puis s'éteint.
> Souvent, l'attente se prolonge. Et seul, à qui sourire
> En silence ? Personne. Et qui voudrait répondrait de loin
> Si l'on criait ? Personne encore. Un jour l'on croit rêver,
> Un autre jour mourir - et vraiment c'est un songe, et c'est
> Aussi la mort. Passent parfois deux lévriers timides
> Et plutôt soucieux qui font mine d'en savoir long
> Sur le sens de la vie. Incidemment, la porte cesse
> De battre et l'on se dresse en criant plus fort dans le noir;
> Ou bien la clarté s'établit, et l'on distingue enfin,
> Pour un instant, ce que l'on ne peut pas dire ni comprendre. [25]

Révélations et épiphanies ne sont que fugaces et encore bien peu substantielles en ce qu'elles ne peuvent être dites ni comprises comme le formule très clairement le dernier vers de ce poème. Au demeurant, Réda, après *Amen* et *Récitatif,* se détache de plus en plus nettement de cette rhétorique de la révélation. Un refus d'aller trop avant vers le fond insondable, vers une limite inaccessible telle la ligne d'horizon toujours inatteignable, se fait jour. L'oeuvre rédienne, au fur et à mesure qu'elle se déploie, est de moins en moins ouvertement travaillée par l'ontologie, comme si elle refusait de transgresser les limites – tenues, on le sait depuis Montaigne[26] mais Heidegger l'a souligné avec insistance – entre poésie et philosophie. Au retrait vis-à-vis de la transgression correspond aussi un retrait par rapport à des poétiques trop attachée au dévoilement de l'être.

Rhétorique du milieu contre rhétorique de la limite

Si la poésie rédienne est travaillée par une expérience des
limites, elle n'est ainsi pas une poésie de la limite et de sa transgression permanente ou systématique. La démarche rédienne est
plus modérée, valorisant le passage plutôt que la transgression
et, de manière fort significative, le milieu plutôt que la limite. A
cet égard, il n'est pas anodin que l'un des recueils de proses
itinérantes qu'est *Châteaux des courants d'air* s'ouvre sur le
chapitre intitulé 'Au beau milieu'. Toutes aussi révélatrices sont
les pratiques d'écriture *in medias res*. Réda choisit en effet le plus
souvent une voie abrupte pour ouvrir le poème. Rien n'est plus
commun dans l'oeuvre de Réda que des poèmes débutant sur des
déictiques qui, en renvoyant à l'*hic* et le *nunc* du discours poétique,
plonge directement le lecteur dans l'univers de référence:

> A six heures il pleut encore, une buée
> Froide sort de la bouche obscure des marronniers,
> A gauche la ville n'est plus un dédale de pierre [27]

Sans parler de tous ces poèmes débutant avec un adjectif
démonstratif qui, perdant alors sa valeur habituelle
d'anaphorique puisque la désignation de l'objet se fait par
rapport à l'espace où se situe le locuteur et non par référence
intratextuelle, fonctionne là aussi comme un déictique:

> Cette lumière, d'une main distraite, m'escamote
> Après chaque virage et puis me restitue ... [28]

Le poème rédien s'ouvre ainsi 'au beau milieu' des choses. Mais
le procédé est plus flagrant encore dans les textes en prose. S'il
dédaigne les orées soignées, les marges graduelles d'entrée dans
le texte, Réda dans ses proses est en effet plus abrupt encore que
dans ses poèmes. 'Que le Nord transcendantal du poète existe, je
m'en convaincs' [29] ou 'Non, ce n'est pas poétique, mais qu'est-
ce qui l'est, et qu'importe si c'est ce qu'il faut dire ?'.[30] ainsi
commencent par exemple deux textes de Réda. Mais remarquons,

pour tenter de dégager des structures introductives récurrentes, que Réda a souvent recours à des conjonctions, des locutions qui ne devraient justement pas être utilisées à ce stade liminaire, que ce soit des termes comme 'ensuite' ou ces chevilles que l'on nomme des connecteurs pragmatiques ou argumentatifs tels que 'car', 'du moins' ou 'd'ailleurs' lesquels s'emploient généralement pour surenchérir sur un précédent argument ou développement:

> Ensuite elle-même a défleuri, la haute plante des décombres

> Car finalement nous ne sommes, me confie ce livreur, que de passage ...

> Du moins il reste de la splendeur cette rouille de novembre, et de la majesté son cafard[31]

Voilà autant d'entrée en matière (qui ne veulent en être) aux proses rédiennes. L'archétype de ces incipits qui se refusent ce statut est cependant indubitablement la célèbre phrase liminaire de *La Tourne*:

> - après cela (je commence, je commence toujours mais c'est aussi toujours une suite)...

Au commencement solennel, la poésie rédienne préfère l'ouverture *in medias res*, de même qu'à la rupture, elle substitue la poursuite et à la limite, le milieu. Plus que de transgression, de rupture inaugurale, l'oeuvre rédienne semble ainsi en quête de jointures.

D'un point de vue métapoétique, la valorisation du milieu est loin d'être dépourvue de sens. En se détachant des rhétoriques de la limite, Réda marque son désaveu de certaines poétiques voyant notamment dans l'exténuation de la parole poétique dans des silences et des blancs typographiques la seule fin de l'art. Réda, attaché à une lisibilité du texte, s'écarte de ces pensées polarisées par l'indicible. L'oeuvre se place alors en retrait des valeurs exaltées par la modernité comme transcendant le langage défaillant à rendre compte de l'intensité de la sensation comme de l'expérience poétique. Au premier rang des valeurs manifestant mais aussi dépassant la faillite du langage se trouve le silence. Revalorisé dans la philosophie de Wittgenstein, dans les esthétiques dramatiques de Beckett comme de Ionesco ou dans le domaine romanesque par Robbe-Grillet, le silence fut longtemps considéré, en poésie peut-être plus qu'ailleurs, comme une forme transcendant le langage, et même lui faisant atteindre son point d'orgue. Car le silence réussirait à dire l'indicible. C'est du moins l'opinion de Mallarmé.[32] Sans nécessairement aller jusqu'à partager la conception mallarméenne de la 'poésie pure', nombre de poètes contemporains, dans la lignée de Mallarmé qui en affirmant 'le silence, seul luxe après les rimes', posaient le silence comme une *forme* poétique, privilégiant une forme poétique de desserrement typographique et de raréfaction des signes sur la page qui élèvent le silence au rang d'Idéal du langage.[33] Rien de tout cela chez Réda. Si le silence est certes apprécié, voire recherché comme un havre de calme et de paix, s'il est valorisé car connotant l'apaisement et la pacification de l'être, il ne constitue aucunement une valeur suprême qui transcenderait le langage incapable de rendre compte d'une quelconque révélation (laquelle au demeurant ne survient pas) ou de l'émerveillement du poète face à la splendeur du monde. Bien au contraire, le silence est souvent associé à l'échec, à la défaillance du poète inapte à s'effacer, à laisser l'impersonnel 's'établir fugitivement dans la parole'.[34]

Pas plus que le silence, la musique n'est valorisée. Certes, on aurait pu s'attendre à ce que ce grand amateur de jazz qu'est Jacques Réda, cet euphoniste qui désigna le *e* muet comme 'le swing' de la langue française, place la musique comme la forme transcendante du verbe. Mais il n'en est rien. Au demeurant le jazz ne peut guère être le devenir de la parole poétique. En effet Réda met en évidence, dans ses ouvrages sur le jazz, sa décadence. Comme la ville, cet univers qu'est le jazz est en ruines. Réda en étudie la lente décomposition, la déplore, tout en reconnaissant lucidement que dès ses origines le jazz était voué à l'éphémère et au déclin, dans la mesure où dès que se constitue ne serait-ce que le soupçon d'un ordre, dès que s'élabore l'ombre d'une règle, le musicien de jazz s'applique à les subvertir. La poésie rédienne n'est tout au plus qu'*à l'image* du jazz:[35] elle suit comme lui 'une courbe convulsive, progressant par une suite de tentatives centrifuges dont chacune porte un nom' - celui des musiciens dans le cas du jazz, celui des livres pour ce qui est de la poésie - et connaît à son instar un cheminement aventureux, des impasses et la quête anxieuse d'une issue. Mais la musique ne constitue nullement un au-delà du langage. Si Réda fait sien le commandement verlainien exigeant 'de la musique avant toute chose', pour autant la musique n'est pas dans la poétique rédienne la forme vers laquelle tend l'oeuvre, forme qui dépasserait les limitations du langage. En cela, Réda rompt avec une tradition séculaire qui, d'Orphée à Ezra Pound en passant par Lautréamont ou Valéry, associe le poète et la lyre, la poésie et le chant. La poésie est tout au plus, comme le titre d'un des premiers recueils de Réda le suggère, un 'récitatif', une forme de chant qui ne diffère guère à la vérité de la déclamation puisqu'il se définit comme 'un chant qui se rapproche, par la mélodie et le rythme, de la coupe des phrases et des inflexions de la voix parlée'.[36] Rien de très étonnant à cela dans la mesure où c'est de la parole ordinaire dont Réda cherche le plus à se rapprocher ainsi qu'il le dit dans un des poèmes de *La Tourne*:

> Ce que j'ai voulu c'est garder les mots de tout le monde;
> Un passant parmi d'autres, puis: plus personne [...]
> Afin que chacun dise est-ce moi, oui, c'est moi qui parle -
> Mais avec ce léger décalage de la musique
> A jamais solitaire et distraite qui le traverse. [37]

Si un 'léger décalage de musique' pare la parole rédienne, si des silences s'établissent parfois, musicalité et silence contribuent tout au plus à l'expressivité de la poésie et ne sont pas donnés comme son point d'orgue et sa fin. En discréditant la capacité du silence et de la musique à abriter mieux que les mots la poésie, en ne cherchant pas à dire l'indicible, Réda transgresse à la sauvette – pour reprendre ici un des titres de ces livres qui dit bien l'attitude clandestinement subversive du poète – quelques autres des grands articles de foi de la modernité poétique.

Telles sont les implications métapoétiques de la substitution de la rhétorique du milieu sur celle de la limite. Mais ce n'est pas la seule. En particulier, en valorisant le milieu et en se détachant de ces arts de la limite, Réda se détache également des poétiques posant le sublime comme fin de l'art. Après avoir souligné le désir rédien de rapprocher le langage poétique de la parole ordinaire, cet implicite désaveu du sublime n'a rien de bien étonnant. Réda, s'il conçoit la poésie comme un état ou un moment de 'grâce', de 'fièvre' ou d' 'exaltation',[38] ne lui donne pas comme but, s'il en est un, le sublime aussi expurgé de la grandiloquence effusive qu'il puisse être dans les poétiques contemporaines. Jacques Réda préfère de loin la simplicité ordinaire. Plus qu'un dédain pour le sublime, il faut voir sans doute dans cette mise à distance du sublime, l'expression de la modestie sans affectation d'un poète dont la seule ambition déclarée est d'explorer, toutefois non sans rigueur et ferveur, une voie moyenne. *Mediocritas aurea*, telle semble être la devise qu'à la suite d'Horace le poète se donne.[39]

Mais sans doute est-il un peu sommaire de définir de l'oeuvre rédienne comme absolument étrangère à la tension vers le sublime. Si les écrits rédiens refusent la solennité qu'infère le sublime, compris dans son acception commune de ton élevé adapté à un objet exceptionnel, ils ne sont en effet pas totalement à l'écart des problématiques afférentes au questionnement sublime. La réflexion sur le sublime et l'oeuvre rédienne comportent en effet toutes deux, sur des modes radicalement différents mais ultimement convergents, une interrogation sur les limites. Comme le montre Jean-Luc Nancy, le sublime ne renvoie en effet pas à un au-delà de l'art mais à sa limite. Le sublime est à la limite de l'art. Mais parce que l'art est suspendu dans et par le mouvement d'élévation sublime, c'est un illimité que le sublime tente de faire surgir à cette limite qui est aussi seuil d'exténuation de l'art. Le sublime est 'l'infini d'un commencement' de dépassement toujours vain des limites. Or les proses et poèmes de Jacques Réda, innervées par le décentrement, revenant inlassablement buter sur les lisières de la ville mais refusant les limites de l'écriture par des pratiques d'ouverture *in medias res* et de fermeture suspendue, rejoignent d'une certaine manière cette recherche de l'illimité au bord externe de la limite qui est le domaine du sublime.

L'art de Jacques Réda, malgré son intelligibilité, son désaveu des questionnements réflexifs ou philosophiques, en un mot malgré la simplicité sereine dont il se pare, n'est pas un art dénué de tension. Et l'on pourrait aisément lui appliquer ces phrases qui referment la contribution de Jean-Luc Nancy sur le sublime et qui renvoient à l'art contemporain:

> Cela n'habite plus les hauteurs ou les profondeurs comme le sublime, mais cela touche, simplement, à la limite, sans excès déchirant, sans exaltation 'sublime' - mais sans puérilité et sans niaiserie. C'est une vibration puissante, mais douce, exigeante, continue, aiguë [...]. [40]

Et peut-être l'oeuvre de Réda est au fond cette offrande, laquelle a trait au sublime mais le dépasse, et dont le critique dit qu'elle

> [...] renonce au déchirement lui-même, à l'excès de la tension, aux spasmes et aux syncopes sublimes. Mais elle ne renonce pas à la tension et à l'écart infinis, [...] ni au suspens toujours renouvelé qui rythme l'art comme une inauguration et comme une interruption sacrées.

Cette citation si elle définit assez bien la position rédienne face au sublime, éclaire également de manière lumineuse celle adoptée par Jacques Réda par rapport aux poétiques de la transgression. De même qu'il renonce aux déchirements sublimes, le poète renonce en effet aux déchirements transgressifs sans pour autant renoncer au caractère inaugural que tout poème possède.

A l'issue de cette étude centrée sur la poésie de Jacques Réda, sans doute convient-il de souligner l'originalité de cette démarche et de cette approche de la transgression. Si les écrits rédiens ne possèdent nullement un caractère nettement transgressifs mais bien plutôt obliquement, subrepticement subversifs, une transgression fondamentale est pourtant à l'oeuvre. Se dessine en effet une remise en question des poétiques de la rupture, de la déconstruction des codes poétiques, de la fragmentation, en un mot des poétiques érigeant la transgression au rang de valeur suprême, poétiques devenues pour le moins sclérosantes pour ne pas dire conventionnelles, voire clichés. Sans rompre à proprement parler ou plus exactement de manière déclarée avec les poétiques de la rupture et de la transgression – ce qui ne serait en fait que s'y affilier – Réda se positionne en retrait. Au cérémonial ostentatoire de la transgression se substitue alors une démarche toute en modestie, en réserve, dépourvue de déclaration d'intentions fracassante et de poétique élaborée ou plutôt formulée. En l'absence de pensée centralisatrice, c'est aventureusement, dans l'ignorance de sa finalité, et au risque de perdre l'équilibre que se déploie l'oeuvre, 'petit pas de danse vers sa limite, son dieu, son précipice'.[41]

University of Kent at Canterbury

1   Roland Barthes, *Oeuvres complètes*, 3 vols (Paris: Seuil, 1995), III, 397.

2   *Les Ruines de Paris* (Paris: Gallimard, 1977), p.156.

3   S'il aime à se présenter comme une sorte de cow-boy en guerre contre
     l'automobiliste (cf. *Les Ruines de Paris*, p.54-55), de Don Quichotte à
     solex, dans le regard d'autrui, le poète se voit 'grand maboul' (*Les
     Ruines de Paris*, p.95) et autres 'énergumène'.

4   'Rétrovisions' in *L'Herbe des talus* (Paris: Gallimard, 1984), p.164.

5   *Beauté suburbaine* (Fanlac: Périgueux, 1985), p. 9.

6   *Châteaux des courants d'air* (Paris: Gallimard, 1986), p.59.

7   *L'Herbe des talus*, p.104 et p.106 respectivement.

8   'Je vais à pied comme un bandit, comme ce réprouvé, là-bas, nègre ou
     kabyle.. ' in *Hors les murs* (Paris: Gallimard, 1982), p.43. Cette pra-
     tique délinquante de la marche n'est d'ailleurs pas sans faire penser aux
     écrits de Michel de Certeau mettant en évidence dans son *Invention du
     quotidien* son caractère de pratique de résistance au sein de l'ordre
     social le plus strict et le plus complexe. La mobilité rédienne appar-
     tient à cette appropriation transgressive de l'espace social.

9   'Des vies, mais telles que la mémoire les invente, que notre imaginaire
     les recrée, qu'une passion les anime. Des récits subjectifs, à mille lieues
     de la biographie traditionnelle' précise, sur le rabat des ouvrages pub-
     liés dans cette collection, l'éditeur.

10   'L'un et l'autre: l'auteur et son héros secret, le peintre et son modèle.
     Entre eux, un lien intime et fort. Entre le portrait d'un autre et l'auto-
     portrait, où placer la frontière ?' lit-on par la suite.

11   Dans *Aller à Elisabethville*, en particulier, l'identité de nom entre l'au-
     teur et le personnage n'est pas établie. Or il s'agit là, Philippe Lejeune
     l'a fort bien montré dans *Le Pacte autobiographique*, du seul critère à
     même de définir avec certitude la nature autobiographique d'un texte.
     Par ailleurs, le sous-titre de 'récit' achève de voiler la dimension auto-
     biographique de l'oeuvre.

12   *Le Sens de la marche* (Paris: Gallimard, 1990), p.104.

13   Dans ce qui lui tient d'art poétique, Réda soulignait en effet: 'Je ne
     sais quoi de viscéral m'a conduit à expérimenter un type de vers
     métrique imitant ce parler (..) qui se trouve être le mien dans les
     échanges de la vie ordinaire. J'ai appelé ces vers *vers mâchés*' in *Celle qui*

vient à pas légers (Montpellier: Fata Morgana, 1985), p.82.

14   Dans son recueil intitulé *Hors les murs*, Réda pratique à diverses reprises ces coupes intralexicales caractéristiques de la poésie de Denis Roche. Ainsi lit-on notamment dans 'Juin à Fontenay-aux-Roses', rimant avec 'nuage' '... tour saugrenue age- / Nouillée entre les pois et les rhododendrons.' *Hors les murs*, p. 48. Cette pratique est abandonnée pour revenir à des vers plus traditionnels, conventionnels, voire des formes de versification archaïques. Réda joue de toute la possibilité de la gamme prosodique. Et c'est ce refus de la transgression systématique qui le rend en fait éminemment transgressif.

15   Stéphane Mallarmé, *Oeuvres complètes* (Paris: Gallimard, 1945), p.368.

16   Jean-Paul Sartre, *Qu'est-ce que la littérature?* (Paris: Gallimard, 1947), p.48.

17   Cf. la magistrale étude de Dominique Combe sur ce sujet: *Poésie et récit: une rhétorique des genres* (Paris: Corti, 1989).

18   *Les Ruines de Paris*, p. 33.

19   Pour Michel Sandras, ce texte s'avère un poème en prose. Commentant cet 'Episode' dans l'anthologie de poèmes en prose qu'il livre à l'issue de son ouvrage, l'auteur de *Lire le poème en prose* souligne en effet que les affinités du texte avec le récit ne sont pas telles qu'elles produisent une indétermination quant à sa définition générique: '[...] notre attention est centrée sur le bref instant d'une intrigue dont les rares indices alimentent notre imagination. Une anecdote en raterait la vibration, une nouvelle devrait nécessairement mettre en oeuvre une histoire. A la manière d'une séquence cinématographique, le poème en prose inscrit seulement le cadre optique d'une blessure qui nous reste inaccessible'. Michel Sandras, *Lire le poème en prose* (Paris: Dunod, 1995), p. 173.

20   *L'Herbe des talus*, p. 127.

21   Cf. Charles Baudelaire, 'Les Fenêtres', pièce n° 35 du *Spleen de Paris,* (Paris: Poésie Gallimard, 1973), p.118.

22   Combe, op. cit., p.185.

23   ibid., p. 186.

24   *Celle qui vient à pas légers,* p.18.

25   'La Porte', in *Amen* (Paris: Gallimard, 1968), repris dans la collection Poésie Gallimard (Paris: Gallimard, 1988), p. 17.

26   'Et certes la philosophie n'est qu'une poésie sophistiquée...'. *Essais*, II, (Paris: Garnier-Flammarion, 1987), p.202.

27   Les deux passages sont extraits de *Retour au calme* (Paris: Gallimard, 1989), respectivement p.99 et p.85.

28   *L'Herbe des talus*, p.41.

29   ibid., p.120.

30   *Le Sens de la marche*, p.47.

31   Les incipits cités sont extraits des *Ruines de Paris*, respectivement p.74, p.59 et p.110.

32   '[..]l'Indicible ou le Pur, la poésie sans les mots !', ibid., p.389.

33   A cet égard, la pratique mallarméenne d'espacement typographique sur la page est plus qu'une figuration du silence, elle est le moule, la structure et l'on pourrait même dire l'ossature du poème. Mallarmé ne dit-il d'ailleurs pas lui-même: 'L'armature intellectuelle du poème se dissimule et tient - a lieu - dans l'espace qui isole les strophes et parmi le blanc du papier: significatif silence qu'il n'est pas moins beau de composer, que les vers', op. cit., p. 872.

34   *Celle qui vient à pas légers*, p.12.

35   Et si Réda a pu dire que le *e* muet constituait le swing de la langue, c'est sans doute plus pour attirer l'attention sur les similitudes entre la musique qu'il promouvoit et sa prosodie que pour établir la précellence de la musique sur le langage qui aurait 'presque' les mêmes qualités rythmiques. Notons au demeurant que Réda semble se repentir d'avoir ainsi défini le *e* muet: 'ce qu'à demi témérairement j'ai parfois appelé le swing', *Celle qui vient à pas légers*, p.88. Dans cet ouvrage, il préfère d'ailleurs définir son effet comme 'pneumatique' et ainsi associer l'emploi qu'il fait du *e* muet au mouvement du poème, à son cheminement souple et rythmé.

36   Cf. définition donnée dans le dictionnaire *Le Nouveau Petit Robert* (Paris: Dictionnaires Le Robert, 1993), p.1887.

37   *La Tourne* (Paris: Gallimard, 1975), repris dans la collection Poésie Gallimard, p.199.

38   Cf. *Celle qui vient à pas légers*, p.12.

39   Au demeurant, le parti pris d'intelligibilité, le style quasi classique que

nombre de commentateurs ont souligné, le recours même à certaines formes versifiées tombées en désuétude, en particulier dans *Lettre sur l'univers*, un grand nombre d'aspects de l'oeuvre rédienne se rattachent à une esthétique classique.

40 Jean-Luc Nancy, 'L'offrande sublime', in *Du sublime* (Paris: Belin, 1988), pp.37-75 (p.75).

41 *Celle qui vient à pas légers*, p.21.

Transgressing Transgression:
the Limits of Bataille's Fiction

Benjamin Noys

How can we define the limits of Georges Bataille's fictional writings? They are most commonly limited to being examples of pornography or erotica, but this doesn't seem quite right. Consider the *Story of the Eye*, probably the best known of Bataille's novels: in the final chapter its polymorphously perverse heroine Simone participates in an orgy in a church. She fellates a priest who is also made to urinate on the host, and then finally strangled to death by Simone while she forces him to have sexual intercourse.[1] Although it has the explicit sexual content characteristic of erotica or pornography, this is combined with blasphemy and violence, and it articulates a systematic challenge to moral, legal, political, religious, sexual and physical limits (which is also true of all Bataille's fiction). Bataille himself attempted, in *Eroticism*, to explain this by arguing that eroticism is 'assenting to life up to the point of death'[2] and theorising this systematic challenge to all boundaries as transgression. This threatens to make it impossible to define the limits of Bataille's work, because transgression is about the breaking of limits, including those of genre and literature. One solution to this problem is to argue, as Susan Rubin Suleiman does, that Bataille's fiction is putting into practice the work of his theory.[3] This makes Bataille's fiction into a privileged exemplification of the practice of transgression by the theorist of transgression, and so we can define Bataille's fiction as transgressive.

It is Julia Kristeva who has developed the most theoretically sophisticated and influential version of this argument, treating Bataille as part of a tradition of radical writing: 'I have in mind the major writers of polyphonic novels over many centuries – Rabelais, Swift, Sade, Lautréamont, Kafka, and Bataille – to mention only those who have been and still remain on the fringe of official culture.'[4] I want to challenge the argument that

Bataille's fiction is an example of transgressive writing, which locates him in a history of radical writing, and makes his transgressive literary 'practice' the most radical part of his work. To do this I use the more 'theoretical' arguments that Bataille makes about transgression to disrupt the logic that defines the limits of Bataille's fiction by transgression. I want to show that seeing Bataille's fiction as inherently transgressive or radical actually ends up producing a *limited* version of transgression, a limitation that runs counter to Bataille's own exploration of transgression. The irony is (and transgression will produce multiple ironies), which Bataille himself is not always aware of, that a writing which appears to be *most* transgressive can, in fact, be the *least* transgressive.

The advantage of selecting Kristeva as the example of this tendency in the reading of Bataille is that she doesn't just assert that Bataille is a radical writer but attempts to justify it. In *'Bataille, experience and practice'* she does this by arguing that what is radical about Bataille's writing is the way it presents violent and disruptive pornographic images as themes.[5] These images 'evoke a radical heterogeneity' (p.247) which uses the theme against its usual function of being 'that thetic moment around which the process [*procès*] crystallises' (p.246). Kristeva is drawing on the theory developed in *Revolution in Poetic Language* where she sets up an opposition between the semiotic, which is the pre-verbal domain of the materiality of the body's drives, and the thetic, which is the organisation and imposition of structure on the semiotic by language.[6] For Kristeva what Bataille does is to take up the semiotic, through his violent images, and use it to de-stabilise the thetic moment of the theme. This does not mean that Bataille destroys the thetic moment, because in the context of Kristeva's theory this would lead to psychosis and regression, but he opens it up to the process of the subject's constitution. She pairs Bataille with Joyce: 'Within the perspective of the avant-garde literary adventure, Bataille is perhaps the only one, with Joyce, not to have modestly or disdainfully renounced this thetic moment of the process [*procès*] of producing meaning that creates the subject as subject of knowledge and as social subject' (p.239).

Bataille and Joyce form a complementary couple: Bataille exploring a transgressive *content* while Joyce explores a transgressive *form* (although Kristeva ignores the fact that *Finnegans Wake* does contain its own thematic transgressions, like the father exposing himself to the daughter[7]). In both cases the two orders of the semiotic and thetic are brought together: 'carnal organicity, erotic orgies, and obscenity exist only as contradictions, as struggles, between the violent materiality external to the subject and the affirmed authority of the subject' (p.245). Bataille does this by '*representing through themes*' (p.250) the semiotic and transgressive. Kristeva has some justification for identifying Bataille's fiction by its explicit thematisation of violent eroticism, and her reading also provides a means for explaining why this should be radical. This is not just a mis-reading of Bataille, Bataille himself encourages the idea that his fiction is radical in its explicitness. Therefore what Kristeva allows us to do is to identify three common, and linked, moves in the reading of Bataille:

1)   Bataille's fiction is overtly shocking or pornographic in its thematisation of transgression, transgression is its content or subject matter.

2)   It is this directness that makes Bataille a radical writer, because he opens up our language to a new and violent representation of sexuality: 'What characterises modern sexuality from Sade to Freud is not its having found the language of its logic or of its natural process, but rather, through the violence done by such languages, its having been 'denatured' – cast into an empty zone where it achieves whatever meagre form is bestowed upon it by the establishment of its limits.'[8]

3)   This means that the best place to find transgression, to see it at work or in practice, is in Bataille's fiction.

Contrary to this positive interpretation of Bataille's fiction I want to suggest a more negative evaluation of it, and its reception. The receptions of Bataille which emphasise the shocking effects of his representations of transgression all depend on limiting transgression to a certain content or certain themes.

Here we have focused on how these shocking effects are narrowed down to Bataille's fiction. This not only happens with theorists like Kristeva, but also with writers who look to Bataille's fiction as a model of violent transgression, for example the gay American writer Dennis Cooper. There are also exactly the same problems if these shocking effects are found in Bataille's 'theory' rather than in his fiction. Perhaps the most obvious example of this sort of gesture is Nick Land's *The Thirst for Annihilation*,[9] which although it shows some scepticism about transgression (e.g., pp.58-74) still develops from Bataille the importance of a radical and shocking rhetoric: 'Bataille may be praised or condemned in terms of his erudition, but this scarcely matters when compared with his sanctity as a voyager in sickness ...' (p.xiii). It does not matter whether it is in fiction or theory that the shocking effects of Bataille's writing are found because by trying to present Bataille in a way which is as overtly shocking as possible these readings actually covertly refuse the radical effects of transgression, and this also applies to Bataille's fiction itself.

This can be seen in the irony that Bataille's violently blasphemous eroticism can end up supporting what it is supposed to disrupt, as Gilles Deleuze recognises, '"Transgression", a concept too good for seminarists under the law of a Pope or a priest, the tricksters. Georges Bataille is a very French author. He made the little secret the essence of literature, with a mother within, a priest beneath, an eye above'.[10] Bataille's blasphemy retains all the props of religion, Catholicism in particular, in order to produce the enjoyment (*jouissance*) of transgression. What Deleuze does not note or discuss is how Bataille went beyond this infantile blasphemy by analysing the operation of transgression, and this involves returning to Bataille's more 'theoretical' work, *Eroticism*. The concept of transgression describes the act or activity of breaking a rule, law, taboo, border, limit, etc. To take transgression as a theme involves fixing it around a specific content. Although this may shock us or break some norms of decency, it still fixes transgression as content. The problem for this thematic reading is that transgression may appear as the breaking of a *particular* rule but as a concept it implies the potential breaking of *any* rule. It is just this dual function that disrupts the logic of the presentation of Bataille as a transgressive writer, because transgression would fail to be transgression if it was limited to specific themes or content.

How does transgression 'work'? Bataille identifies an opposition at the heart of transgression, between the fact there is no taboo which cannot be transgressed and that taboos also seem to forbid transgression (p.63). The result is that taboos are indifferent to logic because they invite their own violation (p.64). This invitation to be violated takes two forms:

1) An 'Organised transgression' which is part of our social life: 'The frequency – and the regularity – of transgressions do not affect the intangible stability of the prohibition since they are its expected complement' (p.65). This explains the commonly noted effect that phenomena which appear to disrupt and shatter social norms, such as carnival, festival or saturnalia, actually lead to the reinvigoration and reinforcement of those norms.

2) An 'Unlimited transgression': 'once a limited licence has been allowed, unlimited urges toward violence may break forth' (p.65). So, once taboos start to be broken all taboos start to lose their stability. Bataille describes this unlimited transgression as 'a return to violence, an animal violence' (p.65).

This looks like an opposition between two types of transgression, and what Bataille calls organised transgression can be identified with the problem of thematic representations of transgression that appear radical but actually result in conservative effects. I want go beyond this opposition, *not* by arguing, as Bataille so often appears to, that unlimited transgression is better than organised transgression but instead by exploring how Bataille can help us to deconstruct this opposition and so move toward a more complex thinking of transgression.

Already these two forms or types of transgression are mutually implicated: any act of organised transgression is haunted by the possibility of unlimited transgression, *and* unlimited transgression only appears as a possibility through organised transgression. Bataille shows this double functioning with religion, one the one hand 'the recoil that inevitably follows the forward movement is constantly being presented as the essence of religion' (p.69) but on the other hand religion is also 'the moving force behind the breaking of taboos' (p.69). However, although transgression has this double function it is conceptually incoherent and inadequate to describe this through organised and unlimited transgressions. Firstly, although organised transgression operates as the temporary breaking of a social norm which ultimately leaves that norm intact and even strengthened, its capacity to break the norm in the first place depends on the fact that the concept of transgression implies that *any* taboo can be broken. Organised transgression can never be as organised as it would desire to be, it is haunted by unlimited transgression, which it figures as the possibility of all taboos being swept away. Secondly, the problem with seeing this conceptual capacity of transgression to break any rule (including that of the concept) as unlimited transgression is that it too would be incoherent. This is because if unlimited transgression swept away all rules and taboos it would be left with nothing to transgress and so cancel itself out. In both organised and unlimited transgression the disruptive force of transgression is controlled within limits that actually destroy that force. The double function of transgression is reduced to a choice between a transgression that aids the law and a transgression that is beyond the law, in both cases transgression finds its destination in law.

The incoherence of the two types of transgression is why we cannot remain in the opposition, as Bataille does by making unlimited transgression another, more radical, type of transgression. In so doing Bataille may appear to step beyond the problems of organised transgression, but the idea of unlimited transgression as unlimited violence is only the result of the perspective of organised transgression. It fits with the fantasy of returning to an animal state that preoccupies Bataille, what he calls in the *Theory of Religion* 'the unconscious intimacy of animals'.[11] Therefore, although we can see that the thematic representation of transgression in Bataille's fiction can be criticised for defining that fiction by *one form* of organised transgression, this doesn't mean going beyond it to a reading from unlimited transgression. The power of Bataille is that his texts offer resources for deconstructing this structure and this fantasy by undoing the opposition. Instead of two types of transgression we just have transgression, appearing unlimited because it could disrupt any rule and appearing organised because it only exists in the limited act of rule breaking. This allows us to account for both how this opposition comes to be set up and also how it fails: there can be no unlimited transgression as such and no organised transgression as such, each forecloses the other. Although we seem to lose the possibility of unlimited transgression we can actually more radically re-think the way law and transgression relate and so avoid simply making transgression something that is always derivative of the law.

Usually we suppose transgression follows on from the law, and Bataille's attempt to find a pure transgression leads him to an unlimited transgression that is after and beyond the law. What Bataille also does, by exploring the operation of transgression, is suggest a rupture of the derivative status of transgression secondary to the law. He approaches a thinking of transgression as the origin and possibility of law, a law would only be possible if it could be transgressed; if it could not be transgressed then there would be no need for it as a law, it would not be thinkable because it could never be transgressed. This does not mean that transgression just replaces the law, because then transgression itself would become a sort of law. It would be a paradoxical and self-contradictory law because transgression would imply that a law demanding transgression be transgressed. Rather the difference between law and transgression becomes unstable, transgression becomes necessary to the function of law and this makes law unlike what we usually think of as law. We can compare this operation of transgression to the effect of what Derrida calls iterability, which inflicts an 'essential drift'[12] on the function of language, to the point where language becomes part of a general iterability. Transgression would be a similar effect of opening and disruption which means that any law only has a relative stability. Rather than positing an incoherent purity of transgression beyond the law which would keep transgression where the law wanted it, in a position of exteriority, transgression insinuates itself into the law. This makes it more radical than transgression as an act of law breaking and it also means that it is no longer possible to move into a pure space of transgression, whether in fiction or theory.

This can be clarified through Foucault's presentation of Bataille's thought of transgression in 'A Preface to Transgression', where Foucault states that 'Transgression, then, is not related to the limit as black to white, the prohibited to the lawful, the outside to the inside, or as the open area of a building to its enclosed spaces. Rather, their relationship takes the form of a spiral which no simple infraction can exhaust' (p.35). This spiral undoes the idea of a pure space of transgression, of moving from the pre-transgressive to the transgressive, and it also has the consequence that transgression is no longer negative, no longer the negation of a specific law. The result is that the existence of transgression 'must be liberated from the scandalous or subversive' (p.35). This suggests the inadequacy of defining Bataille's fiction by its representations of transgression, which rests on transgression as the negation of law rather than as the affirmation of the limit. The effect of transgression 'is sometimes immobilised in scenes we customarily call 'erotic' and suddenly volatized in a philosophical turbulence, when it seems to lose its very basis' (p.39). We are shifting from the immobilisation of transgression in erotic scenes to a 'philosophical turbulence' produced by transgression. For Foucault this can best be seen as an extension of 'that opening made by Kant in Western philosophy when he articulated, in a manner which is still enigmatic, metaphysical discourse on the limits of reason' (p.38). The problem with Kant's interrogation was that it closed this opening 'when he ultimately relegated all critical investigations to an anthropological question' (p.38), and it is ironic that Bataille's more overtly anthropological discourse in *Eroticism* can actually lead us back to this more philosophical interrogation.

Foucault's reading can show us that for Bataille transgression is not just negative but also the affirmation of the limit, the limit *does not* exist as closed, but as a passage of opening. This affirmation of limits can be related to the Kantian gesture of critique, as Foucault does, but it cannot be reduced to philosophy. It is not the erection of a philosophical universal but the opening up of transgression as the *general* event of the opening of any field, because it is no longer just the negation of a specific law but an act of affirmation of the limits of being, a sort of opening. This general event connects to what Bataille calls 'general economy': 'Changing from the perspectives of restrictive economy to those of general economy actually accomplishes a Copernican transformation: a reversal of thinking – and of ethics.'[13] It is not universal, because it only happens in the opening of a specific field, but general because it inscribes the necessity of any field being open. Here we can see the double function of transgression, this time in a more 'philosophical' register. The difficulty for philosophy is that it does not leave philosophy intact, this opening cannot be controlled by philosophy. Despite *Eroticism* being preoccupied with anthropological data, to the point where a critic like Michael Richardson can reduce it to a renovated anthropology or sociology,[14] its thinking of transgression leads Bataille, in his conclusion, to the problem of philosophy: for Bataille, 'If philosophy were to shift its ground from work and taboo with their complementary accord to take its stand upon transgression, it would be philosophy no longer but a mockery of itself' (p.275). For transgression to be transgression it must resist and de-stabilise any attempt to control it by philosophy, its attempt to make it into a new philosopheme. What Bataille's analysis indicates is the contaminating and contagious effects of transgression on the purity of any discourse, including on itself.

It is perhaps testament to just how difficult this thinking of transgression is that Foucault should also claim that Bataille gives us 'the pure transgression of his texts' (p.40). Here Foucault steps back from the finding that he helps us to make, with Bataille, that transgression *cannot be pure*. Although, as with Bataille's desire for unlimited transgression, it is possible that transgression always generates as a sort of transcendental illusion the desire for and fantasy of a pure transgression. This is also how the concept of transgression provides resources for its division into organised and unlimited, which is one way of resolving its unstable conceptual duality and also preserving the dream of a pure transgression. We have already seen that this must be a dream, because if transgression where to be pure or unlimited it would destroy itself, and so it is necessarily parasitic on law. Purifying transgression involves a violent misreading in which transgression is assimilated to a discourse of breaks and absolute divisions between the pre-transgressive and the trans-gressive. However, it is only through the opening and ruptures which transgression produces that it is possible to construct a discourse of the break: both making it possible for such a discourse to exist while also marking out the impossible limit which that discourse cannot think. Often these sorts of arguments have often been applied in the domain of the political, where a discourse of revolutionary breaks has been countered with a discourse of subversive transgressions. Whatever the critical and strategic value of this critique, which is certainly important, it becomes naive if it in turn attempts to limit transgression to the political. Nowhere can lay claim to transgression but it haunts us with the possibility of grasping it, claiming it, being transgressive.

The persistence of this desire for a pure transgression can also help to explain why Bataille's fiction should be so often identified as the site of this fantasy of being transgressive. Where Bataille does so much to put the concept of transgression in play, to open up its disruptive forces to the point where the concept is shattered, perhaps he, and his readers especially, have reeled back in this force through localising it in his fiction. What the re-thinking of transgression as a general event of opening and away from its immobilisation in erotic scenes can allow us to do is to return to the problematic status of Bataille's fiction in a new way. This does not mean an act of re-reading which would simply insert this argument about transgression into one of a series of methods of criticism. Instead it involves rupturing through transgression the limitations which were put on transgression to produce a pure transgressive text. This results in an opening up of Bataille's fiction to new effects and new possibilities that have been previously foreclosed. It also opens up new possibilities for criticism in general, transgression resists confinement in the text or 'genius' of any writer while opening up a text in singular ways. Transgression is an effect of *general* opening that only appears in the singularity of a text's *specific* openings, which is why it is also a patient practice of reading.

This can be seen in its effects upon the organisation of Bataille's texts. One consequence for Bataille's fiction of this loosening up of transgression is that it is no longer possible to simply assert that what is radical in that fiction is its explicitness, its erotic or pornographic imagery and themes. Transgression can function in places we did not expect, and perhaps to be transgression can only function in places we did not expect. It operates more generally at the limits of texts and across those very limits, opening up the text to its Others. The effect of this transgression is also to blur those limits and make them more unstable, it becomes harder to be sure where the limits of and between texts lie. In particular with Bataille it makes it harder to police the difference between Bataille's fiction and his more 'theoretical' works. In fact it may be possible to suggest, paradoxically, that Bataille's 'theoretical' works can have moments that are more literary than his literary writings (I am thinking of *Inner Experience* and *On Nietzsche* especially).

Another major consequence is that as well as shattering the image of Bataille as a radical writer this thinking of transgression also shatters the idea that Bataille is a matter of literary theory. Since Kristeva Bataille has often been taken as the image of a radical *post-structuralist* writer, and in this way Bataille and post-structuralism are reduced to matters of literature and literary theory. Also literature is often then seen as being clearly separate from and more radical than philosophy. For example in the recent argument of John Lechte: Even if his more philosophical analyses and statement (e.g. on Hegel) in the end connect Bataille to restricted economy, as Derrida proposes, his fictional and poetic writing (not interpreted by Derrida) comes to disrupt the tranquillity of conformist equilibrium and – as Barthes, Foucault, Sollers, Kristeva and others realised – raises again the unanswerable question about where to draw the boundary between madness and sanity.[15] Lechte completely misreads Derrida's argument about Bataille to draw up a firm boundary between philosophy and literature which would seem to complicate the instability he is trying to argue lies in the boundary between madness and sanity. Lechte draws on Kristeva, on whom he had already written a book,[16] but in so doing vulgarises her work even further. In the name of a theoretical radicalism literary criticism retains all its old privileges, leaving its own relationship to philosophy and its philosophical presuppositions intact.

These sorts of arguments depend on the security of the boundary between literature and philosophy, which the generalised effect of transgression puts into question. Barthes confronts this problem through the example of how we could define Bataille's writings: 'literary manuals generally prefer to forget about Bataille who, in fact, wrote texts, perhaps continuously one single text'.[17] This doesn't mean that transgression results in an (infamous) textual free-play, or makes everything textual, because transgression is both the breaking of a limit and the attention to that limit, in that sense it multiplies differences and distinctions. It also leads to an insecurity of the limit, we can no longer be so sure where the limits lie, or on their fundamental stability. The problem of text and writing becomes allied with the problem of transgression through the questioning of the limits of the text as book, and within the various organisation of texts into genres. This does not entail the elimination of literature, or its absorption into theory, but its *transformation* from being a container for transgression to something different, for Derrida, 'when I speak of literature it is not with a capital L; it is rather an allusion to certain movements which have worked around the limits of our logical concepts, certain texts which make the limits of our language tremble, exposing them as divisible and questionable.'[18] This makes it impossible to think of Bataille as a radical writer if we leave the concept of literature untouched, transgression cannot be limited to literature but disrupts the limits of literature.

This new possibility of reading through transgression can be examined through Bataille's own literary criticism in *Literature and Evil*.[19] There he develops the concept of communication as the definition of literature (p.viiii), and communication is a way of thinking about similar problems to those raised by transgression, although it lacks the associations with criminality and crime of transgression. Both are about the opening of limits and both provide a way of thinking about literature that does not presume a stabilised essence of literature. The difficulty is that Bataille is ambivalent in *Literature and Evil* between seeing literature as radical because it represents evil, and seeing literature as an effect of a communication that is more complex and neutral. It is possible to see that Bataille's own fiction is structured by the same ambivalence, up to now we have had far more emphasis on how it *represents* transgression or evil, and little, or none, on its capacities for a more neutral transgression, or communication, beyond the limits of the literary itself. It may also be that Bataille's own literary practice would not necessarily measure up to his critical thinking of communication. This starts to disrupt the stable identification between a 'theory' and 'practice' of transgression in Bataille. Transgression and communication are therefore only just starting to be thought through in relation to literature, Bataille challenges the assumptions that we already knew what they are and what they mean, and the assumptions that have been made about Bataille's own writing.

The various attempts to define Bataille's fiction, or his theory, as being representations of transgression are flawed. They are flawed because they limit transgression to particular representations, when the effect of transgression is to potentially disrupt any limit. Through Bataille's more 'theoretical' analysis of transgression we saw how he grappled with the way transgression escapes from limits and definitions, producing a complex structure that his fiction often doesn't deal with directly in its commitment to the effect of shock through representation. By taking up Bataille's tentative deconstruction of transgression I showed how transgression exists through a limit and as disruptive of any limit, and this includes the limit between the literary and philosophical. This operation cannot be reduced to literature or literary theory, but it does re-open a new way of thinking about literature as part of a general *writing*. We should not think that this is just Bataille's problem, it's a problem for any attempt to 'use' the concept of transgression. The value of the concept of transgression is that in its self-disruption it reveals a general effect of all attempts at the foundation of a discourse although, as we have seen, it is possible even to attempt to secure and stabilise transgression. Any such attempts have to be in direct conflict with transgression's own conceptual resources.

This can also explain why this analysis may appear to be very traditional, it is returning to tradition to excavate resources within it, but that shaking and opening of the concept of transgression means that tradition itself becomes unstable. The tradition that is returned *to is no longer traditional*. This creates a strange temporality where transgression is an opening of the *future*, we can agree with Foucault that 'in spite of so many scattered signs, the language in which transgression will find its space and the illumination of its being lies almost entirely in the future' (p.33) as long as we don't think of this in terms on a simple progression forward (which Foucault's language suggests). Instead, transgression as an opening is also an opening to the future and to future possibilities of thought. These possibilities also exist in the past, in tradition, in its very openness that is the possibility of thinking something new. What transgression signals is an opening and freedom that does not just belong to it but which is *general*, at the root of any concept, any foundation, any law. It is also what makes transgression liberating, and liberated itself from its own limits as scandalous or subversive. This is how to approach the claim to transgress transgression, which is not to produce a purer thought of transgression or to finally find the real and true transgression, although it is certainly difficult not to feel or act on this desire, and this desire is itself an effect of transgression. Transgressing transgression is to feel the intangible opening and freedom of transgression, a freedom that it opens everywhere but which exists through a demand of reading.

University of Sussex

1 Georges Bataille, *Story of the Eye*, trans. by Joachim Neugroschal (Harmondsworth: Penguin, 1982), pp.59-67.

2 Georges Bataille, *Eroticism*, trans. by Mary Dalwood (London, New York: Marion Boyars, 1987), p.11, further references in text.

3 Susan Rubin Suleiman, 'Like Water in Water', *London Review of Books*, 12 July 1990, 22-23 (p.23).

4 Julia Kristeva, *Desire in Language*, ed. by Leon S. Roudiez, trans. by Thomas Gova, Alice Jardine, and Leon S. Roudiez (Oxford: Blackwell, 1980), p.86.

5 Julia Kristeva, 'Bataille, Experience and Practice', in *On Bataille*, ed. and trans. by Leslie Anne Boldt-Irons (Albany: State University of New York Press, 1995), pp.237-264, further references in text.

6 Julia Kristeva, *Revolution in Poetic Language*, trans. by Margaret Waller, intro. by Leon S. Roudiez (New York: Columbia University Press, 1984), pp.25-30.

7 James Joyce, *Finnegans Wake* (Harmondsworth: Penguin, 1992), ed. and intro. by Seamus Deane, based on 3rd edition (London: Faber, 1939).

8 Michel Foucault, 'A Preface to Transgression' in *Language, Counter-memory, Practice*, ed. And intro. By Donald F. Bouchard, trans. by Donald F. Bouchard and Sherry Simon (New York: Cornell University Press, 1977), pp.29-52 (pp.29-30), further references in text.

9 Nick Land, *The Thirst for Annihilation: Georges Bataille and Virulent Nihilism (an essay in atheistic religion)* (London and New York: Routledge, 1992), further page references in text.

10 Gilles Deleuze and Claire Parnet, *Dialogues*, trans. by Hugh Tomlinson and Barbara Habberjam (London: The Athlone Press, 1987), p.47.

11 Georges Bataille, *Theory of Religion*, trans. by Robert Hurley (New York: Zone Books, 1992), p.53.

12 Jacques Derrida, *Limited Inc.*, trans. by Samuel Weber and Jeffrey Mehlman (Evanston: Northwestern University Press, 1988), p.9.

13 Georges Bataille, *The Accursed Share. An Essay on General Economy*, trans. by Robert Hurley, 2 vols (New York: Zone Books, 1991), I, 25.

14 Michael Richardson, *Georges Bataille* (London and New York: Routledge, 1994).

15 John Lechte, 'An Introduction to Bataille: the impossible as (a Practice of) Writing', *Textual Practice*, 7.2 (1993), 173-194 (p.184).

16 John Lechte, *Julia Kristeva* (London and New York: Routledge, 1990).

17 Roland Barthes, *Image Music Text*, trans. by Stephen Heath (London: Fontana, London, 1977), p.157.

18 Jacques Derrida, 'Dialogue', in *Dialogues with Contemporary Continental Thinkers*, ed. by Richard Kearney (Manchester: Manchester University Press,1984), pp.105-126 (p.112).

19 Georges Bataille, *Literature and Evil*, trans. by Alastair Hamilton (London and New York: Marion Boyars, 1985), further page references in text.